M000280632

SOLDIER'S POCKET BOOK

Author
Major (Retd) John Hobbis Harris

LEWIS

INTERNATIONAL, INC.

First published in the United States in 2000
by Lewis International, Inc.

ACKNOWLEDGEMENTS
Where applicable, information contained in this publication is produced
with the permission of ROYAL ORDNANCE plc and © copyright/MOD,
reproduced with the permission of the Controller of HMSO.

MINISTRY OF DEFENCE DISCLAIMER
"The Ministry of Defence takes no responsibility as to the contemporaneity
of the contents especially the weapons drills section and that the publication
does not negate the individual's responsibilities to check such
drills in the appropriate Army pamphlet".

© Copyright 1999 Military Pocket Books
ISBN 1-874528-02-0

Lewis International, Inc.
2201 N.W. 102nd Place #1
Miami, Fl 33172 USA

Tel: 305 - 436 - 7984/800-259-5962
Fax: 305-436-7985/800-664-5095

CONTENT

i

CONTENT

Subject	Page No's

PERSONAL DETAILS

Surname .... No ....

Other Names ....

Home Address...

.... Post Code ....

Next of Kin Relationship ....

Address ....

....Post Code.....................................

Blood Group........... Colour of Eyes............. Colour of Hair ....

Nat Ins No .... Date of Birth .... Religion ....

Relevant Medical Information ....

....

....

Date Attested .... Date Passed Initial Training ....

1

INTRODUCTION

This Pocket Book brings together, in one cover, much of the basic information that you, the soldier - either Regular or TA needs to know. However it should not in any way be construed as superseding what is taught by the officers and NCO's in your unit. In the Army of today, we find that both Regular and TA Soldiers take part together in training exercises. This is part of the 'One Army' concept, ensuring that in times of a general mobilization for any reason, that they are already integrated as an efficient, professional Army to defend the nation or be part of a United Nations Force in a peace keeping role.

We can only assume that you are a British Soldier reading this, as such you are a Volunteer Soldier either as a Regular, or a member of the Territorial Army.

As a member of the British Armed Forces, you have joined an Army which is admired and respected the world over. All three services have traditions and experience which is reflected in almost all that they do. The Army is no exception to this, and a large part of the Territorial Army has a history which can be traced back through all major conflicts, to its formation in 1908, and before that to the 11th Century when civilians were embodied, with their own weapons, in Anglo-Saxon times.

Many of you in different Regiments or Corps, will be proud to be able to relate that your forefathers fought in famous campaigns or took part in specific events, where gallantry and examples of leadership will always be remembered as part of the tradition of the Regiment or Corps.

The same traditions will be true for your unit today, your officers and instructors will no doubt tell you about the history and traditions of your particular Regiment or Corps.

Certainly a modern war of the scale of those "wars to end wars" cannot be fought without a general mobilisation of the whole population. The role for which you have volunteered either as a regular soldier or member of the TA is a very important one, with considerable responsibility and trust, ensuring that you are worthy of upholding the traditions of the service and maintaining the respect of the nation.

To be an effective soldier, either as a regular or territorial, you must be fit, well trained and experienced. Your training will be carried out by the officers and NCO's of your unit.

You will only gain experience through the amount of time and effort you yourself put into your training. Skills are only improved by consistent practice and a determination to keep on learning. The aim of this pocket book is to make a contribution towards that end.

RESPECT OF THE NATION

At this time in its existence the Army serving Queen and Country, is under severe pressure from the changing attitudes towards previously accepted standards of personal and social behaviour. It is not surprising that those who join the Army today bring with them the 'on-going' standards of society today.

In the past the Army has always expected *you* the individual, without question, to fulfil the Army's needs, regarding *your* personal standards of behaviour, irrespective of the situation or occasion in which you found yourself.

Today we are expected to ask the reason *'why'* a particular rule or occasion is brought to light. The Army has become aware of the need to more closely define the high standards of personal conduct and respect for the law demanded of those in military service, in this respect it applies to both the Regular and Territorial Army.

The basis for these standards is the LAW of the nation and the overall operational efficiency of those serving in the Army.

You work and live within the Army environment — where team work, the need to do your best and mutual trust are of vital importance. Any individual(s) whose actions or behaviour threatens this team work is failing in their prime duty and will not be accepted.

The role of the British soldier in 'peacetime' has taken them into many different parts of the world, to cope some times with very difficult, 'tricky' and frustrating situations. Their patience and restraint has been tested to the limits of their ability. Yet, there have been no incidents where they have been found wanting for the correct action.

Against this background it is necessary to remind ourselves that the soldier is a person with the common strengths and weakness we all have. The standards that society appear to be setting are not those that the soldier can go along with and as a result of this some very clear rules in the form of a Code of Conduct were produced. We have in turn written a synopsis of them for your guidance. Detailed explanations of them and their implications are the responsibility of your own officers to discuss in some depth with you.

This Code of Conduct applies to everyone — including yourself. It is not just the responsibility of your CO or unit Sergeant Major or NCO's, but relies on you and every other rank in the Army. Remember the basis of discipline is SELF DISCIPLINE. Your own self respect and the high standards expected of you by the Army will ensure the continuing support of the nation.

CODE OF CONDUCT

THE REASON WHY

The British Army has a long tradition and reputation for high standards of behaviour, high morale and strict discipline has stood the Service in good stead in both peace and war.

The ending of conscription, and the introduction of the "professional" army, with their overseas tour commitments, and in more recent times due to strict security, the physical separation from the civilian environment, have all tended to cut off the Army from society at large. This however, has meant that the Army has been able to maintain high moral and ethical standards largely unaffected by changes in the pattern of behaviour in society in general.

In more recent times, this difference between the standards expected in the Service, and what many may take as acceptable behaviour within our civilian society, has been called into question — due to a lack of understanding of the military's strict code of conduct.

Therefore it becomes important to define and justify the standards which the Army regard as essential to maintain, in order that those standards are easily recognised and fully understood at all levels in the service and in society at large, especially those who are seeking to join.

These standards will maintain the reputation of the service and apply equally to both Regular and the Territorial Army.

EXPLANATION

In the following pages we have set out under various headings some aspects of personal behaviour that come under particular scrutiny by the public. In some instances they are the most sensitive and the most difficult to deal with.

CODE OF CONDUCT

Remember there is a requirement for high standards of personal conduct and respect for the law demanded of all those in military service irrespective of rank.

Some examples are given of the standards required. The consequences of failing to maintain those standards are briefly set out. It is the intention that you will be able to identify with all aspects of this section of the Pocket Book. It will no doubt be referred too on many occasions and provoke many lively discussions, thus achieving an important role in talking through the right's and wrong's of personal behaviour, your role in maintaining a good reputation, both as an individual and the service at large.

THE DRIFT OF SOCIETY

Over a number of years, religion, education and the family no longer always provide the framework of behaviour, social structure, and responsibility they have in the past. More liberal uncaring attitudes hold sway leading some groups of society to reject or reduce in importance those values which the Armed Forces seek to maintain and regard so highly: sense of duty, loyalty, self-discipline, self-sacrifice, respect and concern for others.

The rights of the individual are increasingly preserved and protected by Laws which have been passed to stop discrimination on the grounds of race, colour, beliefs or gender.

Other minority groups have sought to permit what they believe to be their rights where these are viewed to be identified not by physical characteristics, place of birth, or beliefs, but by individual behaviour. The rights and freedom of the individual tend to be promoted over attitudes of society generally. Where individuals fail in their responsibilities to society there is an increasing tendency to take the easy way out and blame this on the failure of government.

Individual freedom now available has in many cases led to decline in both individual and collective responsibility. This has led to an increasing lack of respect for the law, for example, in attacks on the Police, violent street crime, car theft, burglary, and drug misuse. The promotion of individual freedom has contributed to an uncaring attitude towards their responsibilities to society and a total lack of any self discipline.

The Army cannot remain isolated from the society it serves, and from which it recruits, obviously it cannot allow itself to follow trends which might undermine its traditional values.

CODE OF CONDUCT

The Army recognises that keeping to its standards must be upheld on their importance rather than on emotional or traditional grounds, but it must also be mindful of being kept well informed of the changing scene and attitudes of society in general, and if required change its own attitude to meet the needs of the service.

It must recognise that where reform is appropriate, this must be carried out as a policy rather than action taken in the face of events that have already happened.

Society demands high standards of personal behaviour from those in public positions, including the Army.

When those standards are relaxed or seen to be compromised, the trust and confidence of society risk being lost.

TERMS AND CONDITIONS

Naturally terms and conditions of military service are very different from those of civilian life. The Service aims to foster personal and team commitment within a clearly defined chain of command, but by its very nature, such cooperation can be destroyed where there is a loss of trust or confidence.

Most military communities comprise of young, robust, heterosexual people. They live in close proximity with others often in single-sex accommodation, often working under great stress and in close contact with one another. They do not have a chioce with whom they work or share accommodation which may have only limited privacy.

Unlike civilians they do not have the opportunity to leave their jobs if the conduct of their work mates causes offence.

The effectiveness of the Army depends upon the efficiency and contented service of these individuals, who make up the greater majority.

To allow any element to affect adversely the morale, team spirit, and hence the operational efficiency of any unit would be detrimental to its role and would not be tolerated.

THE OPERATIONAL OBLIGATIONS

Society expects the Armed Forces to place the interests of the nation before self. It is the soldier's obligation to follow orders in the face of an enemy and to do his duty despite the risk of death or injury. It is that operational liability, with the possibility of self-sacrifice (accepted by every soldier on enlistment), that marks the

CODE OF CONDUCT

Armed Services out as being essentially different from the rest of society. In order to meet these demands, the Army insists on a more exacting code of conduct.

Operational effectiveness demands a high standard of discipline and the most effective discipline is that which is self-imposed.

Self-discipline is the core of all discipline, and the foundation on which leadership, motivation, courage, morale and corporate discipline, are built. Without these qualities no Army could be deployed on operations with any degree of success.

The operational obligations of the Army puts the importance of the group over self-interest. Armed conflict is, by its very nature, a group rather than an individual venture.

A sense of unity, team spirit and loyalty are decisive factors in any armed conflict. Nothing must be allowed to detract from the forging of close bonds, based upon mutual trust and respect, between members of the group, and between the group and its leaders, be it a section or a brigade.

This applies equally to low-intensity conflict, such as working with the UN, where stress upon the individual can be considerable.

All ranks must have trust and confidence in their comrades, and in their superiors. Without this trust and confidence, sound personal relationships will not withstand the severe pressure imposed by the battlefield.

THE LAW OF THE LAND

When enlisting, servicemen and women remain subject to the criminal law applicable to civilians. They also become subject to military law, which in a number of respects makes certain conduct a criminal offence, where in civilian life it would be lawful. The law thus imposes further obligations and demands on Service personnel.

Following a military or civil conviction for an offence, administrative action may be taken against an individual.

Such action may also be taken for misconduct even if the individual has not been convicted of an offence.

Administrative action may result, in the case of an officer, in being called upon to resign or retire, or, in the case of a soldier, in being discharged.

CODE OF CONDUCT

MAINTENANCE OF STANDARDS

EQUAL OPPORTUNITIES

"The Army is fully committed to Equal Opportunities for all personnel regardless of sex, race, marital status ethnic origin or religion."

GENERAL

It is the duty of all ranks to uphold the standards of conduct and respect for the law which are essential to military service. The behaviour and example of those in positions of authority must be outstanding, otherwise their usefulness, effectiveness and proper relationship with all ranks will be impaired.

The Queens Commission. First and foremost an officer is a leader, required to uphold and enforce discipline fairly and without bias. Officers are expected to set an example, give advice and guidance to their juniors, and to show moral courage in dealing with undisciplined incidents or misconduct.

For these reasons an officer's personal conduct must be beyond reproach. Integrity is essential to leadership in that it implies honesty, sincerity, reliability, unselfishness, moral courage and consistency of approach.

If an officer's conduct calls into question his or her integrity, or brings the Army into disrepute, the trust and respect of those he or she is privileged to command is placed in jeopardy, and the right to hold the Queen's Commission may be forfeited.

ALCOHOL

Social Drinking. Team spirit, mutual respect and self confidence are forged through hard and demanding training, which in turn brings about the will to do the job properly.

Team spirit is further developed by fostering a social identity within the unit.

Social drinking is an accepted part of service life. There is, however, a clear difference between socialising and drunken behaviour and whilst the former is to be encouraged the latter will quickly destroy discipline and erode team spirit.

Organised social functions must, therefore, always take place in a regulated and controlled environment. It is of concern that the average consumption of alcohol by service personnel remains very

CODE OF CONDUCT

high and is a major cause of impaired efficiency, disciplinary
problems, accidents and poor health. Not to mention the adverse
affect on personal finance, marital relations and disharmony in the
home. Moreover, alcohol remains the single highest contributory
factor to violent crime in the Army. One of the most effective
methods of preventing the abuse of alcohol is the moderate and
responsible behaviour by officers and senior NCOs in the unit.
All in authority are expected to set an example and an instance of
drunken behaviour, particularly in front of junior ranks, is viewed
seriously as a matter calling into question an individual's integrity.

Drunkenness: Drunkenness is in certain specific circumstances a
military offence. The Army Act states that a person is guilty of the
offence, owing to the influence of alcohol (or any drug), whether
alone or in combination with any other circumstances, if the
individual is unfit to be entrusted with any duty, or any duty they may
be reasonably expected to perform, behaves in a disorderly manner,
or behaves in such manner that may bring discredit onto the
Services.
It is not normally an accepted defence for a person charged with
other offences to plead that he was drunk at the time. A conviction
for drunkenness against an officer or NCO will call into question
their fitness to retain their rank and responsibilities.

Driving Under Influence: Driving under the influence of alcohol is a
serious criminal offence. It displays irresponsibility and a lack of judgement
and self-discipline.
A conviction for driving whilst under the influence of alcohol will almost
certainly affect an individual's employment and career.

Alcohol Abuse: Alcoholics and heavy drinkers are an operational
liability. Individuals who fail to co-operate or respond to
rehabilitation are to be considered for discharge.

DRUG MISUSE

The misuse of controlled drugs is illegal. It undermines trust and
mutual respect, impairs efficiency, judgement and reliability and is
therefore detrimental to operational effectiveness.
Drug misuse has a insidious effect and wherever it takes hold will
undermine quickly a unit's discipline, morale and cohesion.
Drug misuse will not be tolerated and the Army's sentencing policy
for drug offences is based upon dismissal.

CODE OF CONDUCT

To that effect the Army Board are committed to Compulsory Drug Testing. Drug misuse, which includes prescription drugs, such as anabolic steroids, and solvents as well as controlled drugs, may result in administrative discharge (or a call to resign or retire in the case of an officer) even when charges are not preferred.

DISHONESTY

All forms of dishonesty involve deceit and a lack of integrity which call into question whether an individual may continue to be trusted and relied upon.

Acts of dishonesty cover a wide spectrum and include behaviour which raises doubts about an individual's character, as well as criminal offences, such as fraud and theft.

An individual who, by his dishonest actions or behaviour shows that he cannot be trusted, has no place in the military community where mutual trust between all ranks is vital.

INDEBTEDNESS

Persistent indebtedness displays a lack of judgement and poor control over one's personal affairs. It can also lead to an individual becoming a security risk.

The mismanagement of personal financial affairs calls into question whether a leader is suitable to oversee the welfare of his subordinates. Failure to ensure that there are sufficient funds in an account to honour a cheque is one example of the type of personal mismanagement which will discredit an individual, and may bring the Army into disrepute.

Such cases are viewed as particularly serious when involving an officer and may culminate in disciplinary action; a review of vetting status may also be required.

BULLYING AND INITIATION CEREMONIES

The responsibility for and wellbeing of subordinates rests with commanders at all times. Any abuse of, or disregard to, this responsibility amounts to neglect. Illegal punishments, unauthorized initiation ceremonies, and physical abuse are unacceptable; in particular, junior commanders are to be supervised closely in this respect.

Bullying: Operational effectiveness requires the Army to train to be physically strong and robust and, when needed, to display controlled aggression.

CODE OF CONDUCT

However, the abuse of physical strength, or of a position of authority, to intimidate or victimise, will quickly lower morale and undermine confidence in the chain of command.

It is the responsibility of commanders at all levels to protect individuals from both physical and mental intimidation and to report any instances of bullying promptly. Cases of bullying do great harm to the Services and to all units involved and bring the Army into disrepute.

Initiation Ceremonies: Initiation ceremonies involving assault, humiliation, intimidation, or the abuse of alcohol, will not be tolerated.

RACIAL & SEXUAL DISCRIMINATION & HARASSMENT

All personnel, irrespective of their racial origin or gender, have the right to live and work in a environment free from prejudice, humiliation, or intimidation.

It is unacceptable that their performance, career development, and job satisfaction should be affected by behaviour on the part of others which draws attention to their racial origin or gender.

This includes actions which in any way create feelings of offence, unease, or distress: for example by offensive jokes, or language or by abuse; graffiti; literature or posters; gestures or remarks. Discrimination, prejudice and harassment by an individual can amount to misconduct and a disciplinary offence.

Racial Discrimination: Racial discrimination will not be tolerated. As an employer, the Army has certain legal responsibilities under the Race Relations Act 1976, and may be liable for acts of discrimination by Service Personnel.

WHAT IS HARASSMENT?

Harassment, even if unintentional, is any behaviour you feel is:

UNACCEPTABLE, UNWELCOME, UNREASONABLE

It may be **physical**, e.g. touching, patting. **Verbal**, e.g. offensive comments, e.g. about gender, race, religious belief, physical appearance. **Non-verbal**, e.g. offensive material or suggestive actions.

Harassment may take the form of bullying, victimisation or misuse of authority. It may extend to physical assault, which may be an offence under criminal law.

Serious cases of harassment may lead to dismissal.

CODE OF CONDUCT

WHERE DO YOU GET ADVICE?

INTERNALLY.	EXTERNALLY
CO/OC	The Equal Opportunities Commission
A trusted friend	The Commission for Racial Equality
Unit Equal Opportunities Officer	Local Citizens Advice Bureaux
Unit chaplain	
Unit Medical Officer	
The Army Legal Services	
The Confidential Support Line	
The Army Welfare Services	

CONFIDENTIAL SUPPORT LINE

(Totally confidential, you do not even have to leave your name if you do not wish to). See Soldier Magazine for telephone numbers.

Sexual Harassment: Sexual harassment is unacceptable behaviour. There can be no simple definition of sexual harassment but it may be described as unwelcome conduct of a sexual nature, or other conduct based on sex, which degrades the dignity of an individual of the opposite sex.

Sexual harassment can be persistent unwanted sexual attention which continues after the recipient makes it clear that he or she wants it to stop.

A single incident, however, can also constitute sexual harassment if sufficiently serious. Sexual harassment is not a criminal offence itself, though certain forms of sexual harassment can result in criminal charges: for example, indecent assault.

SOCIAL MISCONDUCT

The Army operates within a close-knit organisation where teamwork and team spirit are of the greatest importance and therefore, cannot allow any conduct on the part of its members which compromises the integrity of its disciplined structure or of those within it, or which is harmful to the security of those who are part of the military community generally cannot be allowed. In this context, liaisons, whether of a sexual or non-sexual nature which nonetheless involve intimacy or excessive familiarity, can damage that integrity or security and can amount, in service terms, to misconduct by the military individual concerned.

CODE OF CONDUCT

Adultery: Adultery is likely to prejudice the position of an individual and may bring the Army into disrepute:

Adultery Within the Military Community: The most serious cases of social misconduct involve adultery within the military community. It is essential that military personnel are not worried about the integrity of their marriages at any time, but especially whilst the unit is deployed away from its peacetime location any extramarital relationships will be considered unacceptable.

Adultery Outside the Military Community. Married or single officers who enter into adulterous affairs outside the military community jeopardise their status as an officer should the circumstances of the affair become public, and if it brings either the officer or the Army into disrepute.

Other Sexual Relationships: The Army is based on a clearly defined rank structure, with distinctions between the different ranks that are well understood and accepted, as is the particular division between officers and noncommissioned ranks.

Sexual relationships which undermine this well-ordered structure cannot be tolerated. While there would be no objection to a consensual liaison between a junior noncommissioned officer and a private of the opposite sexes, the same would not be true of a similar liaison between an officer and a noncommissioned rank. Such relationships diminish the authority and standing of credibility and trust.

While marriage between an officer and a noncommissioned rank cannot be prohibited, such relationships will inevitably cause difficulties, as the couple will not be permitted to serve in the same unit, and therefore it is discouraged.

SINGLE PARENTS

Retention in the Service of single parent is dependent upon their ability to continue to be operationally effective. There are proper and supportive arrangements for those married personnel who become single parents by change of circumstances, for example, by bereavement or divorce. However, those who become single parents through circumstances within their control and who are unable to meet their operational liability will not be retained.

CODE OF CONDUCT

FORMS OF PUNISHMENT

General standards of conduct apply to all soldiers, but those in the chain of command are expected to set a proper example. Each case will be judged on its merits and action taken will be graded in severity dependent upon the incident and its effect on the Army; the censure awarded will reflect with the level of command, experience and rank of the individual reported.

Officers: For minor incidents young officers may receive a warning from within their unit. More serious or repeated incidents may be reflected in the officer's confidential report.

Experienced officers, or those whose cases are not dealt with by the Commanding Officer, may receive a verbal or recorded rebuke from their formation commander. Some matters may warrant a warning as to future conduct. The officer may also be liable for a move from the unit where the misconduct took place.

Formal warnings and awards of displeasure are recorded on the individual's confidential report book, and may have a detrimental effect on the officer's career.

Soldiers: Standards expected of senior noncommissioned officers are as high as those expected from junior officers. The degrees of censure, as for officers, will reflect the seriousness of the incident and the rank of the individual.

Soldiers may be warned as to their conduct and placed on a 3 month warning under Chapter 9 of Queens Regulations.

The lowest form of administrative censure is a "Recorded Rebuke"; this is recorded for 2 years on a soldier's record.

The next level of censure is an award of "Displeasure"; this is recorded for 4 years and prevents the individual being considered for promotion for one year from the date of the censure.

Next is the award of "Severe Displeasure" which is recorded for 5 years and prevents the individual from being considered for promotion for 18 months. A soldier can also be reduced in rank administratively. In most severe cases a soldier can be discharged.

"ATHELETE'S ARE SUBJECTED TO RANDOM DRUG TESTS"
. . . . **SO ARE SOLDIER'S**

MILITARY LAW

In this section we are not attempting to emulate the 'barrackroom lawyer', but purely give you some background information in the hopes that it might keep you clear of being 'on orders' tomorrow morning

Should you be a member of the TA, whilst serving you are expected to behave like a soldier and for the most part have an element of self-discipline which makes the rule of law unnecessary. In all probability this is due to the fact that the majority of people in the UK are law abiding citizens.

Naturally there are always exceptions to the rule and occasionally a commander will have to invoke Military Law, perhaps Section 69, for some minor indiscretion.

During wartime, the Army Act 1955 and Military Law in general might take on a different *mantle* and be more rigorously applied. However, it is true to say that like most laws they are there for a reason and are as much for the protection of the individual as they are a means of discipline.

Your rights as a soldier charged with an offence under the Army Act 1955 are many and varied. For instance, when charged you might be placed into close arrest or open arrest. If you are in close arrest you have the right to know the name rank and unit of the person who is charging you and to have a copy of the charge report as soon as it is received.

If you have been placed in open arrest as a private soldier you may be ordered to perform all duties. In close arrest or if you are an NCO (who must hand over his duties to another NCO) you would not be required to attend parades or carry out any duties except for keeping your room and your belongings clean.

As soon as possible after you have been charged you should be brought before your company, etc., commander who will investigate the charge.

You may if you do not understand the charge ask for it to be explained to you. You have the following rights if the investigating officer decides to hear the evidence:

a. to be present while the charge is being heard.

b. to ask for the evidence of witnesses to be given in person instead of in writing.

c. to ask for the evidence to be given under oath.

d. to ask the witnesses questions.

e. to give evidence under oath, make a statement or remain silent.

f. to call witnesses in your own defence.

There are many more rights which would apply in different circumstances including the right to have an officer represent you and explain to you your legal rights. Obviously it would be best to pick an officer who you know and respect and who knows you.

Some examples of charges you might encounter are shown below and make interesting reading. Examples of maximum punishments under the act are also shown, mostly two years imprisonment or less, some are more, all will depend on the circumstances and may only involve a reprimand or a small fine. Having a drink is OK; take it to far and you may meet this one.

87654321 Pte Bloggs J is charged with DRUNKENNESS CONTRARY TO SECTION 43(1) OF THE ARMY ACT 1955, in that he, at .... , on 23 July was drunk.

On conviction by court-martial a term of imprisonment not exceeding two years or any less punishment provided by the act. This is unlikely isn't it, you did volunteer, so you must like soldering - mustn't you. However, don't skive or you might face this one:

87675434 Pte Bloggs.B is charged with MALINGERING CONTRARY TO SECTION 42(1)(b) OF THE ARMY ACT 1955, in that he, at .... on 5 July falsely pretended to Captain J Brown, Royal Army Medical Corps, that he was suffering from a sprained ankle.

On conviction by court-martial a term of imprisonment not exceeding two years or any less punishment provided by the act. We have all heard of those who have gone AWOL.

87342145 Pte White.B is charged with ABSENCE WITHOUT LEAVE CONTRARY TO SECTION 38(a) OF THE ARMY ACT 1955, in that he, at .... absented himself without leave from 15 June to 18 June. On conviction by court-martial a term of imprisonment not exceeding two years or any less punishment provided by the act.

The rule to avoid the next one is do as you're told at the time and argue it out afterwards. Note that the charge includes the phrase *LAWFUL COMMAND*, you cannot be ordered to break the law and being in the army does not relieve you of responsibilities under normal civil laws.

87656565 Pte Black C is charged with DISOBEYING A LAWFUL COMMAND CONTRARY TO SECTION 34 OF THE ARMY ACT

1955, in that he, at .... on 16 May did not stand to attention when ordered to do so by No. 12345678 Corporal Green P.

On conviction by court-martial a term of imprisonment or any less punishment provided by the act.

We all lose things and in most cases we can replace or pay for them without the need for being charged, however if you do lose kit and are put on a charge - this is it.

89876432 Pte Brown G is charged with LOSING HIS EQUIPMENT CONTRARY TO SECTION 46(1)(a) OF THE ARMY ACT 1955, in that he, at .... on 6 Jan lost a sleeping bag of the value of £65.87, equipment issued to him for military purposes

On conviction by court-martial a term of imprisonment not exceeding two years or any less punishment provided by the act.

It is an offence to strike a superior officer be he a Junior NCO, Senior NCO, Warrant Officer or Officer.

87234516 Pte Thump. U is charge with STRIKING HIS SUPERIOR OFFICER CONTRARY TO SECTION 33(1)(a) OF THE ARMY ACT 1955 in that he, at .... on 31st Dec struck No 12345566 Sergeant Hurt T.M

On conviction by court-martial a term of imprisonment or any less punishment provided by the act.

It is also an offence to strike a subordinate, so note that your superiors are not allowed to abuse you or hit you in any way.

123456 Captain I Hithim is charged with STRIKING AN OFFICER OF INFERIOR RANK CONTRARY TO SECTION 65(a) OF THE ARMY ACT 1955 in that he, at .... on 4 Sept struck 2nd Lieutenant S.Lapped, an officer of inferior rank.

On conviction by court-martial a term of imprisonment not exceeding two years or any less punishment provided by the act.

This one is the charge that seems to cover a *multitude of sins*, and it does.

87687654 Pte Anyonelse.F. Is charged with CONDUCT TO THE PREJUDICE OF GOOD ORDER AND MILITARY DISCIPLINE CONTRARY TO SECTION 69 OF THE ARMY ACT 1955 in that he, at ...... on 14 Oct neglected to clean his rifle for a weapon inspection.

On conviction by court-martial a term of imprisonment not exceeding two years or any less punishment provided by the act.

You can be charged under this section for all sorts of things, such as; writing dud cheques, 'borrowing' someone's bike, using a vehicle incorrectly, failing to repay a debt, a negligent discharge of your rifle, crashing a vehicle, in fact anything which does not *"uphold the standards and good reputation of the service"*.

As said in the opening pages of this Pocket Book, as a member of the TA you are equally responsible for upholding the traditions and maintaining the respect of the Nation for the Army as is the Regular Soldier, and may we again remind you of the Code of Conduct in this respect.

DRILL & DISCIPLINE

INTRODUCTION

When a civilian thinks of the Army their immediate thoughts turn to well disciplined, smartly dressed soldiers in uniform. Part of your training to be a soldier involves teaching you to be a disciplined, well turned out and organised individual.

As a soldier you must be trained to obey orders instantly, since the speed at which you respond to orders in battle can mean life or death to you or your comrades.

As volunteers it would seem to be a difficult task to instill this sort of discipline in someone, who, in the case of the TA, is essentially a civilian in uniform.

However, this is not really the problem it seems since, after all, the soldier does what he does because he is a volunteer, and more importantly, his officers and NCOs will rely much more on the form of discipline we have already dwelt upon - SELF DISCIPLINE.

The traditional way of instilling discipline in an army has been through the use of drill, a method which is still very effective.

Another way is through the use of a uniform. Both methods require you to pay attention to detail, in the first case so that you can march correctly and not draw the Sergeant Majors wrath and in the second so that you will look smart.

You will no doubt be told that you can enjoy learning to carry out good drill movements in a squad, you may think that the instructor is 'out of his mind', but you will find that there is more to drill than you first thought, it is a team effort more precise that the most highly trained football team.

The concentration of individual effort and self discipline will be hard to find in any other situation. Once you have perfected this better than most others in your unit and taken part in parades, you will feel the pride in your unit and yourself that takes some beating. If you are fortunate to have an experienced drill instructor learning drill can be an interesting subject.

PAYING COMPLIMENTS - SALUTING

Throughout our history the tradition of saluting with the hand, or the present arms with a rifle and the salute with the sword were the methods by which the person paying the compliment, could show to the recipient that no offence was meant. The salute, no matter in what form it was given, became accepted as a symbolic gesture of loyalty and trust.

Today it is accepted that a salute is the normal greeting between comrades in arms. That is of course provided, that when you meet an officer and do give a salute, it is given in a smart and soldierly manner, that is a matter of your personal discipline and good manners.

That you give the salute properly and smartly is a matter of training, which reflects upon your Regiment or Corps.

Failure on the part of an officer to correctly return your salute shows a lack of personal discipline and courtesy on his part. All compliments derive their origin from the Sovereign, to who the highest compliment, the Royal Salute, is paid.

All officers in the Armed Services, including the Territorial Army, and Cadet Forces are holders of the Queens Commission, therefore when you pay compliments to an officer, it is in recognition of the Sovereigns Commission held in trust by that officer.

DRESS

There are various forms of dress/uniform used in the forces for different parts of the world, conditions and different jobs. Which ever form you wear it should always be clean, in good condition and pressed. In some cases you will be told pay particular attention to your dress, for a parade perhaps, in which case boots should also

be highly polished.
The types of dress you will most likely come across are:-
a. Barrack Training Dress. b. Combat Dress. c. Shirt Sleeve Order
You will always be told by your unit which form of dress to wear and
when to wear it. However, bear one thing in mind, while units may
dress slightly differently, those within one unit should all be dressed
the same, as laid down in their orders. The following is a guide to
each form of dress:-

BARRACK TRAINING DRESS

Regimental Headdress - usually a Beret with Cap Badge. Some
units wear a hackle in this form of dress. Shirt KF. Trousers
Lightweight. Socks. Boots Combat High. Combat jacket and Belt.
Some units replace the Combat jacket with a Jersey Heavy Wool.

COMBAT DRESS

As above with the following changes and additions. Steel Helmet
may replace Regimental Headdress. Combat Trousers may replace
Trousers Lightweight especially in winter.
The following may also be worn; T-shirt, Jersey Heavy Wool and
Long Johns. In summer some units wear only a T-shirt under the
combat jacket.

SHIRT SLEEVE ORDER

This form of dress is usually worn during the summer in place of
barrack dress. Regimental Headdress, Shirt KF - sleeves rolled up
to just above the elbow and highly pressed. Trousers Lightweight.
Socks. Boots Combat High. Belt - Plastic, web or if your regiment
allows a stable belt in Regimental or Corps colours. Your unit PRI
will have items which are approved by your Regiment or Corps, so
pay them a visit.

FOOT DRILL

Words of Command on the March in Quick Time.

HALT - Given as the left foot is on the ground.

ABOUT TURN - Given as the left foot passes the right.

SALUTING ON THE MARCH - Given as the left heel strikes the ground.

SALUTING TO THE FRONT - Given as the right foot passes the left.

MARK TIME - Given over a left pace.

HALT AND FORWARD - (when MARKING TIME)

SQUAD HALT - given when left knee is at it's highest point.

RIGHT TURN or RIGHT INCLINE - Given as the right foot passes the left.

LEFT TURN or LEFT INCLINE - Given as the left foot passes the right.

PAYING COMPLIMENTS - SALUTING

SALUTING TO THE FRONT

Common Faults

a The body and head not remaining erect.

b Allowing the elbow to come forward.

c Hand not straight and in an incorrect position.

d Allowing the left arm to creep forward.

e Left fist not clenched with thumb to front.

As a aid to good saluting, remember your right hand - with the palm of your hand flat, thumb on top, travels the - longest way up and the shortest way down - when saluting correctly.

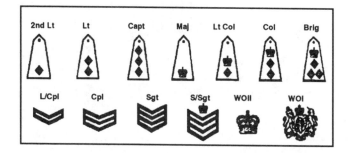

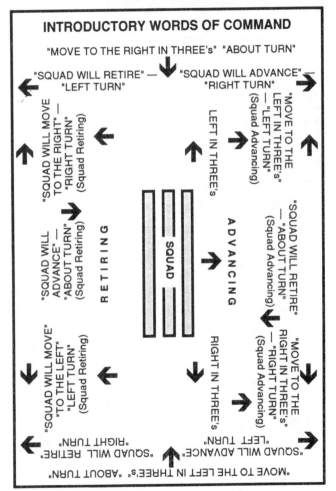

INTRODUCTORY WORDS OF COMMAND

"MOVE TO THE RIGHT IN THREE's" "ABOUT TURN"

"SQUAD WILL RETIRE" — "SQUAD WILL ADVANCE" —
"LEFT TURN" "RIGHT TURN"

"MOVE TO THE
LEFT IN THREE's"
— "LEFT TURN"
(Squad Advancing)

LEFT IN THREE's

"SQUAD WILL MOVE
TO THE RIGHT"
"RIGHT TURN"
(Squad Retiring)

"SQUAD WILL RETIRE
— "ABOUT TURN"
(Squad Advancing)

RETIRING

ADVANCING

SQUAD

"SQUAD WILL
ADVANCE" —
"ABOUT TURN"
(Squad Retiring)

"MOVE TO THE
RIGHT IN THREE'S"
— "RIGHT TURN"
(Squad Advancing)

"SQUAD WILL MOVE"
"TO THE LEFT"
"LEFT TURN"
(Squad Retiring)

RIGHT IN THREE's

"SQUAD WILL RETIRE"
"RIGHT TURN"

"SQUAD WILL ADVANCE"
"LEFT TURN"

"MOVE TO THE LEFT IN THREE's" "ABOUT TURN"

DRILL AND DISCIPLINE

MARCHING AND DRESSING OFF

DIAGRAM OF A SQUAD CORRECTLY DRESSED AND COVERED OFF

REAR
Rank

X   X   X   X

ONE
ARMS
LENGTH

CENTRE
Rank

X   X   X   X

ONE
ARMS
LENGTH

FRONT
Rank

X   X   X ONE ARMS LENGTH X

CHANGING DIRECTION - WHEELING ON THE MARCH

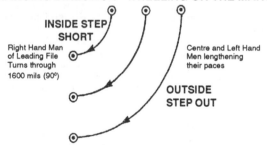

INSIDE STEP SHORT

Right Hand Man of Leading File Turns through 1600 mils (90°)

Centre and Left Hand Men lengthening their paces

OUTSIDE STEP OUT

"STEPPING OUT" and "STEPPING SHORT"

The term "Step Short" means reduce the length of your pace, "Step Out" means slightly lengthen your pace. By doing this while Wheeling you keep your Dressing in each file as it changes direction.

A common fault when giving the "Left or Right Wheel" is for the command to be given sharply, when in fact it should be drawn out - "WHEE-EEL", allowing the files to slowly change direction, keeping their dressing in threes.

23

CUSTOMS and TRADITIONS

The history of the Army goes back a great many years as a result of this many of the traditions that have evolved are still held in great awe and respect by Regiments and Corps. They are closely preserved and at the appropriate time and circumstances brought out for all members of the Regiment or Corps to be reminded of the occasions which are to be commemorated

As a serving soldier you should be fully conversant with all the customs, traditions and practices of your particular Regiment or Corps. Having said that , those of you who are members of amalgamated Regiments and Corps will no doubt be on the receiving end of many new traditions, customs and practices that will be brought forward into the new Regiments and Corps.

These customs, traditions and practices are an important part of the pride that we feel in belonging to a particular Regiment or Corps. It gives us a lot of pleasure to know that we are upholding the spirit of those who have gone before us, it increases our desire to do a good job and in so doing maintains the standard of the Regiment or Corps which we serve.

It would be impossible in this Pocket Book to give you all the Customs and Traditions and include some of the practices of the British Army, and perhaps we would not get it right as there are so many variations to contend with. What we will try and set out in the following pages are some of the generally accepted Traditions and Customs.

Your Regiment or Corps will have established Standing Orders covering a great many of the routine organisational and administrative practices, plus many Standard Operational Procedures (SOP's). In addition your unit will have its own standing orders to control 'local conditions' and operations.

Standing Orders usually cover the following subjects:

Unit Administration.

Duties

Fire Orders

Unit Detention Centre

MT Orders

Health, Medical and Welfare Orders

Financial Orders

Orders for Messes

CUSTOMS AND TRADITIONS

It is your responsibility to make yourself conversant with these orders at all times, not forgetting that they may be changed quite often.

Your Regiment or Corps will have copies of its Regimental or Corps History from its very beginnings up to recent times, again you will be expected to have a good knowledge of the history sufficient to enable you to relate some of the specific battle honours and deeds of the past.

The 'make-up' of the people that form every Regiment or Corps can be roughly divided into three particular groups. Firstly there are the youngsters who have a particular interest in your Regiment or Corps who will be members of the Army Cadet Force or Combined Cadet Forces who will be wearing your cap badge. Like you they are volunteers, they are the future members of your Regiment or Corps and need encouragement and support whenever it is possible.

Secondly, those serving with the colours, either as regular soldiers or as members of the Territorial Army. If serving with their own Battalion or Unit of a Corps they are said to be carrying out Regimental Duty. If employed away from their normal unit for example with a training unit or serving on the staff of another unit then this is termed as being on Extra Regimental Duty.

The third category are those who have served and now left the colours, who hopefully will join their Regimental or Corps Associations, whose members play an important part in the promotion of the Regiment or Corps and are often called upon to assist with the families of the serving members when they are in difficulties. The serving members of many Regiments support their Regimental Associations through the Days Pay Scheme. This is where a days pay is deducted annually and paid into Regimental Association Funds. These funds are mostly used in support of those ex-members of the Regiment who fall on hard times.

It is said that the British Army is the largest "family" in the world, true or false the fact remains that many Regiment and Corps have always drawn their members from a particular County or area of the Country. This has always been one of the strongest traditions and many generations in a family have served in the same Regiment or Corps. It is important that we preserve this family spirit within the Army and must always support any of the three groups of people that make up our Regiment or Corps.

CUSTOMS AND TRADITIONS

THE COLOURS
Colours are blessed in a religious service before being taken into use. When they are "laid up" they are usually returned to a church and become a part of the fabric of that church.

The colours are always held in great reverence and embody the spirit of a Regiment or Corps therefore they are of great importance to the Regiment or Corps.

For their protection they are held in a case, but when paraded are said to be 'un-cased'. They are usually taken on all regimental church parades. In church the colours are placed upon the altar. If a service is held outside a church it is a tradition in some regiments to pile the drums to form an altar and the colours are laid on the piled drums, hence the term drumhead service.

The Queens colour being the senior is always carried on the right, when on a stand or piled on drums or on an altar it appears on the left, but this represents the right of a colour party facing toward the observer.

Except when on display or safely secured in the Officers Mess the colours are always in the custody of a commissioned officer. Colours may not be removed from the Officers Mess without the authority of the Commanding Officer or the Adjutant.

Regimental and Corps Badge
The origins of your Cap Badge will no doubt take you into the realms of your own Regiment or Corps history which you will no doubt have had taught to you during your early training.

REGIMENTAL & CORPS ASSOCIATIONS
You may be familiar with your own Regimental or Corps Association if only through the 'Days Pay Scheme' where you contribute a days pay each year to your Associations funds.

You should be fully aware of the good work carried out by your Association in helping those members of your Regiment or Corps who have fallen on hard times. You should not need reminding that when on leave do take some time out to visit your local Association Branch, as they will always be pleased to see you while you are serving. Keep it in mind, it is always a good idea to know people in your home locality as you may need their help yourself one day.

FITNESS & HEALTH

To become an effective soldier most people who join the army will have to become physically fit. It is one thing to do a jog in PT kit and quite another to march ten miles in boots carrying thirty or forty pounds of equipment and complete an assault course at the end of it. To be realistic, nobody expects you to be as fit as an SAS trooper, but if you are reasonably fit you will get more out of your training and feel much better for it.

Time is generally in short supply for training so most units will suggest that you carry out some fitness training each week in your own time. All you need is the Self Discipline to do it. The following is what you ought to be able to do and make no mistake about it, getting fit hurts.

1. Run 3 miles in boots, lightweight trousers and sweat shirt in less than 29 minutes. If you are reasonably fit you should take between 20 and 24 minutes depending on age. You should do this at least once a week.
2. Complete a full assault course.
3. Jump in to water from a height of 6 feet tread water for two minutes and then swim 100 m.
4. Cover 10 miles, surmount a 6ft wall, jump a 9ft ditch and then carry a man 200m.

You may have decided that this does not apply to you, perhaps because you believe that it only applies to the infantry or perhaps you have a job in the infantry that is not physically demanding. If so, you are mistaken for we are all soldiers first and specialists second. In any case you will find from experience that when you are fit your whole outlook on life changes, you will do more and enjoy more of what you do.

Most of us can find very good reasons why we do not have the time to do fitness training. However when you think about it the excuse is pretty thin you will not make much of a soldier if you don't have the self discipline to keep yourself fit.

The following is a programme which will not get you into an Olympic squad and certainly not into the SAS, but will keep you in trim and will improve your general fitness. Start easily and slowly build up. Remember *'no pain is no good'*, getting fit involves stretching tight muscles, unfortunately this usually hurts, especially when you get up the following morning, no pain means you probably have not been

FITNESS & HEALTH

trying hard enough, reasonable pain in the form of aching muscles the following morning is to be expected, but severe pain may mean something is wrong, so seek advice.

EACH DAY

Carry out some exercises perhaps when you get up in the morning or at a gym at lunch time or in the evening. This should not need to take more than 10 to 20 minutes, but will improve your overall condition. The following is a list of things which you might do in a period of this length. Alter what you do each day to fit in with your normal routine and keep a record of your progress (this is very important, more later).

a. Run a set route which you know the length of, one and a half mile should take you between 10 and 15 minutes depending on your fitness. Make a note of the time you took. Next time you do this try to beat your time. As you get fitter your times should improve, though you will find that the amount you can knock off your time will lessen.

b. Sit ups - sit down, tuck your toes under a convenient position, place your hands behind your head, lay down then sit up, then repeat. Press ups down on your chest, place the feet together with the toes touching the floor, place your hands on the floor by your shoulders. Keeping your body straight push up on your hands then lower your body to the floor, then repeat.

c. Swim for 10 to 15 minutes, more if you can spare it. If you can obtain a set of weights or use a multi-gym at your local Sports Centre, then carry out a sequence of training to improve your upper body strength.

Be sensible about how you start with easily manageable weights and carry out a number of repetitions, counting how many you can do in one minute. Do this three times with a rest of thirty seconds in between, then move on to a different exercise. After a while you should be able to do more repetitions in the same period of time. It is important to carry out a selection of exercises — even if one hurts more than another — to ensure that you develop a general improvement in your muscle tone throughout your body.

RECORD YOUR PROGRESS

However you decide to train keep a record of your progress. For instance write down the time it takes you to run one and a half miles, count the number of press ups you can do in 2 mins. These measurements will always give you something to beat next time and will act as an incentive.

Each *week* complete the Battle Fitness Test.

Each *month complete* a ten mile hike with a pack weighing between 13Kilo (30lbs) and 22Kilo (50 lbs) depending on your own fitness. Do this with a friend or fellow soldier and plan it well in advance. Use it as an opportunity to practice your Map Reading and Navigation skills and also for 'living out' an important new skill for many city dwellers who are not aware of the countryside nor used to walking.

> *"HE WHO HAS HEALTH, HAS HOPE;*
> *HE WHO HAS HOPE, HAS EVERYTHING"*

AIDS AND RELATED SUBJECTS

INTRODUCTION

It would be irresponsible for us to produce this Pocket Book without some reference to this subject which we have kept to basic facts and the most up to date information/guidance that there is available. We do not wish to over react or be taken for prophets of doom .

GENERAL INFORMATION

Infection with the Human Immunodeficiency Virus (HIV) usually results in a severe and as yet irreversible breakdown in the body's defence system. It leaves its victim liable to infections and certain cancers. The body thus affected develops the condition we call AIDS (Acquired Immune Deficiency Syndrome). At present there is NO KNOWN CURE and the majority of people who develop it will eventually die.

Infection is caused by the transfer of the virus in body fluids blood, semen and vaginal secretions. Originally, as the disease was identified in homosexuals, it was considered that homosexual practices were responsible for infection. Later it was realised that infection could be acquired by other means such as blood transfusion or the sharing of needles by drug abusers. Increasing evidence is now showing that the virus is being spread through heterosexual activities with an affected partner, this fact causes great concern in trying to prevent the increasing numbers affected. In the UK over 9000 cases of AIDS have been reported at this date.

After initial infection an individual will be a *silent* HIV carrier for a period of time. It is not known what proportion of HIV carriers will progress to AIDS.

There is no evidence that AIDS is spread by any other means than sexual intercourse, the transfusion of contaminated blood or blood products, the use of contaminated needles and from infected mother to infant.

It is NOT spread by coughing or sneezing, or by sharing washing, eating or drinking facilities, toilet facilities or articles commonly in general use.

There is no evidence of the virus being spread by blood sucking insects such as mosquitoes.

Blood donated under normal circumstances is screened for the virus and if positive is discarded. A significant risk does exist in time of conflict, accident, or if there is a need for blood transfusion in an isolated area of operations. Screening of donated blood cannot be carried out under these extreme situations.

PREVENTION IS BETTER THAN CURE

None of us should need reminding that for any individual member of the Armed Forces where HIV infection or AIDS has been contracted through intravenous drug abuse or homosexual activity, disciplinary action would be taken against them and may well result in them being discharged.

On the other hand should infection be through other circumstances, then the Armed Services would deal with the individual and care for them in the same manner as the National Health Service.

Where soldiers serve in parts of the world known to be at risk, it would be expected in everyone's interest for screening to be carried out through blood tests of those who are returning from an at risk posting.

Screening is not (yet) compulsory for those already in the Armed Services or recruits who join, but any member of the services men or women who may consider themselves to have been at risk should, in their own interest consult their medical officer on a confidential basis to undergo voluntary screening for HIV.

DON'T DIE THROUGH IGNORANCE

The most effective ways of reducing the risk of infection are:
1. By restricting sexual intercourse to only one partner and using a condom.

FITNESS & HEALTH

2. By avoiding sharing ANY device that punctures the skin unless it has been properly sterilised. THIS INCLUDES: TATTOOING, EARPIERCING AND ACUPUNCTURE

DRUG ABUSE

Some misguided soldiers especially the youngest, i.e. recruits; believe that smoking is less addictive than injecting drugs and of course carries less dangers in respect of contaminated needles and the risk of AIDS.

Within the Army the dangers of DRUG ABUSE are quite clear and the risks apart from your health and wellbeing are clearly set out in the beginning of your Pocket Book under the Code of Conduct.

The self discipline required to *JUST SAY NO TO DRUGS* should be well within your capability, if not :

YOUR NOT MUCH OF A SOLDIER — ARE YOU

SYMPTOMS FOLLOWING HIV INFECTION

Some people infected with the virus will initially suffer no symptoms, others may have symptoms, which will be noticed 6 weeks following infection. Its severity varies from a mild illness with fever, sore throat and a non-itchy rash, to a severe illness associated with ulcers and neurological symptoms that require treatment in hospital.

There are several stages in the progression of the illness following the initial bout, which may take anything from 2 to 6 years or even longer to develop.

The collection of symptoms which make up AIDS occur towards the end of the illness and result finally in the persons death.

AIDS is characterised by feeling unwell, with a variety of possible ill-defined symptoms as the virus weakens the body's resistance to a whole range of infections.

A loss of appetite and consequently rapid loss of weight, night sweats and unusual infections especially of the lungs and bowels occur.

In some victims the virus seems to infect the cells in the brain which results in poor coordination and mental instability. It is usually the inability of the persons immune system to deal with the infection by other unusual organisms, and the lack of effective drugs which cause the ultimate demise of the person.

YOURS IS THE RESPONSIBILITY

As already stated homosexuality and drug abuse are contrary to military law. Apart from this military aspect you should now be fully aware of the dire consequences of the medical risks that such activities involve.

You have a responsibility to your unit and in fact your family to be constantly on the alert to those involved in these activities and ensure that it is brought to the notice of the proper authority.

The standards of discipline of the Army and TA are recognised by the public at large and has been well documented elsewhere in this Pocket Book, nevertheless — it is a matter for you as an individual to have the Self Discipline to protect yourself and your family — the choice is yours.

THE SPORTSMAN

A Sportsman is one who:

Plays the game for the games sake.

Plays for the team and not for themselves.

Is a good winner and good looser, i.e. modest in victory and generous in defeat.

Accepts all decisions in a proper spirit.

Is chivalrous towards a defeated opponent.

Is unselfish and always ready to help others to become proficient.

As a spectator applauds good play on both sides.

Never interferes with judges or referees - no matter what the decision.

The above definition although published by the Army Sports Control Board many years ago, is perhaps a poignant reminder of how the services in general and the Army in particular uphold this definition in their sporting activities.

We point out that the term "Sportsman" today applies to both genders, more correctly referred to as "Sportsperson".

FIRST AID

INTRODUCTION

As a British Soldier you have the reputation to cope with any situation no matter what the conditions. This is put to the test when called upon to carry out First Aid . It may be a 'buddy' under active service conditions, a civilian when serving overseas or at home with a member of your own family.

The information in this section must be read with *two hats on* - civilian and soldier. We switch from one to the other with no apologies, after all they both can bleed to death or be saved.

Some standard procedures have now been adopted for the initial treatment of casualties in a peacetime environment and on the battlefield. Obviously it is not possible nor desireable to have the same approach to first aid in a battlefield situation as in a civilian peacetime environment.

In the battlefield you will no doubt be isolated from immediate expert medical advice, be in a dangerous situation or have very little equipment. Therefore your ability to adapt to a given set of circumstances, making use of what help you can get and learning how to improvise will add to your ability to render effective first aid. Your skill in first aid could decide the extent of the casualties injuries and their chance of survival. Many casualties die needlessly between injury and admission to hospital. You must be able to give effective first aid to wounded or injured comrades, but remember — to be of any use as a first aider, you must avoid becoming a casualty yourself.

THE AIMS OF FIRST AID ARE:

To save life.

To prevent the casualty's condition from becoming worse.

PRINCIPLES OF FIRST AID

To assess and treat casualties in the following **A B C D** order of priority as below:

A = Airway   B = Breathing
C = Circulation   D = Disability

FIRST AID

PRIORITIES.
1. Remove danger from the casualty or the casualty from danger.
2. Check each casualty, as you come to them, for :-
    Airway   Breathing   Circulation   Disability
3. Where breathing needs treating do so immediately. Leave all other injuries until you have checked each one for breathing.
4. Return to the most seriously injured casualty.
5. Stop severe bleeding.
6. Immobilize fractures.
7. Cover Burns
8. Reassure the casualty.
9. Treat for shock.
10. Do not delay by treating trivia.
11. Do not be distracted by noisy casualties.
12. Remember to send for help, giving location, number of injured and the seriousness of the injuries.

SHOCK.
Shock kills. It is very important that *'wound shock'* should be recognised quickly and treated as soon as possible. In these cases the use of intravenous fluids can be life saving. In addition, while protecting the casualty from the elements is important, do not overheat, since this will cause the patient to lose more body heat and dehydrate.

RELIEF of PAIN
Morphine and other drugs are available in the field for the relief of pain. However careful treatment of a casualty will often relieve pain before drugs need to be applied. If morphine is available it should

be injected into a muscle, normally in doses of 15mg.
A record of all drugs administered should be kept and in the case of morphine the casualties forehead should be clearly marked with a letter **'M'**.

PRIORITIES for EVACUATION
a. Those with breathing problems.
b. Those whose pulse is more than 100 per minute.
c. Those with open wounds.
d. All others.

FIRST AID

ACTION IN AN EMERGENCY

Before carrying out FIRST AID treatment it is necessary to FIND OUT
WHAT IS WRONG - *"DIAGNOSIS"*.

LISTEN to the story of how it happened - it may help you to work out
what the likely injuries are.

ASK the injured person where it hurts.

LOOK at the injured person and examine him quickly, but
systematically;

LOOK for bleeding to indicate wounds (remember that bleeding may
be from the underneath of the patient).

FEEL the scalp gently for "lumps "and "bumps".

ASK if they can feel their fingers/feet. If they are numb or have no
feeling there is a possibly of spinal injury.

ASK casualty to lift each limb separately. If they cannot move a limb,
run your hand gently along it looking for areas of swelling or
tenderness.

ASK the them to take a breath and cough. If this can be done without
pain it is unlikely there are broken ribs or serious chest injuries.

FEEL gently down the centre of the neck. A tender spot may mean a
broken spine.

DO NOT lift the head or give a drink before examining the casualty.

DO NOT ask the casualty to try and move the head and neck.

DO NOT move him unnecessarily. When examining an injured
person it may be necessary to remove some clothing. Do not do
this without good cause, but do not hesitate to cut clothing if it is
necessary. When you remove clothing always take the clothing off
the sound limb first, then the injured limb.

GENERAL RULES

In carrying out FIRST AID there are some GENERAL RULES, which
are applicable in every case, they are as follows;

REST - it is wise to keep the injured person lying quietly at rest. If the
casualty is in a dangerous or an exposed position, move to safety.

FIRST AID

WARMTH - blankets, coats, etc, should be used to prevent the casualty from becoming chilled. Remember to place blankets under the casualty as well as over.

REASSURANCE - a casualty is always frightened and anxious. Words of comfort by themselves will not help much, but the calm, methodical, gentle handling of the casualty will go a long way to inspire confidence and relieve fear.

FLUIDS - never give fluids until you are sure it is safe to do so, it is better to wait until the casualty has been seen by a doctor. If and when it is safe to do so, water is always acceptable.

ORGANISATION - the efficient first aider will always take charge of the situation, and will organise the patient's treatment.
Bystanders should be sent for the doctor, ambulance etc. In the case of road accidents organise traffic control and prevent further accidents.

SEND FOR MEDICAL AID - When dealing with severely injured casualties send for medics early, move the patient to hospital as quickly as you can. Don't waste time by bringing the doctor to the scene of the accident. The main factor in saving lives and limbs is early surgery. So get casualty to hospital immediately.

EFFECTS OF EXCESSIVE HEAT - If you are not used to very hot weather and are working in the sun or a hot climate heat exhaustion or heat stroke can occur. This is due to the loss of fluid and salt from your body through excessive sweating.

SIGNS AND SYMPTOMS - Casualty is exhausted. Face is pale and cold, and the body is in a clammy sweat. There may be a sudden loss of consciousness. Pulse and breathing rapid. Casualty may complain of headache, dizziness and feeling sick. Sudden movement may cause fainting.

TREATMENT FOR EXHAUSTION

1. Place casualty in cool surroundings.

2. If conscious give cold water to drink and if there is sweating, has cramps or diarrhoea or is being sick, add half a teaspoon of common salt to each pint of water.

3. Obtain medical aid as soon as possible.

FIRST AID

CLEAR AN OBSTRUCTED AIRWAY AT ONCE

If a casualty has: Noisy, bubbling, gasping or whistling breathing or his breathing has ceased or something is tight round his neck or foreign material in the mouth and throat - such as dentures, blood clot, vomit , froth, YOU MUST - remove anything from around the casualty's neck. Remove all foreign material from his mouth and throat with your fingers.

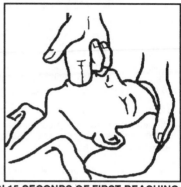

YOU MUST DO THIS WITHIN 15 SECONDS OF FIRST REACHING THE CASUALTY - OR IT WILL BE TOO LATE.

AN UNCONSCIOUS PERSON

If you have a casualty who cannot be roused - clear their airway and place them in the 3/4 prone position. YOU MUST DO THIS WITHIN 20 SECONDS.

3/4 PRONE POSITION.

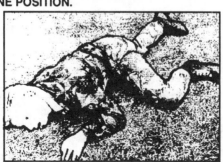

FIRST AID

ARTIFICIAL RESPIRATION - THE KISS OF LIFE.

When a casualty does not have injuries to the nose or mouth or if an airway is obstructed by foreign material in the mouth and throat: **YOU MUST** - Clear the casualty's airway, place on back and loosen clothing at the neck and waist. With one hand, lift the neck slightly. With the other hand on the forehead, tilt the head fully backwards.

Clear Airway

Remove your hand from behind the casualty's neck, using the hand on the forehead to retain the head fully backwards.
Close and seal the mouth with your free hand: take a **DEEP BREATH**, seal your mouth over the nose and blow just hard enough to make the chest rise.

Blow just enough to make chest rise

Remove your mouth from the casualty's nose, release the mouth and allow the chest to fall.
Repeat this mouth to nose procedure every six seconds until normal breathing has resumed or medical help has arrived. If the chest does not rise on blowing into the nose: **CHECK** that the airway is clear and that the head is fully tilted backwards, then proceed as before. If the chest still does not rise, **PINCH** the casualty's nostrils shut, **SEAL** your mouth over the casualty's mouth, **BLOW** into his mouth until the chest rises.
Remove your mouth from the casualty's mouth and allow the chest to fall.
Repeat this procedure every six seconds and continue until normal breathing has resumed or medical aid has arrived.

Watch for chest to fall

Chest not rise - check airway

Repeat every six seconds until breathing starts

FIRST AID

ARTIFICIAL RESPIRATION

HOLGER NEILSON METHOD

If a persons breathing has just
stopped and they have **injuries to
the face and mouth:**
YOU MUST - Clear the casualty's
airway and place them fully prone -
that is on their stomach.
Put their hands one on top of the
other under their chin to stretch it
forward. Kneel down with your knees
almost touching their head, facing
their feet. Place your hands on their
back with the heel of each hand just
below the shoulder blade and the
thumb in line with their spine.
Rock forward and press down,
keeping your arms straight; clasp
their arms just above the elbow and
rock backwards, pulling their arms up
and towards you.
Return their arms to their original
position. Repeat this process every 6
seconds, pausing for 18 seconds
every three minutes until normal
breathing returns or medical aid has
arrived.
Place the casualty in the 3/4 prone
position when normal breathing has returned.

Hands under chin

Rock forwards

Rock backwards

STOPPING BLEEDING and DRESSING WOUNDS.

If a casualty is bleeding from a wound or
wounds on any part of his body. YOU MUST Lie
them down. If they have an injured limb, raise
the limb as high as the comfort of the casualty
will allow. Using a dressing press it firmly over
the wound. If the wound is large, make a pad of
the dressing and press it into the wound at the

Apply dressing

39

FIRST AID

point where the bleeding is worst. Cover any wound completely, using any available dressing. Bind the dressings firmly into place whilst continuing to apply pressure with your hands. If bleeding does not stop, apply further dressings over the first as they become soaked with blood. Press firmly on the new dressing for several (up to 15) minutes and bind them securely into place.
DO NOT REMOVE ANY DRESSING ONCE APPLIED.

TO SPLINT AN ARM

IF a casualty has an obvious broken bone or a large wound of the arm **YOU MUST DRESS ANY WOUND.** Place the casualty's forearm across the body with the elbow at right angles. Retain it in position with an improvised sling. Secure the injured arm to the body by binding a piece of broad material around his chest and over the sling. The arm should be splinted within 5 minutes of you reaching the casualty.

Dress wound

Improvise sling

Secure to body

TO SPLINT A LEG.

If a casualty has an obvious broken or a large wound of the leg. **YOU MUST** dress any wound. **IMMOBILIZE** the casualty. Bring the casualty's legs together gently and place padding in the natural gaps between the legs. Tie the feet and ankles together with a figure of eight bandage, then tie their legs together with further bandages above and below the wound or fracture and above and below the knees. Now select improvised

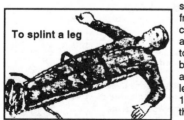

To splint a leg

splints long enough to extend from the lower part of the casualty's chest to the feet and pad them. Tie the splints to the side of the casualty's body with bindings at the ankles, knees and hips. The leg should be splinted within 10 minutes of you reaching the casualty.

FIRST AID

TREATMENT OF BURNS AND SCALDS.

When a burn or scald is sustained the injury must be put into cold water as quickly as possible, preferably under a running tap or stream for TEN MINUTES. A sterile dressing must be applied and bound loosely in place with a bandage. Severe burns and scalds must be seen by a doctor as soon as possible. **Creams and oils must NOT be applied.**

HEAT ILLNESS

During training for your BFT or taking part in exercises you may become a casualty yourself or recognise a buddy who is in difficulties through Heat Illness.

This is always a risk for a soldier who runs in full battle order for any length of time and can occur in quite cool weather conditions.

An NBC suit presents particular problems.

Heat Illness is best prevented by leaving enough skin uncovered for sweat to evaporate.

Leaving the head and forearms uncovered when running will help prevent it.

Any soldier who falls behind on a run or rapid march and is *distressed* should be considered to be suffering from **heat illness.**

The first aid treatment is to remove the casualty to shade, strip them off, sprinkle them with water and then fan them. **ONLY THEN** should they be evacuated.

HYPOTHERMIA or EXPOSURE

HYPOTHERMIA - describes the serious effect which may result from exposure to climatic conditions where the heat content of the body is so reduced to the point where the deep body temperature begins to fall - this is a serious condition. Ignorance of a victims condition can lead to dangerous incorrect treatment. It is not easy to recognise a mild case of exposure, but, just the same very important to do so to avoid a crisis. It is vital to preserve the heat already in the body, but NOT to increase the heat rapidly on the surface of the body.

FIRST AID

SIGNS AND SYMPTOMS.
1. Unexpected behaviour, complaints of coldness and being tired.
2. Physical fatigue - failure to understand questions/instructions.
3. Failure of vision - a usual symptom and serious.
4. Some slurring of speech.
5. Sudden shivering fits.
6. Violent outbursts of unexpected energy, violent language and physical resistance to help.
7. Falling over - stumbling.

Other symptoms may sometimes be muscle cramp, very grey face, dizziness and fainting fits.

TREATMENT - HYPOTHERMIA.
1. Put victim into a sleeping bag or wrap blankets all round body.
2. Put fit companion into sleeping bag with victim or lying close by them.
3. Shelter victim from wind or draught,
4. Get rest of the party to build a shelter.
5. If victim is able to eat, give him sugar in easily digestible form, for example condensed milk.
6. If breathing ceases - perform artificial respiration.
7. When victim recovers he MUST be treated as a STRETCHER CASE, in spite of apparent recovery or protests of being 'all right'.
8. Seek medical aid immediately.

Prevention is better than cure. Better to take action to prevent exposure. Make sure that clothing, including headgear, is windproof and wear it early enough on your journey. Eat small quantities of energy giving food before and while on a expedition such as glucose sweets or Kendal Mint Cake.

WARNING

IT IS A COMBINATION OF CAUSES THAT MAKE YOU VULNERABLE TO THIS DREADED KILLER, WHICH CAN AFFECT YOU IN MANY CIRCUMSTANCES, NOT ONLY IN WILD COUNTRY. SINGLY, THESE CAUSES ARE NOWHERE AS DEADLY, BUT GIVEN THE RIGHT CONDITIONS ALL FOUR "GANG UP" ON THE UNSUSPECTING, WHO RAPIDLY BECOME VICTIMS OF HYPOTHERMIA.
REMEMBER:
COLDNESS + WIND + WETNESS + FATIGUE = HYPOTHERMIA

FIRST AID

FROSTBITE

Frostbite is the freezing or partial freezing of parts of the body, more often than not the extremities of the body, ears fingers toes. If the supply of blood to those parts is sufficient and the tissue keeps warm there is little chance of frostbite. However, if the person is in the early stages of hypothermia, is exhausted or has poor insulating clothing the circulation will drop and parts of the body susceptible to frostbite will cool rapidly. The tissues will freeze and the initial stage of 'frostnip' will show itself in the form of the nose, hands or ears turning white. They must be re-warmed immediately. Feet and hands will feel warm and then cold. This is a sure sign of **'frostnip'** and if not treated will be followed by frostbite.

TREATMENT for 'frostnip'.

Warm affected part on a warm part of the body. Hands warmed under the armpit, ears and nose with hands and feet on the belly of your buddy. Superficial frostbite can be skin deep or surface tissues which are a white/grey colour, frozen on the surface yet soft beneath. Immediate action and the correct treatment can lead to full recovery and no damaged tissue. **Deep frostbite** affects not only the skin, but also the muscles, tendons and bone in a limb. Recovery is a very slow and painful process and **nearly always leads to some loss of tissue or worse.**

TREATMENT - deep frostbite

Introduce warmth to the casualty and maintain the warmth protecting the damaged limb from the weight of blankets etc with some form of rigid support over it, preventing physical damage or contact with the affected limb. Make sure that cooling does not take place. **Immediate evacuation is essential.** If there is any delay treat for exposure, give shelter and continuous warmth.
DO NOT ATTEMPT TO RE-WARM FROST BITTEN PARTS BY EXERCISE OR ANY OTHER MEANS - THIS WILL GIVE THE CASUALTY THE BEST CHANCE OF RECOVERY LATER
Insufficient attention is paid to the relationship between the wind speed and air temperature - the environment in which you are operating. The ambient air temperature combined with the speed of the wind has a very high 'freezing power' for the human body — Wind Chill Factor. Make allowances and take it into consideration if you are looking after a casualty in exposed conditions.

FIRST AID

BULLET WOUND

There will be an entry wound which sometimes cannot be immediately seen and providing the bullet does not lodge in an internal organ or against a bone, there will be a much larger exit wound.

Internal organs, tissue and blood vessels may be damaged during the bullets passage through the body, causing external and internal bleeding.

TREATMENT

1. If available place a large sterile dressing over the wound and apply direct pressure over the area. Place further dressings on the top if blood seeps through.
2. Keep the casualty warm, give them nothing by the mouth until they have been seen by a medics. If unconscious put them in the three quarter prone position. Arrange medical aid.

NOTE. If the injury is in the chest area, do not lie casualty down, prop them in a semi-recumbent position, ensuring that the injured side of the chest is LOWER than the good side to prevent congestion of the sound lung.

APPLICATION OF A FIELD DRESSING

1. To open the dressing, tear the outer cover at the corner indicated by the arrow.

2. Hold the folded ends of the exposed bandages firmly in either hand and gently pull the pad open.

3. Without changing your grip, apply the surface of the pad to the wound. If the wound is bledding very badly press on top of the dressing with the flat of your hand to stop the bleeding.

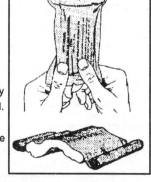

4. Secure the dressing by using the bandage.

FIRST AID

PERSONAL MEDICAL KIT
It is a good idea to have two medical kits, one to carry in your survival kit and is sealed, and a larger version with considerably more items in your Bergen. You can tailor your kits to your own needs and the type of country, climate etc. .

Your Survival Medical Kit
It may consist of the following:
For Minor cuts: antiseptic cream, a roll of heavy duty fabric backed plaster (not assorted waterproof plasters), steri strips to hold together small wounds, micropore tape which is ideal for blisters.
For Gunshot wounds; you'll have your Field Dressing. This is not enough for deep open cuts, its recommended that ordinary tampons (ladies hygiene items) are pressed into the wound and bound into place with a 2" crepe bandage.
For Ailments: pills for colds, headaches, diarrhoea. Beware of antihistamines they can cause drowsiness.. If you are allergic to any drug carry some ID that warns the medics of your allergy.
Instruments: you will require scissors, a scalpel with spare blades and a set of tweezers.

Your Main Medical Kit
As well as the items in your Survival Medical Kit you may require:
Dioralyte - replaces vital salts lost in dehydration, ideal for replacing fluids lost whilst wearing an NBC suit.
Foot Powder or cream. Through experience you should know which is the most suitable for your personal use.
Proplus; to keep you awake and aware, be careful how you use this caffeine product as it plays havoc with your sleep rhythm, but there will be times when there will be no other way to stay awake.
Bradosol, Delaquin or such like for sore throats and mouth infections.
Anti Bacterial Cream for burns, cuts and boils.
Anti Fungal Cream (Canesten) Especially required by the females amongst us.
Insect Repellent and Sunscreen life savers in jungle or desert environments.
Morphine — personal issue in time of conflict.
Magnesium Trisilicate Tablets or any indigestion tablets.
Water Purifying Tablets.

FIRST AID

Your Medical Kit list could be never ending. Most of the items mentioned are easily obtainable from a chemist. In some survival and medical books antibiotics and various other drugs are recommended, we have not mentioned these as they are prescription only medicines.

Remember what you pack is what you carry. In a well organised expedition additional kit like Medics is often split between members of the group.

CASEVAC - THE EVACUATION CHAIN

The diagram below is a rough layout of the Evacuation Chain. This can be varied according to demands and circumstances and is shown for interest.

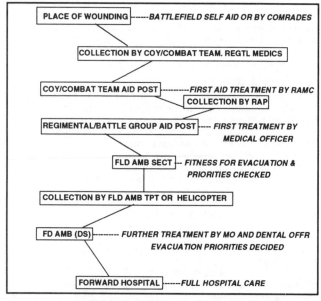

PLACE OF WOUNDING ------*BATTLEFIELD SELF AID OR BY COMRADES*

COLLECTION BY COY/COMBAT TEAM. REGTL MEDICS

COY/COMBAT TEAM AID POST ----------*FIRST AID TREATMENT BY RAMC*

COLLECTION BY RAP

REGIMENTAL/BATTLE GROUP AID POST -----*FIRST TREATMENT BY MEDICAL OFFICER*

FLD AMB SECT --*FITNESS FOR EVACUATION & PRIORITIES CHECKED*

COLLECTION BY FLD AMB TPT OR HELICOPTER

FD AMB (DS) ---------*FURTHER TREATMENT BY MO AND DENTAL OFFR EVACUATION PRIORITIES DECIDED*

FORWARD HOSPITAL ------*FULL HOSPITAL CARE*

NUCLEAR BIOLOGICAL and CHEMICAL WARFARE (NBC)

INTRODUCTION

There is no doubt that the threat posed by NBC weapons in any future conflict is very real. History shows us how effective these weapons can be and although all might agree that their use should be avoided, who can say what a desperate enemy might do.

Weapons of this type have been used for a great deal longer than is usually thought. The soldier who poisoned his enemy's water supply was surely using a form of chemical warfare. Chemicals were used during the First World War and were available; though fortunately not used in the last war. Most people throughout the world will know what happened at Hiroshima and Nagasaki. In recent times Iraq and Iran, in their ongoing Middle East conflict, and the Russians in Afghanistan had resorted to Chemical Warfare.

There is no doubt that the super powers have the capability of both offence and defence in the use of these weapons, but we must always be aware that many of these 'weapons' can be delivered in very small and easily concealed amounts yet have devastating effects upon unsuspecting forces and or civilian targets. However, our policy has always been to only have a defensive capability.

You are trained to use your **Individual Protection Equipment (IPE)**, which protects you - to some extent - from the hazards of these weapons. If you are to survive in this environment you will need to be well practised in the various individual survival drills. The pamphlet called SURVIVE TO FIGHT which you were issued with when you joined gives you all the drills and skills.

The following notes are of general interest and information on the subject.

These weapons will kill you if they get into your body.

They can get through your skin - ABSORPTION -.

Through your mouth - INGESTION, and by breathing -INHALATION.

To survive you must block these routes of entry.

47

NBC

NBC INDIVIDUAL PROTECTION EQUIPMENT (IPE)

The following is a list of the equipment in your IPE.
You must learn to recognise the items, become proficient in their use, wear them and know your respirator drill.
Respirator, Haversack, Canister and anti-dimming outfit. Detector Paper No 2 (1 Colour). DKP1 pad and DKP2 powder.
NAPS tablets (Nerve Agent Pre-treatment Tablet Set).
NBC suit. NBC overboots. NBC gloves -inner and outer.
If you wear spectacles, a pair of respirator spectacles.

NBC DEFENCE RESPONSIBILITIES

Individual.
You must be proficient in all the individual NBC drills.
Commanders are responsible for;
Preparation and testing of NBC defence clothing, equipment, etc.
Posting NBC sentries.
Detecting and reporting NBC attacks.
Warning troops of local NBC hazards.
Surveying, marking and monitoring NBC contaminated areas, vehicles and equipment.
Decontamination of pers, veh, equip and stores.
Control movement in and out of contaminated areas.
Maintain radiation exposure states for own sub-unit.
Passage of NBC information up and down the chain of command and if ordered to flanking units.
All Platoons should ensure that chemical detector paper is deployed throughout their platoon areas.

NBC THREAT STATE

NBC States of Readiness, are used to control NBC defence measures. They are as follows:-
a. LOW — Carry all kit and have it available for immediate use.
b. MEDIUM — NBC suits worn. Collective protection erected and tested. All eqpt under cover. Observe the chemical safety rule.
c. HIGH — Full protection less respirator. Activate collective protection systems.
d. BLACK — Full Protection. Changes in NBC states - These can be raised by any commander.
State BLACK can only be relaxed by the initiating commander.

NBC

COLLECTIVE PROTECTION

As much collective protection must be arranged as possible prior to NBC MEDIUM. Collective protection at company level will include areas for the storage of equipment, large packs, vehicles, ammunition, casualties, personnel. This can take any or all of the following forms. Buildings. Overhead cover to trenches. Tarpaulins. Plastic sheets.

NBC STANDARD DEFENCE DRILLS

CHEMICAL DRILLS

1. THE CHEMICAL SAFETY RULE

All personnel must obey the following rule instantly.

IF YOU ARE:-

a. Subjected to ANY bombardment.

b. Sight hostile aircraft or unidentified low flying aircraft.

c. Observe suspicious, MIST, SMOKE, SMELLS, LIQUID (droplets or splashes), or have SYMPTOMS - see below.

d. Hear the chemical alarm - banging together of two metal objects.

2. CHEMICAL IA, YOU MUST:-

Assume presence of chemical agents and carry out the CHEMICAL IA -Immediate Action Drill as follows:-

Putting on Respirator - (You have nine seconds)

a. STOP BREATHING,

b. CLOSE YOUR EYES.

c. TURN YOUR BACK TO THE WIND.

d. PUT ON YOUR RESPIRATOR. (lean forward with head bent forward, blow out hard, shout GAS,GAS,GAS).

e. CHECK THE ADJUSTMENT OF THE HOOD AND CLOTHING.

f. CHECK THE DETECTOR PAPER AND LOOK FOR OTHER INDICATIONS OF A LIQUID ATTACK.

"Be in time , mask in nine"

3. NOTES. General symptoms of chemical agents are:-

Dimness of vision, difficult to focus on close objects. Irritation of the eyes. Sudden headaches. Tightness of the chest. Running nose. Intense salivation (wet mouth).

Detector paper colour changes are:-

1. One colour paper - NERVE and BLISTER changes BLUE

2. Two colour paper -

    NON PERSISTENT NERVE - YELLOW
    PERSISTENT NERVE - GREEN
    BLISTER - RED

4. IMMEDIATE DECONTAMINATION DRILL

If a liquid attack has taken place, seek cover or wait until the liquid
ceases to fall if no cover is available, then carry out the Immediate
Decontamination drill (ID Drill).
a. The sequence of decontamination. BLOT - BANG - RUB.
b. Prepare DKP No 1.
c. STOP BREATHING, CLOSE EYES, REMOVE RESPIRATOR,
   DECONTAMINATE THE FACE,
   NECK, EARS, HEAD, AND INSIDE THE RESPIRATOR
   FACEPIECE. Replace the respirator
   as often as necessary blowing out hard each time.
d. DECONTAMINATE THE OUTSIDE OF THE RESPIRATOR AND
   HARNESS.
e. REPLACE THE HOOD
f. DECONTAMINATE INSIDE STEEL HELMET AND CHIN STRAP.
g. TEAR OPEN DKP No1 AND DECONTAMINATE BOOTS WITH
   CONTENTS.
CANISTER DAMAGE - if dented change with spare. Replace spare.

CHEMICAL REPORTING

All sentries are responsible for chemical alarms. They must also be
able to recognise when chemical agents are present and give the
alarm. In addition they must also know the IA drill and how to use the
detectors. The sentry must make the following observations and pass
to CSO as soon as possible.
a. Time of attack and duration.
b. Location of attack.
c. Means of delivery.
d. Type of agent.

NUCLEAR DRILLS
EFFECTS OF NUCLEAR EXPLOSION
1. FLASH.
2. HEAT.
3. THE NOISE-EXPLOSION.
4. PRESSURE WAVE.
5. IMMEDIATE RADIATION.
6. FALLOUT.
7. ELECTRO MAGNETIC PHENOMENON. (EMP).

NBC

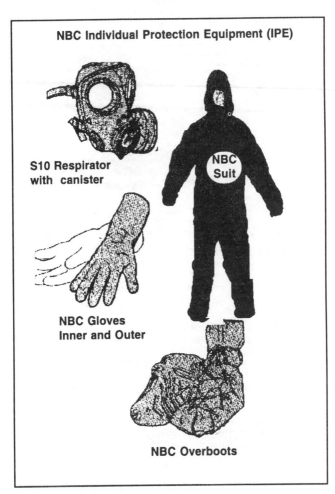

NBC Individual Protection Equipment (IPE)

S10 Respirator
with canister

NBC Gloves
Inner and Outer

NBC
Suit

NBC Overboots

NBC

NBC Individual Protection Equipment

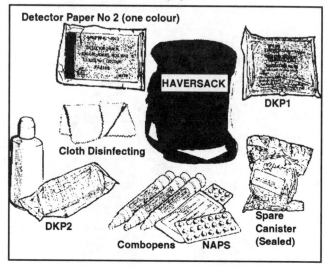

Detector Paper No 2 (one colour)

HAVERSACK

DKP1

Cloth Disinfecting

DKP2

Combopens   NAPS

Spare Canister (Sealed)

THE IA DRILL - NUCLEAR

a. ON SENSING THE FLASH - CLOSE YOUR EYES AND KEEP THEM CLOSED.
b. FALL FLAT, FACE DOWN WITH HANDS UNDER THE BODY.
c. STAY DOWN UNTIL ALL THE EFFECTS HAVE PASSED.
This will give some protection against the immediate effects.

On receipt of a FALLOUT warning.
a. COVER ALL EXPOSED SKIN.
b. PLACE PROTECTIVE COVERS OVER EQUIPMENT.
c. SHUT ALL OPENINGS TO SHELTERS AND BUILDINGS.
d. TAKE COVER.

NBC

After FALLOUT.
a. STAY UNDER COVER UNTIL YOU ARE TOLD TO MOVE.
b. KEEP SKIN COVERED.
c. COVER UP CUTS AND WOUNDS.

Moving in a FALLOUT area
a. WEAR PROTECTIVE CLOTHING.
b. NO EATING, SMOKING, OR DRINKING.
c. KEEP HANDS AWAY FROM MOUTH.
d. AVOID STIRRING UP DUST, BRUSHING AGAINST HEDGES
   ETC.
e. WEAR RESPIRATOR.
f. DO NOT KNEEL, SIT OR LIE ON THE GROUND.
g. KEEP A CHECK ON DOSIMETER READINGS.

NUCLEAR REPORTING

Report all nuclear explosions so that nearby units can be warned and fallout paths predicted and monitored.

Report the following:-
a. The time between the flash and the bang.
b. The width of the cloud in degrees or mils 5 mins after the bang.
c. Type of burst (Air, Surface or Subsurface).
d. Time of the burst.
e. The bearing of the burst.
f. Position of the observer.
g. The angle of the cloud top or bottom 10 mins after the bang.

DETECTION

After an attack or the warning that an attack has taken place sentries and observers should deploy to vantage points upwind of the coy position.
Contamination Control - Limit of spread.
a. Movement of pers and eqpt.
b. CASEVAC.
c. Back loading of vehicles and eqpt that may be contaminated.
d. Resupply.

Marking Contaminated Areas

a. The nature of the contamination is to be indicated by the colour of the signs. These include;

(1) Primary colour for both sides of the sign.

(2) Secondary colour for additional markings.

b. **These colours are:**

DANGER	PRIMARY		SECONDARY	
	Markings		**Inscriptions**	
Radiation	White		None	Black
Biological	Blue		None	Red
Chemical	Yellow		None	Red
Chemical (Mines)	Red		Yellow (stripe)	Yellow

c. SIZE AND SHAPE OF SIGNS

1. The signs will be in the form of a right angled isosceles triangle, made of some adequate material.
2. The type of contamination is to be written on each sign, stating if persistent or non-persistent, the type of agent used, the date and time detected.
3. In the case of radiological contamination the following is to be inserted on each sign:-
a. The dose rate.
b. Date and time of reading.
c. Date and time of detonation if known.
4. Positioning of signs. The signs should be mounted above ground level with apex downwards and the front of the sign facing away from the contaminated area, or the area with the highest dose rate or contamination.

ADVENTURE TRAINING

INTRODUCTION

This subject is often used as a part of recreational training when you might find it called "Adventure Training", canoeing, abseiling, white water rafting, climbing, and many other outdoor activities come under this umbrella.

It is one of the best recognised methods of bringing individuals together giving them experience in learning to plan, organise, carry out instructions, some simple others complicated. Very often under contrived, stressful and physical conditions.

Individuals given tasks for their team learn how to motivate them, give orders, seeing that they are followed through to their logical conclusion.

It tests attitudes in accepting orders, and the spirit in which they are carried out. Finds out those who make a decision and stick to it. Highlights the example they are setting, how others judge their contribution to achieving the tasks set.

Gives an indication - it might be you, of who has any of the characteristics required to get their foot on the bottom rung of the promotion ladder.

It is considered to be an enjoyable, yet important aspect of military training and development of the individual.

The importance is because it brings into practical use so many of the other skills and training that you will have already been taught.

THE COUNTRY CODE.

Taking part in activities in the UK will inevitably involve you in moving over parts of the country that are not Military Training Areas, but land to which the public have access or perhaps privately owned land.

This will require you to observe the normal courtesy expected when in contact with the public or moving over other peoples private property.

The MOD have a well recognised conservation policy. We must all try and preserve the natural beauty of our countryside and the wildlife living there. If we don't then areas of the country will not be available for us or the public to enjoy.

We remind you of the COUNTRY CODE is a series of ten rules based on common sense - and common failings as illustrated over page.

ADVENTURE TRAINING

THE COUNTRY CODE

KEEP TO THE FOOTPATHS

SAFEGUARD WATER SUPPLIES

PROTECT ALL WILD LIFE

KEEP DOGS UNDER PROPER CONTROL

LEAVE NO LITTER

SECURELY FASTEN ALL GATES

GUARD AGAINST THE RISK OF FIRE

USE GATES AND STILES

GO CAREFULLY ON COUNTRY ROADS

RESPECT THE PEOPLE AND LIFE OF THE COUNTRYSIDE

ADVENTURE TRAINING

The Country Code applies to everyone who uses the countryside no matter what time of the year, there is no need to break it, lack of thought and care can cause untold trouble and prevent you and others from using a landowners ground.

Currently, farmers in the UK are facing serious financial losses due to their animals being killed by eating the metal ring fasteners from tins of drinks, condoms disposed of thoughtlessly, and litter dumped in the countryside. No better slogan can be used in this respect than;

"YOU LEAVE NOTHING BUT YOUR FOOTPRINTS"

DISCIPLINES OF PERSONAL HEALTH and HYGIENE
HOW TO WALK — FEET and BOOTS

You only get one pair of feet, therefore they are worth looking after. Some of you may have had the experience of sore feet through badly fitting shoes, or maybe you have in the past worn a pair of trainers and developed *floppy civie feet*.

Your feet do need support, and when it comes to BOOTS then it is more important than ever that you are comfortable in them and that they give you the correct support .

Should you get your boots wet, they should be dried out naturally not over or close to heat. Stuff them with paper to draw out the damp, changing it often.

Leather boots dried by heat will go hard and crack, making them unserviceable.

FITTING BOOTS

When you require a new pair of boots take a *thick pair of socks* with you or two pairs of normal socks to wear when trying on your boots. Make sure you can wiggle your toes and they must not be touching the toe of the boot.

A method of testing the fitting is to be able to get a finger down between your heel and the back of the boot, if you can do this and your toes just touch the toe of the boot that is a good fit.

Fully lace up the boot to check that the uppers have enough room for your foot and that it's comfortable.

Remember, your feet have some of the most delicate bones in your body they need protection.

Your issue boots are of a good quality and you will appreciate that

well fitting shoes or boots for your personal use is a wise
investment, not only will they last longer, but will protect your feet
and prevent problems later on in your life.

If you are to take part in any expeditions etc., and get the most out
of it, make sure that your boots are in a good and serviceable
condition.

CARE OF YOUR FEET

To go with you boots you need clean, well fitting woollen socks,
without holes in them and a similar spare pair in your pack, plus a
darning needle and wool to mend them if required.

Woollen socks ventilate your feet and keep them happy. Always
remember that the extra weight you carry on your back is equivalent
to more than three times the same weight on each foot.

Your balance is more critical and therefore you have to adjust to a
different 'gait' with the weight of your body transferred onto the flat
part of your foot rather than your heel. This will become more
apparent when you carry all your kit on your back.

Don't halt for more than five minutes or your muscles will stiffen up.

BLISTERS

You can help to prevent blisters - as already stated if your boots are
well fitting and "broken in", you are wearing well fitting woollen socks.
You need to harden the skin on your feet. This can be helped by
rubbing them with surgical spirit during your training and preparation
period well before any planned long
expedition.

Every morning when on a march dust your
feet with an anti-fungal foot powder. The
main thing is to keep them clean and
change your socks as often as is practical
to do so.

Wash your feet every night, preferably in
hot salted water - if you can get it - rub
them **DRY** and check your toe nails that
they are cut reasonably close.

Never soak your feet when on the march,
wash them if you wish — quickly and dry
them well, changing socks from one foot to
the other.

SEVERE BLISTER
DRESSING

ADVENTURE TRAINING

Should you experience any discomfort, it is as well to immediately examine them. If a blister has formed, initially cover it with a broad plaster.

TREATMENT of BLISTERS

If a blister has formed improvise a ring plaster which serves to keep the direct pressure off the blister and given time the fluid will be absorbed back into the blood stream. However, if the blister is enlarged *through not treating it early enough*, then it will be necessary to open it to drain the fluid. It should be opened in the right way, so that the skin is not rubbed off and becomes infected.

RING PLASTER DRESSING

Sterilize a needle by holding it in the flame of a match. When it has cooled, prick the blister, not directly, but through the skin at the side, and gently press out the fluid until the blister is flat.
Cover it with a small sterilized dressing secured by two strips of plaster crossing over it. A raw blister would be treated with a dressing adding a smear of antiseptic cream to the raw blister

WET FEET

Should you get your feet wet, if possible dry them and your boots, putting on fresh socks, do not "march to dry them" it will make your skin tender which will then rub off, and you will then become a casualty.
This stresses the fact that you must always carry spare pairs of clean woollen socks.

WATER SHORTAGE

There may be a shortage of water and a requirement to ration it carefully. Should water not be available for any long period and then you have plenty of it, be careful, sip it slowly, to prevent stomach cramps
If you drink ALL the water you are carrying, you may not be able to replace it for some time. To be without it would be courting disaster if an emergency situation came up.
Never try to satisfy thirst by swallowing snow or ice; melt it first by heating it in the mouth - if no fire is available.
It is best to eat a biscuit or something with it as snow or iced water is bad for the stomach. Always treat water with purification tablets if it

ADVENTURE TRAINING

is from a 'foreign' source, i.e., not part of rations drop. If tablets are not available, then boil water for at least three minutes before drinking.

CRAMP

If you have been walking for a long period, without any warning you may get "CRAMPS", this is very painful spasm in your leg muscles which are best treated by massage, which after a few minutes relieves the pain.

THIRST

In hot weather, after the first few hours on a march you may find that you develop a great thirst, not caused by your stomach's demand for water, but by your mouth feeling parched.

The immediate thought is to drink more water, but this is not the answer. It is better to chew a piece of grass, or carrying a non-absorbent pebble in the mouth; a much better thirst-quencher is to suck a prune or carry a bit of raw onion in the mouth.

You can go on a long time without drinking at all if you have an onion with you and it helps to prevent your lips from cracking.

DANGER OF ALCOHOL

The consumption of alcohol in any form increases the rate at which your heart beats, thus increasing the flow of blood through the body, it follows that during cold weather veins near the skin surface cool at a quicker rate, thus increasing the speed at which exposure (hypothermia) may set in.

Another disastrous affect of alcohol is that it slows down your reactions and impairs your thinking, this could only lead to a disaster.

CLOTHING & EQUIPMENT

You are never certain what sort of weather you may be faced with in the UK, in a matter of an hour it can change from bright warm sun to a cold damp wind and rain.

This makes it difficult to be dressed in the right gear.

If we remember that what ever we wear needs to:-

      " **Keep water out** " - keep our body heat in. "

Allowing any water vapour to escape.

ADVENTURE TRAINING

COMBAT JACKET/ANORAK

If your Combat Jacket/Anorak lets in water, your pullover, shirt and under clothing will get wet/damp. Wet clothing will not insulate your body, in fact it will help it cool quicker, as a result your chances of becoming a casualty through Hypothermia increases.

The answer is to have a fully waterproof Combat Jacket/Anorak, but if you did it would be too hot because your body heat cannot evaporate, which in turn would produce condensation making your clothes wet !!

Fortunately modern materials are now available that are fairly waterproof and at the same time do allow your body to breathe.

This material is called GORTEX, it is expensive, but if you want to save up for anything - save up for a GORTEX Anorak.

Another useful waterproof outer garment is a CAGOULE, this is ideal for wet weather and has a ventilated yoke at the back. It packs into a very small space, and can be neatly rolled on top of your kit for quick access.

SHIRTS and UNDERWEAR

On an Expedition it is always advisable to wear clothing made of wool, as this has the best insulating/breathing properties.

Many of you will not normally wear a vest, but we assure you that it is good advice to do so "when out on the hills", it is easy to take it off and "prevention is better than a cure"

BALACLAVA - WOOL HAT

One third of our body heat is lost from our heads, therefore it is very good sense to cover our heads.

The easiest garment is a BALACLAVA hat which can be pulled well down over your ears if it is very cold.

A SKI hat would be ideal, but not so practical and makes it a great deal more difficult to hear.

PERSONAL KIT LIST

Wear your personal Combat Jacket and kit as issued.
A wool cap comforter. Underclothes - loose fitting for good insulation.
To be carried on you personally:-
Map. Compass. Pathfinder Protractor/Romer. Whistle on lanyard.
Matches in a waterproof container. Elastic adhesive dressings.

ADVENTURE TRAINING

Pencil and notebook. Small personal first aid kit.
Packed in your Ruck Sack:-
Mess Tins with knife, fork & spoon, plus reserve food such as raisins, chocolate, Kendal Mint Cake.
Mug - metal preferred - plastic would do, but it cannot be heated up!. A water bottle with secure top. Towel and washing kit.
Groundsheet and a Length of strong string.
Spare pair of thick wool socks. Small Torch. Survival bag or blanket. A sleeping bag liner.
In a kit bag or equivalent to be delivered to camp site -
Two blankets or a sleeping bag. Spare change of clothing. Spare boots/shoes if available. Gym shoes or light weight trainers. Wool Pullover. Six blanket pins.

HILL WALKING SKILLS

Any walk over a reasonable period of time requires you to have a rhythm in the way you walk. This is especially so when HILL WALKING and carrying a heavy rucksack. You should start out at a speed that you feel capable of keeping up for at least a few hours. While walking you should be able to talk or sing, if you cannot due to being short of breath, then you are walking too fast.
To get to the top or where you planned to stop for a "bite", means that you must keep going, if you keep stopping it will break your rhythm. The best way it to have a slow, plodding pace, it will get you there without undue effort. If you use too much effort it will make you overheat and sweat, making your clothes wet and dehydrate you.So if you are wise; conserve your energy, stay in good condition, not getting tired , too hot or too cold.
Climbing a hill
If you place you feet properly when going up hill it will prevent your calf muscles from aching.

This is mainly caused by pointing your feet directly up the hill, which puts strain on your calf muscles and Achilles tendon.
Walk in a "zig-zag" fashion across the slope, your feet will be happier, being in full contact with the ground , with less chance of slipping, this may be slightly further, but far less tiring.

| WRONG | RIGHT |

ADVENTURE TRAINING

Going down a hill
You don't need telling that running down a hill can be dangerous and

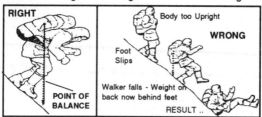

tiring. When descending a slope carrying a full rucksack it requires
some skill to do it safely. It is a matter of confidence and adopting the
right attitude to tackling a decent.
Your balance plays a great part, important to remember is bend
both knees and lean well forward.
By adopting this stance your legs act as springs and absorb the
shaking-up your body would have had.
NEVER attempt to slide down a hill — it will end in disaster as you
cannot control yourself.
If you descend by traversing across the slope, keep your hand on
the uphill side and near to the ground for support should you slip.
Keep off any slopes with loose stones or scree, and if any slope
frightens you too much — find another way down.

Crossing rivers or streams.

Never attempt to cross a river or mountain stream in flood. Water is
very powerful and easy to under estimate its force. It may often be
reasonable to cross streams or small rivers, but , if you do so in your
boots you will regret it, better to take them off first, not forgetting your
socks!.

PACKING YOUR RUCKSACK

As a part of your preparation for any expedition/exercise the
planning of what is to be taken and who takes what is essential.
There is no point in needless duplication of many items, which will
give you spare carrying capacity across the group.
Packing your RUCKSACK correctly can make or break your comfort
on a journey.

ADVENTURE TRAINING

The type of RUCKSACK and capacity you are able to use can make all the difference to the way you pack it.

If it does not have a frame that fits the shape of your body, you will have to be careful not to overload it. The reason being that in trying to pack everything into it you may have hard or odd shaped items that will stick into your back when carrying it. The emphasis is on packing "into" the Rucksack - not hanging boots or other odd items on the outside until you look like a Christmas tree on the move.

Pay attention to LOAD CARRYING and the DISTRIBUTION of the load as illustrated in the diagrams at the bottom of the page.

Practice PACKING and LOAD DISTRIBUTION then wear/carry it to ensure that it is comfortable to carry on a journey.

LOAD CARRYING - the RIGHT and WRONG methods

ADVENTURE TRAINING

Stove Fuel should be packed in a well sealed polythene bag stored well away from rations.
All clothing and your sleeping bag should also be kept in polythene bags and the **rucksack itself** would benefit from a strong quality polythene bag as a liner.

CHOOSING A CAMP SITE - in the first place you will have to get permission if you are to camp on private land or in fact any area that you might think of using. It is only good manners and common courtesy to ask permission to use someone's property.
Make sure that is carried out as part of your pre-expedition

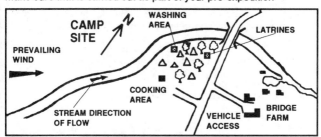

preparation, and you are positive that permission has been given before you arrive to set up camp for the night.
An ideal site, is one offering shelter from prevailing wind, on well drained fairly level soil, facing East to catch the early morning sun.
It should be as far away as possible from any houses, be close to a good clean water supply, be in the open, and not directly under trees.

CAMP SITE LAYOUT

Having chosen a suitable site, the following points should be considered and then if satisfactory, the camp should be laid out in accordance with the following

SAFETY FIRST - is it safe?

1. Is the site below the level of a river, lake, dam or reservoir, whose banks could burst or overflow in the event of a severe storm, or in a dried-up stream which "comes to life "in a storm.

ADVENTURE TRAINING

2. Is the site under overhanging rocks or cliffs.
3. Ensure that the ground does not slope down from the bivi area to where the fire or cooking area is set out, and that the tents are not close enough to be a fire risk.
4. Ensure ground is safe for cooking, heat radiating down through leaf-mould or peat can spread undetected fire many hours later.

CAMP LAYOUT

a. Can the Tents/bivi's be correctly pitched in the area and sheltered from the wind and not under trees.
b. If a platoon or section camp, a COOKING AREA properly set out for the purpose to be conveniently close to the bivi's, but again, not too close in case of fire risk.
c. Latrine/washing area defined and sited down wind and away from tent site and cooking area and afforded some privacy.
d. Where there is running water, a drinking water point upstream from a washing water point.
e. Some access for a vehicle if possible.

LATRINES

One of our normal, everyday occurrences is the use of a latrine, you sit in solitary confinement, with the door secure, not disturbed and very often in a cosy situation, with a chain or handle as the final act of the operation.

It's not quite so civilised living in the field, but there are a few important things to remember. **Hygiene;** in spite of being "in the field" you have to exercise more care in your personal hygiene, especially washing your hands before handling food

The digging of a hole in the ground is essential as any exposed excrement will attract flies who then can quickly spread disease.

The whole idea of this might not be to your liking, but the alternative could lead to a disaster with everyone going down with a serious illness.

ADVENTURE TRAINING

CONSTRUCTION OF A FIELD LATRINE

You must make provision for a latrine by digging a hole not less
than 44cm (one foot six inches) deep.
Some form of seat or bar if time permits the making of it.
The earth taken from the hole is piled up ready to be used by each
individual to cover their excrement, and finally to fill the hole before
leaving the site. All ground used in this way must be marked with a
sign 'Soiled Ground'.
In an operational situation it may not be possible, nor in some
instances desirable, but living in a "bivi site", in the open air, it must
be recognised that privacy is important to every individual, therefore
some form of screen or concealment is desirable and a simple
method introduced to effect some form of control.
If you are an NCO in this situation, the most simple form of
"discipline" is to have a small portable container which holds the toilet
paper (and keeps it dry), left in a prominent position. ALL those when
using the toilet take the container with them - remembering **to return
it after use**.
The message - when the toilet is "engaged" the container is not
there, simple, and effective.

PERSONAL HYGIENE

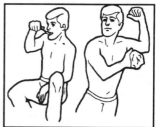

This would appear to be of low
priority when you are in the field,
yet the reverse is the fact.
It requires considerable self
discipline to maintain a high
standard of personal cleanliness
when "living in the field". **Strict
Routines** and personal discipline
are essential if you are to
maintain your health and energy,
and keep friends.

WASHING

Regular washing and drying of all parts of your body with soap and
water - even if it is cold water.
Particular attention should be given to those parts which collect
sweat, such as armpits, crotch area, the waist and feet.

ADVENTURE TRAINING

Dirty hair can harbour lice and cause skin diseases. Teeth and gums must be brushed properly every day with tooth paste (or salt as a substitute) to avoid decay, clean and dry your tooth brush and keep it in a special holder

Take care of your washing kit, keep your towel clean and dry.
Use a container for your soap to keep it dry and not waste it.
They are best kept in a plastic bag to help keep them clean and dry.
Wash out your underclothes and socks (weather and time permitting) clean socks and pants are essential to have spares of at all times.

PREPARING FOOD IN THE FIELD

During cold weather, it is essential to stop and "brew-up" for the whole group on an expedition.

Once you get into a camp site, one of the first duties to be performed must be to "brew-up", it boosts morale and gets the group working.
Your body needs well cooked, hot food to sustain it.
There is no excuse to eat food out of a tin not having cooked it.

COOKERS

You may use butane gas cookers, or more probably 'tommy cookers' which use small blocks of solid fuel in a folding tin container.
They are best used by scraping a hole in the ground to keep any draughts away to prevent them being blown out.
The hole needs to be deep enough to shield your mess tins when they are on the 'tommy cooker' to prevent cooling.

OPEN FIRES

The problem of cooking on an open fire is not so much the actual cooking, but finding a place where you can safely light a fire.
You will be aware of the dangers of fires in the countryside, where woods, forests and crops can be destroyed, causing untold damage taking years to replace. Therefore UK landowners are not at all keen to give you permission and the Forestry Commission strictly forbid fires on land that they look after. The warmth of a fire, the thought of hot, well cooked food is something to look forward to on an exercise, especially if the weather has been bad and you are wet through and cold!!, in which case you will certainly have to know how to produce hot - good food on an open fire.

ADVENTURE TRAINING

STRICT RULES TO BE OBEYED

In the UK you will only light a fire for cooking when it is cleared with
the landowner or when authority has been obtained by your unit and
you are on a recognised and organised exercise - not something you
have set up between yourselves.

You will observe all safety rules - cooking area away from bivi's or
any other fire hazards.

That all fires are out before going to sleep.

BUILDING a "COOKING FIRE"

If you rake together a pile of leaves, cover it "higgledy-piggledy"
with dead twigs and fallen branches off the trees, and set a match to
it, you will have a roaring fire that apart from being useless to cook
on, will be a serious danger, as well as letting everyone know
exactly where you are.

If you are to have good meals cooked in the field and wish to save
time and "hassle", you must learn how to produce a quick, hot little
fire that will boil water in a jiffy, and that will soon burn down to HOT
EMBERS with no smoke.

To light this type of fire you need small dry twigs, that will blaze up
quickly and give you the heat to burn larger twigs and set your fire
going to give you the correct hot bed of embers for cooking.

It is as well to remember that all trees are, in some sense, in the
process of dying, and upon any tree it is possible to find dead twigs
and sometimes dead branches.

Even in the wettest weather dead wood from a tree or hedge row
will be found to be dry inside and easily lit.

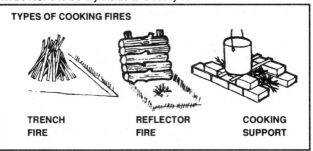

TYPES OF COOKING FIRES

| TRENCH FIRE | REFLECTOR FIRE | COOKING SUPPORT |

If you build a fire on grass, carefully cut and remove the turf and soil, keep it to one side.

When you move out, clean out the fire ashes, water the ground well - make sure it is **not still warm** - replace the soil and turf.

Leave no litter behind you, ensure that the whole camp site has no trace of anyone being there. If you do this you will have no problems if you want to use the site again.

MESS TIN COOKING

Mess Tin cooking is usually carried out with two of you "teaming up", as a small fire or cooker is very efficient in producing hot food for two.

To build a small cooking fire, look for a "rut" made by vehicles in soft ground, or make a "scrape" in the ground, see the diagram at the bottom of the page

It needs to be deep enough to light a small fire that will quickly burn down to embers, at the same time rest your mess tin below the surface of the ground on the embers.

If you are able to do so, have your "scrape" with the breeze blowing through its length, this will keep the embers glowing, giving you a gentle heat — the best possible heat to cook on.

The points to remember are :-

Check the direction of the wind, make a small trench in the ground about the size of your mess tin and six inches deep, with one end facing the wind.

The draught will blow along the length of your "trench" and help to keep the fire alive.

Build up a fire with plenty of **dead wood**, let it burn until all the smoke has disappeared, the trench filled level with the ground with hot embers.

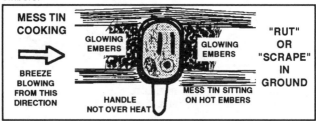

MESS TIN COOKING — BREEZE BLOWING FROM THIS DIRECTION — GLOWING EMBERS — GLOWING EMBERS — "RUT" OR "SCRAPE" IN GROUND — HANDLE NOT OVER HEAT — MESS TIN SITTING ON HOT EMBERS

ADVENTURE TRAINING

GET ORGANISED

The deep - hot ashes do not smoke, never cook on a fire with a lot of smoke, it makes hard work in cleaning your mess tins.
The heat is gentle - not so likely to burn your food and without smoke much more pleasant to work with.
Without any system or thought of getting properly organised to do this simple job, you will waste an hour messing about over a smoky fire, getting your eyebrows singed, finishing up with a 'burnt offering' for your meal.
Prepare your food while the fire is settling down - don't sit there watching it burn.
Make maximum use of the heat once it is the correct fire to use. Put a mess tin of water on while you are eating to make a hot drink, at the same time provide the hot water to wash your mess tins.
The use of cooking foil on an open fire is very efficient, by wrapping the food in foil and then raking the hot embers over the top of the wrapped food. Baked potatoes (in their jackets) are good cooked like this and also banana splits.

SAFETY

You will now realise there is no need to light a "bonfire" to cook in the field.
The last word on this must be to stress the need for safety precautions at all times and we repeat, keep fires well away from bivi's and be sure the fires are out before settling down to sleep for the night.
Should you set up a camp site for a section or platoon , then you may need a larger fire - or several small ones to cook with, the same principles apply, removing the turf and replacing it, **and watering it well when clearing the camp site etc.**

POST EXPEDITION ADMIN

Returning from any exercise, when you are tired, exhausted, cold hungary there is work to be done - then not later.
Kit to checked for damage (fair ware and tear excepted), losses to be accounted for if someone has been careless.
Equipment to cleaned and check. Tents, sleeping bags, clothing cleaned, hung up to dry,preventing costly damage or replacement.
Spare rations, other stores to check, sorted and hand in

ADVENTURE TRAINING

Following these tasks; Showers, Food, Foot Inspections and debriefing on the Expedition or Exercise — in that order.
This is all part of your contribution to the Team Effort, you will be wise to work at it - especially if you have signed for some of the kit !!
It **will be noticed how** *you* **go about the Post Expedition Admin**

"Any fool can rough it, but a good soldier will make himself comfortable under any conditions"

"Leave nothing — but your footprints"

ADVENTURE TRAINING

FOOD-RATIONS

The need for a balanced diet becomes more important as the distance you travel increases and the 'going' gets harder.

If a journey is to take several days you will have to plan your menus giving variety and a balanced diet.

The amount of food you require daily will depend upon the type of country you are moving over and how much you are carrying.

If it is mountainous then your body will use more energy for you to replace by more energy producing food.

Food has to be carried, too much will add unnecessary weight to your load; too little and you will go hungry and that will cause problems.

The use of dehydrated foods (*Pouched Foods*) are very useful, especially as emergency rations.

If you can take dehydrated food with you select the items that give you the most carbohydrates (sugars, starches and fats).

Only take food that you like and enjoy eating. Keep all your meals simple to prepare and eat food hot as often as you can

'All in' stews are very good as you only need one mess tin to cook it in and it will be hot which is important.

Ensure that you have sufficient to drink. In the hot weather water in small quantities should be taken, but not if it is freezing cold.

24 HOUR RATIONS

The General Purpose Pouched Food Rations are issued to you while carrying out Field Training or in an operational situation. These rations have been developed to give a high quality, balanced diet to ensure that you are in the peak of fitness under field conditions.

Unfortunately many soldiers were not easily motivated to actually cook the content of their old style tinned compo rats, perhaps that is why they were already well cooked and fully prepared as issued!!

All pouched foods may be eaten hot or cold. If required hot, the reheating instructions are given on the wrapper of each pouch. These wrappers should not be removed until the pouches are about to be consumed. The water used for heating them may be used again for making beverages or shaving.

The contents of each pouch can be identified, when the wrappers have been removed, as follows;

     a. Breakfast (B) 1-7.   b. Main Meal (M) 1-7. c. Sweets (S) 1-7.

These figures are on the top of the pouch, the last two figures are the manufacturers code.

ADVENTURE TRAINING

24 Hour Menu Ration General Purpose   Menu Sheet

Menu 'A'
Breakfast
Oatmeal Block
Porridge
Bacon & Beans

Snack
Fruit Biscuits
Brown Biscuits
Cheese Spread
Milk Chocolate
Choc Caramels
Boiled Sweets

Main Meal
Soup
Beef & Dumplings
Fruit Cocktail
Fruit Cocktail

Menu 'B'
Breakfast
Oatmeal Block
Porridge
Hamburgers

Snack
Fruit Biscuits
Brown Biscuits
Meat Pate
Milk Chocolate
Confectionery Bar
Boiled Sweets

Main Meal
Soup
Chicken, Pasta
& Mushroom
Creamed Rice

Menu 'C'
Breakfast
Oatmeal Block
Porridge
Pork Sausage
  Beans
Snack
Fruit Biscuits
Brown Biscuits
Cheese Spread
Choc Caramels
Choc Biscuit
and Fruit
Boiled Sweets
Main Meal
Soup
Lamb Stew &
Potatoes
Fruit Dumplings
in Butterscotch
  Sauce

Menu 'D'
Breakfast
Oatmeal Block
Porridge
Corn Beef Hash

Snack
Fruit Biscuits
Brown Biscuits
Meat Pate
Milk Chocolate
Confectionery Bar
Boiled Sweets

Main Meal
Soup
Chicken
Casserole
Peaches in
Syrup

Menu 'E'
Breakfast

Oatmeal Block
Porridge
Bacon & Beans

Snack
Fruit Biscuits
Cheese Spread
Confection Bar
Choc Biscuits
  and Fruit
Boiled Sweets

Main Meal
Soup
Meatballs
Pasta in Tomato
Sauce.
Mixed Fruit Pud

Menu 'F'
Breakfast

Oatmeal Block
Porrrdge
Hamburgers

Snack
Fruit Biscuits
Brown Biscuits
Meat Pate
Milk Chocolate
Confectionery Bar
Boiled Sweets

Main Meal
Soup
Steak & Veg
with Potatoe
Fruit Cocktail

Menu 'G'
Breakfast

Oatmeal Block
Porridge
Pork Sausage
& Beans
Snack
Fruit Biscuits
Brown Biscuits
Cheese Spread
Choc Caramels
Choc. Biscuit &
Fruit. Boiled
Sweets
Main Meal
Soup
Lancashire Hot
Pot. Pears in
Choc Sauce

Drinks
Chocolate Drink
Beverage Whitener,
Sugar, Tea, Coffes,
Beef Stock Drink
and Orange or
Lemon Powder.
Sundries
Chewing Gum,
Matches, Water-
proof Matches,
Toilet Paper, Water
Puritication Tablets
& Menu Sheet

Note
Contents may vary
from Printed menu
sheets, depending
on items availabls
at time of packing.

ADVENTURE TRAINING

COOKING INSTRUCTIONS

ROLLED OATS for PORRIDGE - Oats contain MILK already mixed.
ALL MENUS - Add the Rolled Oats mixture to a little cold water until it makes a paste, add a little more water and bring it to the boil, let it simmer and stir for 4 to 5 minutes. Add sugar to taste.
May also be flavoured with some Chocolate Drink Powder if desired.
INSTANT SOUP Empty the contents of one sachet into your mug. Add half a pint of boiling water and stir well. The variety of soup will depend on the availability at the time of packing.

DRINKS There are sufficient beverage ingredients to make three pints of tea, two pints of coffee, one pint of Drinking Chocolate, one or two pints orange/lemon drink and one third pint of Beef Stock.

PRE COOKED RICE Put rice in mess tin, cover it with boiling water, bring it back to boil and let it simmer for FIVE minutes. Allow it to stand for TWO minutes, during which time it will soak up the water.
APPLE FLAKES and APPLE/APRICOT FLAKES Put sachet in mess tin, pour boiling water over the flakes and leave for TWO minutes - while the flakes are soaking up the water. The flakes are then ready to eat.

TO HEAT CANS

Just in case you get lucky and are issued with the old style tinned Compo Rats, it is as well to remind you that when cooking COMPO rations "in the can" pierce **TWO** holes in the lid of the can, stand the can in your Mess Tin with holes at the top, fill the mess tin with water until half way up can. Bring water to the boil, let it boil for TEN minutes. Handle carefully when opening the hot can.
Although this is an easy method of heating the can, the food does not taste quite as good as if you cook it in the way suggested, bearing in mind that this is a good method to use if you have to cook under difficult conditions.

NOTE: DO NOT drink the water used for heating cans, it is not safe, use it for washing/washing up.
SAFETY - BE SURE YOU MAKE TWO HOLES IN THE CAN AT THE TOP BEFORE BOILING THEM IN YOUR MESS TIN.

ADVENTURE TRAINING

WATER PURIFICATION TABLETS

These are a part of your Ration Pack and it is important that you
know how to use them.
For Drinking Water, add one purification tablet to each litre (ONE and
THREE QUARTER pints) of water.
Leave for TEN MINUTES before use.
Leave for at least THIRTY minutes if using to make up your Lemon or
Orange Drink.

WINDPROOF/WATERPROOF MATCHES

These matches MUST be kept for lighting your Hexamine blocks in
bad weather conditions.
Don't use them for any other reason or you will be in great difficulty if
bad weather sets in and you have:-

USEFUL MEASURE TO NOTE

Examine your small mess tin, if you fill it up to the bottom rivet that
holds on the Mess Tin Handle hinge, you will have a PINT of water in
the mess tin.

IMPROVED SHELTER

Construction of improvised Shelters for use when BIVI'S are not
available. There will be occasions when you do not have a tent to
shelter in. The British soldier has a reputation to be able to
improvise, it is said that "any fool can rough it, but a good soldier will
make himself comfortable under any conditions", the illustrations give
you a few ideas of how to put up improvised shelters.
A shelter with two ground sheets constructed on the same principle
as a BIVI for two.
A groundsheet shelter against a fallen tree
trunk for one person. The ground sheet
must be on the side of the trunk away from
the prevailing wind.
Another groundsheet type of shelter for one
person. The rope must be strong and the
open side of the groundsheet away from
the prevailing wind.

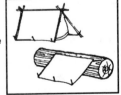

76

ADVENTURE TRAINING

IMPROVISED TENT

Using a string between two
supports, tie groundsheets over the
string, pegging the bottom edges to
the ground. This type of "tent" can
also be put up against a fence or
wall using one half of the tent as
shown on the right as a triangle A -
B - C

To make a Basha for two you need
two groundsheets, string or
bungees (6 at least), meat skewers
or tent pegs are useful (6 or 8 are
needed).
A length of strong string is always
useful to have in your kit.

ADVENTUROUS TRAINING PHYSICAL ACTIVITIES

You must have a responsible attitude to all activities you take part in,
to prevent yourself and others becoming casualties through your own
lack of care and preparation.
The rescue services invariably report that "the party was totally
unprepared for the expedition" or they "had not been trained in map
reading", or even worse the Coroner at the inquest reported "they
had no idea that the deceased was suffering from Hypothermia".
There are many activities that you may take part in as a group, but
they will only be 'official' provided those who are the organisers and
or supervising the event *on the ground* are currently qualified in that
activity or other people who are to assist hold a valid certificate to
organise and run that activity.

OFFICIAL PERMISSION and SUPPORT

On No Account will you organise activities without the knowledge
and assistance of your unit.

ADVENTURE TRAINING

This is not to "spoil your sport", but to make sure that you are properly organised, authorised, prepared, and having the correct equipment, and what is more, that it is carried out to the highest standards.

**REMEMBER - YOU ARE PERHAPS ONLY COVERED BY
INSURANCE IN THE EVENT OF AN ACCIDENT,
IF IT IS OFFICIALLY PLANNED AND ORGANISED.**

ADVENTUROUS & PHYSICAL ACTIVITIES

To remind you, the activities that are considered as adventurous and physical are as follows:-

**Mountaineering - including Hill Walking, Rock Climbing,
Abseiling, Skiing, Caving, Canoeing, Off Shore Sailing, Rafting,
Swimming, Gliding or Hang-gliding, Para-cending, Sub - Aqua
Diving and all activities involving the hazard of water.**

There is no substitute for good training and planning to ensure that you will be able to cope with any crisis.

At an early stage you must carry out fitness and specific skills training related to the activity you are taking part in.

Practice using and testing equipment, practice cooking. .

Make sure that you ARE properly organised and DO have the correct equipment, have a "dress rehearsal" - doing it to a high standard and safely - leave nothing to chance

PREVENTION OF ACCIDENTS ON OUTDOOR ACTIVITIES

Before you set out:-

Don't overdress, leave off that woollen pullover - carry it on top of your pack until the harder part of the march is over.

Do not carry too much kit.

Plan the kit you will carry, reducing non essentials like two sweaters where one will do.

As an individual, always carry a map, compass, protractor, pencil, whistle, first-aid kit and a torch.

Always carry spare warm clothing.

Carry emergency rations such as chocolate, glucose tablets, dried fruit etc. with you, and don't eat them except in an emergency.

Always leave a detailed Route Card showing your intended route out and back, check points, RV's, camp sites and your Estimated Time of Arrival (ETA), all supported by accurate Map References.

ADVENTURE TRAINING

Know the location of local mountain rescue posts and their procedures and map references of telephone boxes. Report to the local Rescue Post letting them know your route and ETD and ETR, give them a copy of your route card.

Decide on a Lost Drill e.g., *"go West until you strike the main road"* or *"keep walking down-stream"*.

BACKUP

If your expedition warrants a 'backup' team, they MUST be fully involved right from the start of your planning and certainly with you on a recce and during any rehearsals you have.

It is not sufficient to say "you thought they knew where the RV was" - make sure they **KNOW - EVERYTHING.**

PLANNING YOUR ROUTE.

If at all possible do a 'recce' well in advance . Plan your route and ensure all members of the group are fully briefed , all to have copies of the route, map refs, check points and RV's.

Take into account weather conditions and the forecasts for the duration of your exercise.

Treat hills and mountains with very great respect.

OUT ON THE HILLS

Always stay together, unless there is an injured person, in which case half of the party should stay with the casualty, while the other half goes for help.

Walk at the pace of the slowest person.

Remember to observe the Country Code.

If you go out as a group, never travel in groups of less than FIVE.

Carry at least one polythene survival sack or sleeping bag per two persons.

Stick to the route you agreed with the local Rescue Post.

Make one decision among the group as to the direction to take. If a compass bearing is used, have others check it, then trust your compass.

PRECAUTIONS —

DO NOT SPLIT UP - DON'T LEAVE ANYONE BEHIND.
If weather conditions deteriorate - DON'T PRESS ON - TURN BACK.

ADVENTURE TRAINING

Do not throw stones; these can dislodge bigger ones and you could cause an accident.

IF YOU DO GET LOST :-
1. **DO NOT SPLIT UP.**
2. **DO NOT PANIC.**
3. **DO NOT FORGET TO USE YOUR MAP, COMPASS AND YOUR COMMON SENSE.**
4. **REMEMBER THE INTERNATIONAL DISTRESS CALL - SIX BLASTS ON YOUR WHISTLE OR SIX TORCH FLASHES PER MINUTE.**

PREVENTION OF ACCIDENTS.

Walking by day or night as an individual, when moving on foot you must:-

Use a footpath or pavement or, if there is not one, walk on the side of the road facing the oncoming traffic (normally the right hand side) and keep as close to the side as possible.

Cross motorways by bridges and railways by bridges or level crossings.

When dark, keep an extra sharp lookout and wear a high visibility jacket or white arm band or white patch (a handkerchief if nothing better is available) which will show up in the lights of a vehicle.

WIND CHILL FACTOR

Not sufficient attention is paid to the combined effect that the air temperature and the speed of the wind has on the human body, especially exposed surfaces, such as the face, head and hands.

The wind speed is often given during weather forecasts and you would be well advised to take note of this if you are to embark on an expedition or extended hill walk.

These factors, the combined effect of the wind speed and air temperature on your body reduces the natural heat.

As the as the wind speed increases it reduces your body temperature more quickly.

This is most apparent at lower wind speeds between 0 to 24 k.p.h. (15 m.p.h.) at these speeds even a small increase in wind speed causes more rapid cooling of the body. Wind speeds above 24 k.p.h. (15 m.p.h.) cool the body slower, but this does not mean that you can ignore high wind as in addition to the wind chill factor it makes you

ADVENTURE TRAINING

THE WIND CHILL FACTOR

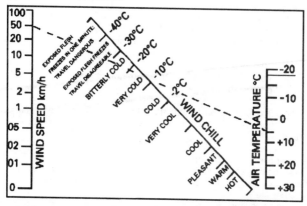

use a lot more energy and can blow you over the edge off a path or hillside.

The diagram on above is reproduced from the book Mountaincraft and Leadership by Alec Langmuir and illustrates graphically how important it is to be aware of the Wind Chill Factor. In the diagram as an example it shows:-

The air temperature at +5 degrees C, at a wind speed of 50 k.p.h. (31 m.p.h.) it crosses the Wind Chill Line at "very cold".

Protection from wind alone is not sufficient, you must try to keep yourself dry, as wet clothing combined with the Wind Chill Factor can rapidly bring on the conditions for you to suffer from Hypothermia (exposure), you will then most certainly become a casualty.

See the First Aid Section for treatment of Hypothermia

ADVENTURE TRAINING

SAFETY and EMERGENCY PROCEDURES
Emergency Messages
The Police are responsible for calling out the rescue services. The information they will require is as follows:-

a. The exact location of the injured person(s), with a six figure grid reference and a description/landmarks of the area for a Helicopter Pilot to identify.

b. The number of persons injured and their name(s).

c. The nature of their injuries.

d. The time of the accident.

Those going for help must remember the area and landscape with any particular reference point to help find the site on return with a rescue party.

Waiting for help to arrive.
Those looking after the injured would set up shelters and carry out emergency first aid, with special reference to the prevention of hypothermia/exposure.

It will be necessary to mark the site with light coloured clothing or bandages on sticks where they can easily attract attention.

There are International **Ground to Air Signals** that can be used to communicate with rescue aircraft. They are shown on the next page. In addition to these signals, **A RED FLARE, A RED SQUARE OF CLOTH** or a **FIRE** are also recognised **International Alarm Signals.** The shape of each signal can be made by setting out clothing or items of kit, or a person taking up the shape of the letter standing up or lying down.

Get help, attract attention in any way you can.

Be alert and watch out for the rescue party to guide them in the quickest route.

Make yourselves comfortable as possible, "brew-up", eat HOT food, keep together, keep warm, keep up the morale.

HYPOTHERMIA or EXPOSURE
SEE THE FIRST AID SECTION FOR FULL EXPLANATION AND TREATMENT - THIS IS PART OF THE PREPARATION FOR ADVENTURE TRAINING

ADVENTURE TRAINING

GROUND TO AIR EMERGENCY SIGNALS

letter	signal	
V		REQUEST ASSISTANCE
↑		WE ARE PROCEEDING IN THIS DIRECTION
X		MEDICAL ASSISTANCE REQUIRED
N		NO WE DO NOT NEED ANYTHING

ADVENTURE TRAINING

SUMMARY

Accidents / injuries ARE CAUSED.

Most accidents and related problems on Adventurous type outdoor activities, no matter where it is taking place, in hills or mountains or even in your local countryside are due to one or more of the following reasons:-

1. Not involving senior, more experienced members of your unit and getting permission in the first place to carry out an "expedition".
2. Insufficient detailed preparation, planning and training - RECCE not done properly, no rehearsals. Menu not planned for type of area travelled and emergencies.
3. Not being properly equipped or dressed - especially wearing unsuitable clothes and useless footwear.
4. Carelessness or casualness by you and those taking part.
5. Over estimating your own and others physical strength and the stamina required.
6. Not having enough practical experience and practice - especially map reading and camp craft.
7. Not paying enough attention to detail, not being observant - failing to notice soon enough to take action due to changes in the weather conditions.
8. Not turning back early enough - when common sense said "turn back".
9. Not noticing a member of the team "flagging"- getting left behind.
10. Failing to work together as a team - getting in a panic.
11. Not accepting advice from experienced people, while en-route.
12. Failing to give Route Cards, Map References of RV's and timings and other information IN WRITING to anyone before departing.
13. Failing to keep to the agreed routes - not advising of changes.
13. Splitting up group loss of use of full compliment of kit, rations and physical resources/skills.
15. Not bothering to cook hot food or make hot drinks.
16. Not taking sufficient care of feet and poor personal hygiene

---

> IF YOU DO AS YOU HAVE BEEN TRAINED TO DO,
> YOU MAY NOT BECOME A
> "DISASTER FOR AN EMERGENCY RESCUE"

MAP READING

INTRODUCTION - MAPCRAFT

Many soldiers are not happy about Map Reading. They find that trying to come to terms with the variety of lessons and the apparent technical detail to be learned, turns it into a boring subject.

The experience of getting lost on a Map Reading exercise and missing out the RV for the rations does not help!.

Sorry, we don't think that its uninteresting. To make the point we have given a lot of space to the subject in this Pocket Book.

We agree that the subject can be ruined by lack of good planning and preparation, but it can also be one of the most interesting and competitive activities for training or on exercise.

You should consider your ability in MAPCRAFT to be as sharp as you are at Fieldcraft or Skill at Arms. It is a pretty useless individual who is unable to find their way out of trouble - especially if their lack of MAPCRAFT skills got them into it in the first place.

Developing the correct attitude towards MAPCRAFT is perhaps the first consideration. Maps today are produced using advanced technology, detail can be infinite, to the extent that it is not just an aerial view of the ground, but can produce answers to virtually any question - from the military stand point - that we might ask.

Skills you have were acquired by constant practice and advanced training, some of which will have been repetitive.

This is not so with MAPCRAFT. Those who are skilled map readers will tell you that it is the ability to look at the ground area - no matter where you go and see it as a map sheet in their "minds-eye". This is practice, but what a variety of material to practice on, there is no repetition of the exact shape of the ground, the width of the river, the climb up or down the hills. They will also tell you that to look at a map and visualise what the ground area is going to be like when they get there, is also a skill acquired through practice.

What if they didn't get it right, landing in a 'bog' or the route they had chosen was impossible and is in full view of the enemy from high ground. You could be the one of those making the wrong decisions - all because of your lack of MAPCRAFT skills.

Orienteering Competitions are a good way of coming to terms with Mapcraft skills (and your physical condition). So, if you have a chance to take part in any competitive exercises you would be well advised to get your name down.

CARE OF MAPS

The provision of maps and other geographical products, less
Hydrographic Charts, to all three services is a function carried
out by Military Survey, a specialist branch of the Royal
Engineers.

A map should be protected either by being folded in a plastic
bag when in use or by being placed on a piece of hardboard and
covered with a transparent sheet, although this is not very
satisfactory if you are walking any distance, but essential to use
for training and route planning.

If maps are not carefully handled they quickly become useless,
it follows that you must not write directly on a map or use it
without protecting it in some way. Your map should be folded
lengthwise and then folded again like a concertina.

RELIABILITY OF MAPS.

A map is virtually a 'birds eye view' of the ground drawn on
paper. It is absolutely accurate only at the time it is drawn.
Today maps are produced by satellite and aerial photography
which ensures their accuracy, but as time goes by much of the
'picture' of the ground soon changes, villages grow, new roads
are made, some woods are cut down and others planted etc.,
For practical map reading purposes this will not affect the
accuracy as far as you will be concerned, any map produced
within the last few years may be relied upon unless specifically
stated otherwise.

MARGINAL INFORMATION.

On most maps you will find a part of it set aside for 'marginal
information', you should find this as soon as you unfold your
map as it provides guidance on how to read the map and how to
interpret the detail.

You will need to constantly refer to this until you have a complete
understanding of what all the symbols (usually called Conventional
Signs) and other information mean.

The number of your map and its scale will be found at the top of
the map. The index to adjoining sheets is shown as a diagram
near the bottom right hand corner of the map. You will need to find
out which sheet number you require to cover the particular area
that you are using and the next sheet if your route goes "off the
map".

MAP READING

Most maps now use metres as the "unit of elevation", check your map by looking in the margin at the bottom of the map as "ELEVATIONS IN METRES".

THE GRID SYSTEM.

The British National Grid System divides the whole country into large squares, which are subdivided and finish up as GRID LINES printed on the maps that you will normally use.

For your purpose the GRID LINES are a method for you to 'pinpoint' a specific spot on a map, by using the numbers of each line as shown in the margins around the outside of the map as coordinates.

Maps are printed with the North at the top of the sheet, one set of GRID LINES run up and down the map (North and South), the others run across the map (East and West).

It is important that you are able to find a point on the map and then be able to go out and find it on the ground, also to be able - at all times - to indicate on the map the exact place where you are standing on the ground.

To assist in the accurate use of the grid system it is advisable to obtain a Pathfinder Protractor/Romer, it provides two of the different scales of GRID SQUARES found on Ordnance Survey Maps.

This Romer is made of rigid plastic which you place on the GRID SQUARE of the map and read off the figures as described below, to pinpoint the exact position.

FOUR and SIX FIGURE REFERENCES

When giving a reference there are a few simple rules to remember:-
1. FIRST - count the figures along the BOTTOM of the map, from left (west) to right (east) these are called **'EASTINGS'**.
   Next count the figures up the sides of the map, from bottom (south), to top (north) these are called **'NORTHINGS'**.
2. A reference must always contain an even number of figures
3. GRID REFERENCES are always given with the **'EASTINGS'** value first, followed by the **'NORTHINGS'** value.

The example in the diagram at the top of the next page, shows a black square, that can be given the reference as square 8040 (a four figure reference). This square could represent a whole square kilometre of ground, not exactly a 'pinpoint' location on a map or ground.

Should you use a four figure reference, you must add a feature to indicate where you mean.

MAP READING

To get an exact position, the square is further subdivided into 10 squares in both directions.

The diagram (centre below) illustrates this subdivision, the black square is **"square 7 - 7**, these figures when added as explained below make up a six figure reference

The first two figures the **EASTING** value, followed by the sub divided square figure, then the two **NORTHING** value figures, followed again by the sub divided figure, making up a six figure reference **807407**

SETTING A MAP WITH (SILVA) TYPE COMPASS

The first essential drill on the ground with a map is to 'set it' or sometimes know as 'orientating' your map. Until you do this it is difficult to establish your exact position on the map/ground. Carry out the following:

1. Lay your map out flat, find the MAGNETIC NORTH ARROW - usually in the margin of the map as shown at 'A' on the diagram opposite.

2. Lay the base of your Silva Compass on the map with the DIRECTION TRAVEL

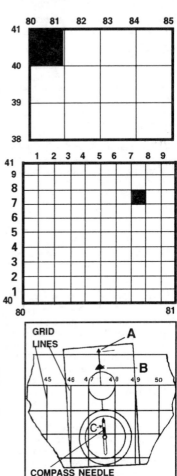

GRID LINES

A

B

C

COMPASS NEEDLE

MAP READING

ARROW (B) in line with the MAGNETIC NORTH (see diagram 'line-up')

3. Carefully turn the map and compass round - watching the compass needle swinging, until the RED MAGNETIC END of the COMPASS NEEDLE (C) coincides with the DIRECTION OF TRAVEL ARROW (B) and the MAGNETIC NORTH ARROW (A) on the map.

Your map is now set or orientated, in relation to the ground.

"FIRST THINGS FIRST - ALWAYS SET - ORIENTATE THE MAP"

SETTING A MAP WITHOUT A COMPASS BY OBSERVATION

This can be easy, once you have identified exactly where you are on the map, and if you are standing on a straight road, line up the road on your map with the road you are standing on. Make certain that the map is pointing in the right direction, i.e. the right way round.

If not on a road, you will need to find other objects on the ground such as a road/track junction, church, prominent hill top or farm buildings. You must also find and identify the same objects on your map, using them as shown in the diagram below by turning your map to set or orientate it in relation to the ground

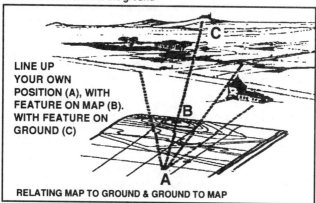

LINE UP YOUR OWN POSITION (A), WITH FEATURE ON MAP (B). WITH FEATURE ON GROUND (C)

RELATING MAP TO GROUND & GROUND TO MAP

MAP READING

THE LIGHT WEIGHT (SILVA TYPE) COMPASS

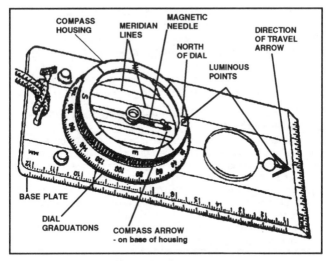

North, East, South and West are known as the cardinal points of the compass.

There are 32 points of the compass, but only 16 of them are normally used in map reading for the description of direction. These 16 are the four cardinal points and 12 intermediate points as shown in the diagram on the next page.

The letters **N, E, S** and **W** stand respectively for **NORTH, SOUTH, EAST** and **WEST**. In the intermediate points these letters are combined, e.g. **SE** is South East. **NNW** is North North West, etc.

These points describe direction only to within one sixteenth of the full circle: for more accurate indication of direction it is necessary to use subdivisions of the circle using "mils" or "degrees".

The mils system is used by the Army to give much greater accuracy than degrees.

MAP READING

CARDINAL POINTS OF THE COMPASS

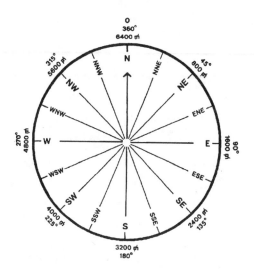

The **MILS SYSTEM** divides the circle of the compass into 6400 MILS, the zero being at the North Point.

The four quadrants or quarters of the circle are each 1600 mils, and so the East, South, and West points fall at 1600, 3200, 4800 mils respectively, as illustrated.

The symbol normally used to represent mils is the character letter m, with a / across it, and appears as m̸ .

NORTH POINTS.

There are **THREE** NORTH points:

1. **TRUE NORTH** - The actual direction of the geographical North Pole..
2. **GRID NORTH** - The direction of the vertical GRID LINES on a map. For all practical purposes TRUE and GRID NORTH are the same.

MAP READING

3. MAGNETIC NORTH -
The direction towards which the compass needle is attracted is the MAGNETIC NORTH POLE, see the diagram on the right.

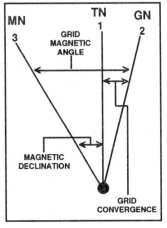

ANGLES BETWEEN NORTH POINTS
Grid Magnetic Angle. (GMA)
This is sometimes called the magnetic variation, is the angle between GRID NORTH and MAGNETIC NORTH and it depends on two factors:
1. **TIME.** As the position of the Magnetic North Pole moves slightly eastwards, so the GMA (Grid Magnetic Angle) changes. This is called the Annual Magnetic Change and must be taken into account when converting magnetic bearings to Grid Bearings and vice versa.
2. **PLACE.** The GMA (Grid Magnetic Angle) also varies from one part of the country to another. These two factors are included in the marginal information on the map.

Magnetic Declination
This is the angle between MAGNETIC and TRUE NORTH as shown on the diagram.

Grid Convergence
This is the angle between GRID NORTH and TRUE NORTH which can, in practice be ignored since for practical map reading purposes TRUE NORTH and GRID NORTH are the same.

BEARINGS - TYPES OF BEARINGS
As there are three types of North points, there are three kinds of bearings, according to the North point from which they have been measured:

MAP READING

1. A MAGNETIC BEARING is one taken with a compass (an accurate compass needle always points towards MAGNETIC NORTH).

2. A GRID BEARING is one measured on a map with the Silva compass used as a protractor or using your Pathfinder Protractor/Romer.

3. A TRUE BEARING cannot be measured direct, but must be calculated from the other two. However this can be ignored for practical map reading purposes.

NOTE. INDIVIDUAL COMPASS ERROR (ICE)

The accuracy of each individual compass is subject to error, it is important that you should check your own compass to establish the INDIVIDUAL COMPASS ERROR (ICE), do this by checking it against other compasses. Having done so make a note of it on your compass base with a small sticky label, don't forget to allow for it.

TO TAKE A MAGNETIC BEARING

1. Point the compass direction of march arrow at the object.
2. Turn compass housing until the red arrow is under the needle.
3. Read off the MAGNETIC BEARING on the compass housing.

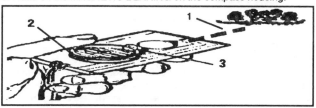

TO TAKE A GRID BEARING

NOTE: IGNORE THE COMPASS NEEDLE.

a. Place the long edge of the compass along the desired line of travel, making sure that the DIRECTION OF TRAVEL ARROW **(1)** on the compass POINTS IN THE DIRECTION of your LINE OF TRAVEL **(2)**

b. Turn the COMPASS NEEDLE HOUSING **(3)**, so that NORTH on the housing rim points to NORTH on the map.

MAP READING

You will notice that the MERIDIAN LINES **(4)** on the COMPASS are parallel to the GRID LINES **(5)** on the map - or they should be.

c. Read the number of mils/degrees against the DIRECTION OF TRAVEL LINE at **(6)**, this is the GRID BEARING. Having taken a GRID BEARING from the map, you must take into account and make allowances for the GRID MAGNETIC ANGLE (GMA)

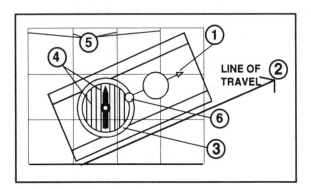

FINDING YOUR
POSITION WITH A COMPASS - RESECTION

There may be times when you need to find your exact position both on the map and on the ground. This could be as a result of being "dropped-off" on an exercise or if you were unfortunate enough to crash land in wild country. You could find your position by using a compass and following the instructions set out below.

You will need to refer to the diagram on this page.

1. Set/orientate your map. Select TWO prominent objects or features which you can be sure of identifying on the map. These objects/features need to be a good distance away, more than 1000 metres and also be separated by an angle of approximately 10 o'clock to 2 o'clock - see diagram on next page.

MAP READING

2. On the "plastic" cover of your map, mark the objects/feature at "**A**" and "**B**". From the position at which you are standing, (call it "**C**") take a bearing on to each of the objects/features in turn, writing down the bearings. As this has to be accurate, don't move from your position and take a further two bearings on both of the objects/features. Add together the three bearings to each object/feature and divide by three to get the average bearing to each.

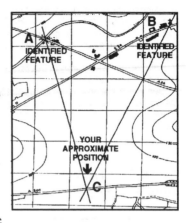

3. These are COMPASS Bearings, they are MAGNETIC Bearings.

As you are to use them to 'plot on a map', they have to be converted from MAGNETIC to GRID Bearings.

NOTE: You will always be best advised to draw a small diagram - until you become familiar with working with bearings - showing the NORTH POINTS as shown on page 212, this will remind you to make an allowance for the GMA (Grid Magnetic Angle).

The current GMA is approximately 100 mils (6⁰) This is the figure that you would subtract from the MAGNETIC BEARING.

REMEMBER: "MAG TO GRID - GET RID"

4. Check the resulting bearing and adjust it to the nearest 25 mils. Remember the settings or divisions on the compass card of a Silva or Light Weight Compass are 25 mils.
5. Now set up the GRID BEARING on your compass for bearing "**A**". Use a wax pencil with a fine point , put the point on "**A**" . Hold it in a vertical position, place the long edge of the compass against the pencil with the DIRECTION OF TRAVEL ARROW pointing in the direction of "**A**", and the NORTH ARROW pointing approximately to the top of the map.

MAP READING

6. Using the pencil still in a vertical position, pivot the compass about the pencil point until the NORTH ARROW points exactly towards the top of the map, with the edge of the compass or any of the red setting lines on the compass base parallel to the nearest GRID LINES on the map.

7. Hold the compass firmly in this position while you draw a line along the side of the compass.

Repeat the same procedure from point "**B**".

Where the two lines you have drawn from "**A**" and "**B**" cross each other is your calculated position on the map/ground. Now work out your exact six figure GRID reference of your location.

CONVERTING A GRID BEARING TO A MAGNETIC BEARING

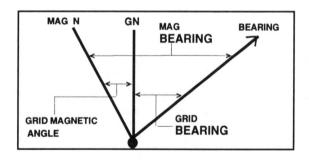

Remember all bearings are measured in a clockwise direction from the NORTH point. A MAG bearing will always be GREATER than the GRID bearing taken, by the amount of the GRID MAGNETIC ANGLE. Therefore to convert **GRID to MAG ADD** the GRID MAGNETIC ANGLE.

To convert a **MAG bearing to a GRID**, **SUBTRACT** the GRID MAGNETIC ANGLE.

MAP READING

IDENTIFYING A FEATURE

Set your map, use the edge of your protractor or a pencil, place it on the map with the edge running through your position, swing it across the map until it lines up with the feature on the ground.

The feature should be easy to pick out, provided it is not too far away and that it is on your map!.

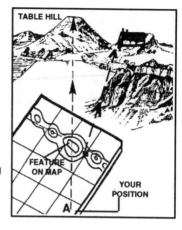

This like so many Map Reading skills need constant practice until you carry it out as a "drill" and second nature.

After a while you will be able to locate and identify features by just looking across the map.

In setting your map, no matter what method you use, it is the constant relating and comparison of the map and ground which will build a good foundation for your navigational skills.

We remind you that this skill above all will go a long way to prevent you getting lost.

GRID MAGNETIC ANGLE

(GMA) in UK
GMA = $6°,15'$ West
or 100 mils West in January 1994
Annual change approx
10' East MN GN GMA

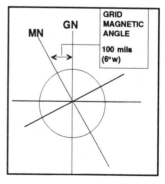

> **REMEMBER**
> "Grid to Mag - ADD"
> "Mag to Grid get RID"

MAP READING

One of the most common uses of taking bearings is to take one from the map to find the bearing to march on with your SILVA type light weight compass or your protractor which is quite simple.

MARCHING ON A BEARING

Having converted your GRID BEARING to a MAGNETIC BEARING, set the graduated circle to read the MAGNETIC BEARING at the DIRECTION OF TRAVEL line.

Then turn the whole compass until the NORTH end of the NEEDLE coincides with the NORTH ARROW and is parallel to the MERIDIAN LINES on the COMPASS HOUSING, holding the compass in front of you, march in the direction indicated by the LINE OF TRAVEL ARROW. So long as the compass needle and the NORTH ARROW are kept together, the DIRECTION OF TRAVEL ARROW will remain on the required bearing.

BACK BEARINGS with a SILVA COMPASS

When marching on a bearing - especially at night - over some distance you may often have a doubt in your mind that you may

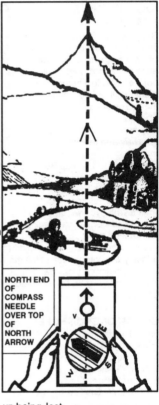

NORTH END OF COMPASS NEEDLE OVER TOP OF NORTH ARROW

go wandering off course and finish up being lost.

The ability to use your compass and to trust it by taking a back bearing on to the point from which you started, will prevent you getting into difficulties.

The simplicity of the Silva compass makes the use of back bearings an easy navigational aid.

MAP READING

To use the compass for a BACK
BEARING, keep the compass on the
bearing you have taken (as 'X' to 'Y' in
the diagram), rotate the COMPASS
HOUSING through 3200 mils (180º).
The compass is now set to march on the
BACK BEARING (in the direction of 'Y' in
the diagram) of your original **FORWARD
BEARING.**
To retrace your route - (from 'Y' to 'X'
march on the bearing given as your
BACK BEARING.
This is a very important skill - easily
learned with a compass, it is one of the
best methods of preventing yourself from
getting lost.

"Practice makes perfect".

HILLS AND VALLEYS

The method of showing how the ground is
shaped in terms of the hills and valleys
which are expressed as the RELIEF, are
shown by CONTOUR LINES. These
appear as thin brown lines on the map
and are described as "an imaginary line
joining all points of equal height above
sea level".
You must check the information at the
bottom of the map near the scale diagram
to find the "Contour Interval", that is the
height between each contour

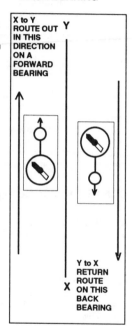

FORWARD AND
BACK BEARING

X to Y
ROUTE OUT
IN THIS
DIRECTION
ON A
FORWARD
BEARING

Y to X
RETURN
ROUTE
ON THIS
BACK
BEARING

To give you a better understanding of contours the following pages
of information and diagrams will explain them.

UNDERSTANDING and INTERPRETING CONTOURS

Contours are quite easy to follow, provided you understand the fact
that they follow the same height, round hills, into re-entrants, and over
the spurs.
They do not provide a picture of the shape of the land, but with
practice and using contours you will be able to interpret the shape
of the ground from the contour lines - mapcraft at its best!.

MAP READING

Until you have mastered your map craft it is difficult to know from a contour whether the ground is rising or falling, whether the feature is a spur or a re-entrant.

A spur projects out from the land mass, while a re-entrant is exactly the opposite - a shallow valley running up into the mass.

It is not always possible, however, to tell which is the top of the slope and which is the bottom, without being able to find the contour figures. When the contour figures can be read with both the map and the figures the correct way up you would be able to tell if the ground is rising or falling.

A general idea of which way the slopes run can be obtained by looking at other features - particularly lakes, ponds, rivers, streams, and railway lines.

A stream running near a set of contours indicates at once which is the bottom of the slope.

Similar features such as railways, villages and large woods are more likely to be found at the bottom of a hill than at the top.

CONVEX and CONCAVE SLOPES

A CONVEX slope is one that bulges outwards, and a **CONCAVE** slope is one that curves inwards - see the diagrams on the right.

Standing at the top of a **CONVEX** slope you would not be able to see all the way down to the bottom, because the outward slope would obscure your view. This is important to recognise as ground that you cannot see - "dead ground" can conceal the enemy or give you cover from view.

When standing at the top of the **CONCAVE** slope, however, there would be a clear view the whole way down the slope.

It is important to be able to recognise these two types of slopes from the map.

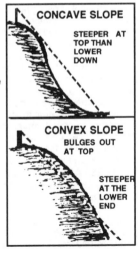

CONCAVE SLOPE

STEEPER AT TOP THAN LOWER DOWN

CONVEX SLOPE

BULGES OUT AT TOP

STEEPER AT THE LOWER END

MAP READING

CONTOUR VALUES

If you had several paths right round a hill, each one keeping at the same level, and were walking round one of them, you would find that where the paths were near to each other the ground would be steep between them, and where the paths were some distance apart, the ground would slope gently, the further they were apart, the less the slope would be.

SPOT HEIGHTS

Apart from contours, height is shown by **SPOT HEIGHTS** which is marked on a map by a dot and number ● 241. This is the exact height in metres or feet above sea level.

You will also find **TRIG POINTS**, shown on the map as a small black triangle with a number next to it ▲ 576, this again is the exact height above sea level. This Conventional Sign will go out of use in future years as advanced methods of map making come into use.

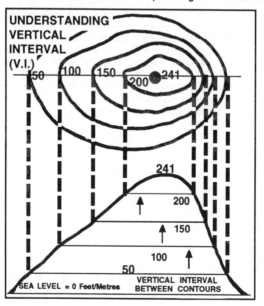

MAP READING

MORE ABOUT CONTOURS

On gentle slopes the CONTOURS are far apart, on steep slopes the CONTOURS are close together.

You do not need to find the figures on the contour lines to give you a 'picture' of the ground in an area, the contour lines show quite simply the comparative steepness of the slopes, the SPURS and RE-ENTRANTS.

If the ground is broken and rugged there will be many SPURS and RE-ENTRANTS and your path will be constantly turning in and out. Broken, rugged country is shown by irregular, sharply turning contours.

Where the slopes are smooth, your path will curve gently, bending out as it follows the line of a SPUR and swinging in at a RE-ENTRANT. On gentle slopes the contours appear as smooth flowing curves.

The contours may appear to wander about all over, but if you follow them they naturally come back to where they started from, the only exception to this is when you find a cliff face with a sheer drop, then all the contour lines are so close together they appear to be one.

Every curve or bend in a contour indicates a SPUR or a valley, a rise or fall in the ground, just as it does on the side of a hill. Remember - the distance apart the contours are still indicates the steepness or flatness of the ground

Heights of Contours - see illustration on previous page

Understanding Vertical Interval (V.I.)

Each contour is drawn at a specific height above sea level and each one is the same vertical height above the one below. The difference in height between contours is called the Vertical Interval (VI).

These heights are written into the contour lines at intervals along their length.

On Ordnance Survey maps the figures showing the height of the contours are always written so as they read facing up hill, it is important to remember this as you can very quickly find out which direction the ground is sloping.

Check the information in the margins of the map to find out if the **VI (Vertical Interval)** is in Feet or Metres.

Whenever you are "out on the ground', you should look at the ground formation in the area, draw those imaginary contour lines around the hills and valleys, make a rough sketch and then get a map of the area and see how well you have been able to interpret the ground.

MAP READING

Contours and the shape of ground

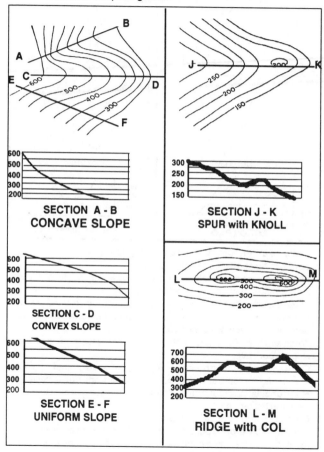

SECTION A - B
CONCAVE SLOPE

SECTION C - D
CONVEX SLOPE

SECTION E - F
UNIFORM SLOPE

SECTION J - K
SPUR with KNOLL

SECTION L - M
RIDGE with COL

MAP READING

KNOW YOUR CONTOUR PATTERNS

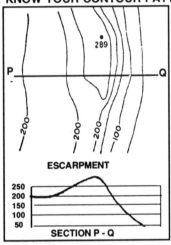

ESCARPMENT

SECTION P - Q

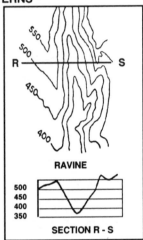

RAVINE

SECTION R - S

1. Contours close together mean steep slopes.
2. Contours far apart mean gentle slopes.
3. When contours are evenly spaced the slope is uniform, thes slopes have small undulations and pockets of dead ground.
4. When the spacing of the contours, reading from high ground to low, decreases, the slope is convex. Convex slopes mean short visibility; dead ground becomes very close.
5. When spacing of contours, reading from high to low, increases, the slope is concave.
   Concave slopes mean good visibility and little dead ground.
6. Wandering contours at various distances apart and never close, mean undulating ground. Important to note the general direction of the fall in the ground.
7. Gently curving contours indicate an area of country of rounded slopes. As the ground becomes steeper the contours come closer together; as it becomes more rugged the curves disappear and the contours take on 'jagged' shapes.

MAP READING

SCALES AND MEASURING DISTANCE

The scale of a map is the relationship between the actual distance measured from one point to another on the ground and the distance between the same two points on a map.

The way that the 'scale' of a map is expressed is by the Representative Fraction.

It used to be expressed in words, e.g., "one inch to one mile", or "four miles to one inch".

This is now being superseded by the **RF** method.

The Representative Fraction (RF) is the standard method used on all continental maps and wherever the metric system is used.

Most British maps are now expressed in metric. It is simple to use if you remember that the RF is 1/X, one unit of distance on the map represents X units of distance on the ground.

For example, a scale of 1/50,000 means that one inch/centimetre/metre on the map represents 50,000 inches/centimetres/metres on the ground.

The essential connection is that the SAME unit of measurement applies both to the map and to the ground measurement.

A distance of 2cms on a 1/50,000 map therefore represents 2 x 50,000 cms on the ground = 100,000 cms = 1000 metres.

All maps are printed with graphic linear scales, usually in the centre of the bottom margin, from which any horizontal distance may be measured on the map in kilometres and metres, or in miles and yards.

A linear map scale is always shown in the form of a diagram as below.

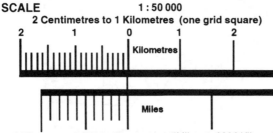

SCALE   1 : 50 000
2 Centimetres to 1 Kilometres (one grid square)

1 Kilometre = 0.6214 mile   1 Mile = 1.6093 Kilometres

NOTE: The above diagram is NOT to scale, but to illustrate the scale found on a 1: 50 000 map.

MAP READING

Referring to the diagram on the previous page, you will notice that the zero mark is set from the left of the scale by one major division, which is then subdivided into ten (or other suitable) subdivisions usually not longer than about 4 mm each. Measurements falling between any of these subdivisions must be estimated.

LINEAR MAP SCALE.
How to measure distance.

Make a mark on the straight edge of a piece of paper, put the mark on the point you wish to measure from and make successive marks along the edge of the paper as you follow the route from your starting point to the final point.

This is easy if you just want to measure along a straight road, but if it means going round corners you will have to pivot the paper and make several marks as you progress.

The total distance is then recorded along the edge of the paper.

Lay the paper along the scale on the map, with the right hand tick against one of the major divisions, so that the left hand tick lies against the subdivision to the left of the zero mark. The total distance is then the number of major divisions plus the distance to the left of the zero.

With practice this is quite an accurate method of measuring distances.

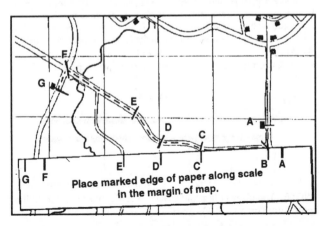

Place marked edge of paper along scale in the margin of map.

MAP READING

MOVING ROUND OBSTACLES

Obstacles are often found on a route and in order to keep a really accurate direction you should make a diversion by going round them. This is done by plotting a series of right angles and measuring by paces as illustrated in the diagram below 200 paces, 500 paces, 200 paces, bringing you back on the original bearing.

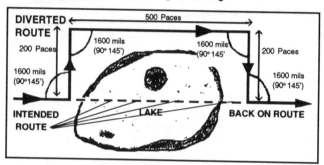

FINDING TRUE NORTH FROM THE SUN USING A WATCH.

When you do not have a map or are map reading without a compass, it can help if you are able to find the rough direction of TRUE NORTH or SOUTH.

The method explained below will give you an approximate direction - not accurate enough for reading bearings or other measurements.

INFORMATION - as the sun rises in the EAST, and moves (in the northern hemisphere) through the southern sky, setting in the WEST, the position of the Sun, when visible, is always a rough guide to the direction of NORTH.

A watch when set to Greenwich Mean Time (GMT) for UK (or to local time for other areas some distance EAST or WEST of Greenwich) may be used. If summertime or other artificial time is in local use your watch should be adjusted to Greenwich Mean Time (GMT) or to the local standard time.

METHOD - lay your watch flat, with the HOUR HAND pointing to the sun.

MAP READING

In the NORTHERN hemisphere, TRUE SOUTH will then be midway between the hour hand and twelve o'clock on the watch - see diagram above. In the SOUTHERN hemisphere, lay your watch with twelve o'clock pointing to the sun. TRUE NORTH then lies midway between the hour hand and twelve o'clock. When the sun is high up in the sky, this method cannot be used with

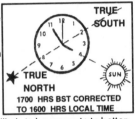

1700 HRS BST CORRECTED TO 1600 HRS LOCAL TIME

any success. In any case the result is unlikely to be accurate to better than five degrees.

THE PRISMATIC COMPASS

In spite of the high technology methods of navigation available to us, there is always the time and place that it does not work and you have to resort to your own devices.

If you are fortunate enough to be able to use a Prismatic Compass and have one in your kit, then what could have been a disaster will be avoided.

The diagrams on the following pages set out the principal parts of the compass, although the illustration shows the COMPASS CARD marked in degrees, it is now used in mils which makes it even more accurate - depending upon your skills at handling it.

The standard Prismatic Compass is an accurate instrument for reading Magnetic Bearings. It is precision made to a very high standard of workmanship and therefore a valuable piece of equipment to be taken care of. That is not the only reason for treating it with care as if it is neglected like any other kit, it will not work accurately when most needed.

It has a double glass cover, one over the compass card, the other in the hinged lid of the compass on which is marked the Lubber Line. The NORTH point is marked on the floating card by a luminous triangle, the card is engraved with an inner and outer circle of mils. The inner circle reads clockwise from 0 to 6400 mils, starting at the NORTH point, each small division being 20 mils.

The outer circle reads clockwise from 0 to 6400 mils, starting from the SOUTH point, each small division being 20 mils.

The compass needle is below the card and fixed to it so that the two swing together.

MAP READING

The box forming the base of the compass is filled with oil to `damp' the movement of the card. Under the upper glass cover is marked with black figures 2 to 64, each division being 100 mils. A small luminous mark is also on the glass, used for night marching. This cover is encased in a brass ring that rotates to any position, and clamped by a screw near the lid hinge.

Opposite the hinge on the lid is a small black triangular block which contains the magnifying prism.

When the lid is open the prism can be flipped over enabling you to look through it and read the figures on the outer circle of the compass card. To improve your focus move the prism up or down on its mounting.

OBSERVING WITH THE COMPASS.

To take a bearing.

1. Open up the compass ready for reading through the prism, make sure the lid is vertical and the PRISM in the reading position.

2. Hold the compass, with a thumb through the HOLDING RING, use other hand to steady it in a comfortable position. Hold the compass level or the card will not swing freely.

COMPASS HELD LEVEL WITH LID VERTICAL

3. Look through the SIGHTING SLIT in the PRISM and line up the LUBBER LINE in the LID with the object on which you are taking a bearing - see SIGHTING PICTURE as illustrated. At the same time, look through the eyehole in the PRISM, and see the readings on the COMPASS CARD below as it swings and settles.

SIGHTING PICTURE

When the card comes to rest, read off the bearing against the LUBBER LINE. This has now given you a MAGNETIC FORWARD BEARING on to the object. With practice you will get very accurate readings, especially if you are able to rest your arms on a wall or against a building.

Watch out for any metal objects that might distort the reading.

NOTE: The LUBBER LINE is sometimes called the HAIR LINE.

MAP READING

NIGHT MARCH

Before a night march, the bearings should be worked out and the
compass set by day. As much of the route should be reconnoitred by
day - even from a distance. Ground studied from Aerial Photographs
if available. Landmarks, roads, hedges, streams etc that have to be
crossed should be noted as a check on distance and direction.
Several compasses may be used with bearings preset for each 'leg'.
If visibility allows pick out an object on the required bearing, as far
distance as can be clearly seen, and march to it. Then select another
object, march on that and so on.

Setting the Compass for a Night March

From a *given* bearing, converted from a map or
taken by a Recce Patrol during the day.
Set the compass by looking through the
EYEHOLE, turning with the compass until the
reading of the graduations against the *lubber line*
shows the required bearing.

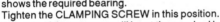

Tighten the CLAMPING SCREW in this position.
The axis of the compass will be at the required bearing when the
NORTH POINT on the COMPASS CARD coincides with the
LUMINOUS STRIP on the GLASS COVER - see diagram below.
Keeping together both the NORTH POINT on the COMPASS CARD
in line with LUMINOUS STRIP on the GLASS COVER will give you
the correct direction of march.

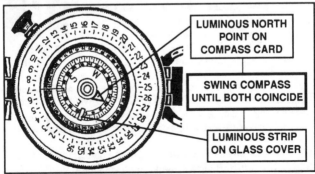

LUMINOUS NORTH
POINT ON
COMPASS CARD

SWING COMPASS
UNTIL BOTH COINCIDE

LUMINOUS STRIP
ON GLASS COVER

MAP READING

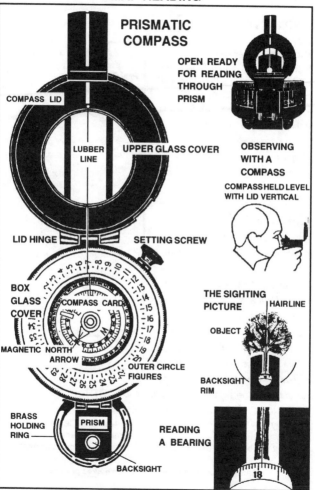

PRISMATIC COMPASS

OPEN READY FOR READING THROUGH PRISM

COMPASS LID

LUBBER LINE

UPPER GLASS COVER

OBSERVING WITH A COMPASS

COMPASS HELD LEVEL WITH LID VERTICAL

LID HINGE

SETTING SCREW

BOX GLASS COVER

COMPASS CARD

MAGNETIC NORTH ARROW

OUTER CIRCLE FIGURES

THE SIGHTING PICTURE

HAIRLINE

OBJECT

BACKSIGHT RIM

BRASS HOLDING RING

PRISM

BACKSIGHT

READING A BEARING

18

MAP READING

FINDING TRUE NORTH
By the stars
(Northern Hemisphere)

In latitudes less than 60° the **POLE STAR** is never more than about 40 miles away from **TRUE NORTH**. The position of the **POLE STAR** is indicated by the "pointers" of the Great Bear or Plough - see diagram.

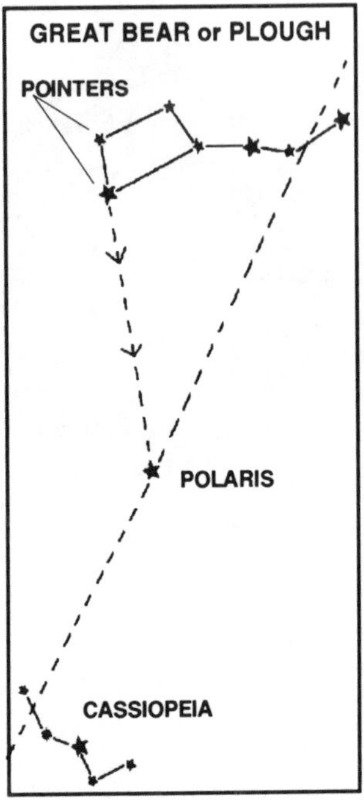

All stars revolve round the POLE STAR and the Plough may be either below it low down near the horizon and "right way up", or above it in the sky and "upside down" or in any position between. If the Plough is obscured or below the horizon, **Cassiopeia** which is shaped like a **W** and is on the opposite side of the POLE STAR from the Plough, may be visible; the POLE STAR is the nearest bright star within the arms of the W.

GREAT BEAR or PLOUGH

POINTERS

★ **POLARIS**

CASSIOPEIA

Above 60° latitude the POLE STAR is too high in the sky to be a good guide to NORTH.

At the NORTH POLE it is vertically overhead.

The only way to learn night navigation is to get out in the dark, identify the constellations shown in the above diagram and practice moving in different directions by using stars and checking with your compass.

"As with all map reading — practice makes perfect."

MAP READING

ROUTE CARDS

The purposes of a ROUTE CARD is to ensure that you plan the route you are taking and from the start become aware of the distances you are proposing to travel, the obstacles that you will encounter, either overcoming them or taking action to find a route round them, RV's and the locations for your bivi sites, also to ensure that in an emergency, assuming you have had the sense to leave a copy - someone will know your approximate position at any given time.

The illustration of the ROUTE CARD below is self explanatory, you need plenty of space in each column to write information. Never be short of detail, it is better to have more than you need than not enough. If you are in a group make sure each person has an accurate copy and leave a copy behind for someone who you will be in contact with during your expedition or exercise.

The importance of CHECK POINTS and the TIMES that you are to be there must be shown on the ROUTE CARD.

ROUTE CARD							
Produced by_____ Start Point Grid Ref_____					Date_____ ETD ___		
Date Finished .... Finishing Point Grid Ref .... ETA							
Leg	From		To		Bearing		Distances	Remarks
	Location	Grid Ref	Location	Grid Ref	Grid	Mag		Landmarks Hazards
			EXAMPLE OF HEADINGS AND LAYOUT FOR A ROUTE CARD					

MAP READING

THE 24 HOUR CLOCK SYSTEM

The hands on the clock face are pointing to quarter past eight. If it was in the morning (Ante Meridian - **AM** - before noon) you would call it 0815 hours. If it was in the evening (Post Meridian - **PM** - after noon) you would call it 2015 hours.

The importance of using the 24 hour clock system cannot be ignored as it avoids any confusion over timings and is explicit in its meaning. The Armed Services use what is known as the date/time group, which includes the date as two figures in front of the time, see examples below.

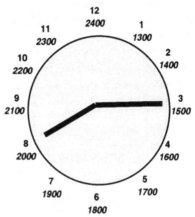

EXAMPLES:-

122200 June would be 2200hrs on the 12th of June, i.e. 10pm in the evening on the 12th of June

This is used when timings cover several days, e.g. START Exercise 170600 END Exercise 201000

The exercise will begin at 6am on the 17th and end at 10am on the 20th.

It is important that you learn how to use the 24 hour clock system as all timings in the services are based on it.

Use it every day until it becomes automatic.

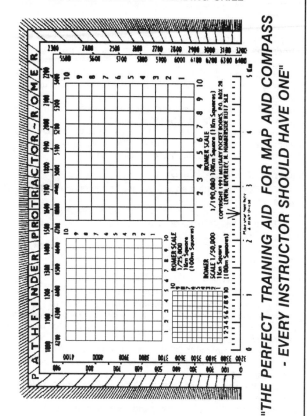

THE PATHFINDER PROTRACTOR/ROMER

IMPROVE YOUR MAP READING SKILL

"THE PERFECT TRAINING AID FOR MAP AND COMPASS
- EVERY INSTRUCTOR SHOULD HAVE ONE"

ORIENTEERING

Orienteering is like a car rally on foot, and as a sport has become well established in the UK. It can be over a mile or two or made to cover a vast area.

It can be a mornings fun, last all day or several days.

It can be toughened up to cross mountains, or be "improved" by introducing rafting or even canoes. It can be a treasure hunt or finding "escaped prisoners".

It can be carried out by day and night. It is a competitive activity putting your map reading skills to the test and your ability to think quickly on your feet.

You need to be fit and have plenty of determination, to safely navigate around a set course laid out by the organisers.

The `event' is judged by the shortest time it takes the competitors to navigate and complete the course with the most points scored.

You have to record your progress on a Control Card.

HOW IT IS ORGANISED

A MASTER MAP of the area in which the orienteering is to take place will be set up for all competitors to see.

Normally you will be given a list of MAP REFERENCES which are the CONTROL points. You will be issued with a map of your own in a plastic cover or Map Case.

You plot the CONTROL references on your map from the Master Map and then set off for your first CONTROL.

CHECK POINTS or CONTROLS

The CHECK POINTS or CONTROLS which make up the route are usually marked in some way to distinguish between them.

In some Forestry Commission areas for instance these markers are diamond shape painted red and white, fixed to posts each one being separately numbered.

In competitions moveable CONTROLS are put out before the competition. This allows the organisers to use different areas and different courses.

To prove that you have been to the CONTROL you have make a note of the number or symbol carved into the top of each post or use a special punch called a Swedish marker punch on your event card.

ORIENTEERING

These will be checked when you return.

The Controls are not easy to find, more often than not they can only be seen from a close distance, usually less than 30m, therefore accurate map reading is essential if you are to find them.

It is a good idea to choose an easily identified point like a track junction near to the CONTROL (this is called an ATTACK POINT) and then to pace the distance on a bearing to the CONTROL.

EQUIPMENT

To orienteer safely you would normally require the following:- Map and map case. Compass (Silva type). Pen. Whistle. Suitable Clothing.

The type of clothing you wear depends to some extent on the time of year, the location of the course and how long the event is likely to last. Your combat kit is adequate, especially in wooded areas or in rough terrain.

Set out in the paragraph below is the minimum kit required. However, you would be advised that experienced people take what they need and nothing more - what you take - you have to carry:-

Wool or cotton shirt or vest.

A lightweight waterproof Cagoule.

Long trousers/track suit bottoms to protect your legs against thorns, nettles etc.

Cotton or wool socks.

Strong walking/running shoes.

A towel for when you return to your transport.

A change of clothing (you may be very wet and or dirty) including shoes.

KEEPING DIRECTION

To orienteer successfully you must be able to keep going in the correct direction. This can be achieved in two ways :-

1. USING A COMPASS.

This will always tell you where NORTH is and by SETTING the compass you can find the direction in which you want to go. This is however only really useful in open country like moorland.

2. USING THE MAP.

This is perhaps the best method since it is hard to get lost if you do it correctly. The compass is also used to set or orientate the map, set the map in relation to the ground.

ORIENTEERING

Once the map is orientated, if possible, always use features you can identify **on the map and on the ground** to get you to your destination.

This involves planning your route in advance and in a number of short easily navigated "legs". If there is a leg with no easily identified features trust your compass.

When either of these methods are used, keep in mind the orienteering techniques mentioned below, they will help you to navigate by the quickest and safest method.

GETTING LOST

Even the best navigators can sometimes get lost, however this is not usually the disaster it may seem, since it is not too difficult to find yourself again.

If you get into a situation where you are lost, **STOP** and **THINK IT THROUGH**, bearing in mind the following:-

1. Don't Panic - a cool head is needed.
2. Use the compass and orientate your map, try and trace your route.
3. Try to identify the ground around you and match it to the map, if you succeed then you have found yourself, plan your route onward.

If you cannot, then try to retrace your route to the previous check point. If this also fails, set your compass and walk toward a road or other easily identifiable line on the ground then stay there until found.

THE ORIENTEERING MAP

The map is a large scale (usually 1:10000 or 1:15000 scale) representation of the land, the information around the margin of the map will tell you what the colours and symbols means.

Study your map and identify all the different markings and colours. Colours on the SPECIAL ORIENTEERING MAPS are used to indicate the speed at which you can MOVE, not the TYPE of GROUND, for instance an area shaded dark green might indicate ground which would be very difficult to move through, - usually known as "FIGHT" because you would have to fight your way through it, whereas a light green area could indicate close woodland or very rough ground through which you could walk.

White may indicate where you could run, perhaps grassland or very mature woodland where the trees are well spaced.

The orienteering map, because of its scale shows great detail and will accurately position depressions in the ground, holes and mounds,

ORIENTEERING

earth walls and embankments which would normally not be shown. Learn these new symbols as soon as you can, identifying them on the ground could be the difference between being 'lost or found'.

As you know, you must know exactly where you are at all times, you will only achieve this by constantly checking the map and always keeping it orientated.

Remember NORTH is at the top of the map, the black grid lines which run up and down the map run approximately NORTH to SOUTH. It will always pay you to set or orientate your map correctly, until your skill in map craft ensures that you know your location at any given time on the map/ground during your journey.

NAVIGATING TECHNIQUES AND CHOOSING A ROUTE

When you choose your route try and find the best way of getting to the first **CONTROL** by selecting a good, easily identifiable **ATTACK POINT** like a track junction and then plan your route to this **ATTACK POINT** using easily followed features like tracks, fence lines, forest edges and streams these features which you will meet on your route are known as **COLLECTION POINTS** (because as you move around the course you can 'collect them').

It is not a good idea to go directly for the **CONTROL** since they are easily missed.

When you begin to select your route start by choosing a good **ATTACK POINT** near to the next **CONTROL**. A track junction or corner of a wood will do but it should be as close as possible to the **CONTROL** and easily identifiable. Next select a route which will have as many **COLLECTION POINTS** on it as possible. The more the better since these are the way in which you will navigate from one **CONTROL** to another, however remember to check direction from time to time with the compass.

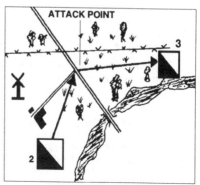

ORIENTEERING

Try to avoid bogs, dense forest and very steep hills as these will slow you down and may even be impassable.

It will often be better to go round an obstacle even if the distance covered is greater because it will be easier and faster.

To help you decide which route you should take remember the following.

The Short Hard Route v The Long Easy Route

Swim across the lake or go round it. Climb up and over the mountain or go round the valley.

There are usually several ways to get from one point to another, two points may be separated by different types of terrain which will take different amounts of time and energy to get through.

A good runner will typically take the following amounts of time to complete 400 metres over different terrain:-

a. Path 2 mins

b. Heathland 4 mins

c. Open Forest 6 mins

d. Thick Firs 10 mins or more

It may be the case that it will be quicker to run twice or three times the distance on tracks, than to try and fight your way through a thick forest.

The Steep Short Route v The Long Flat Route -

You will often find when orienteering in hilly country that the course has a number of CONTROLS at opposite sides of a steep hill or valley.

You must then make the decision whether or not it will be quicker to go over the top or to 'contour' round.

If you remember that a 25 ft height gain will be equivalent to 100m on the flat, in the amount of effort used, you should be able to make the choice.

AIMING OFF

Sometimes the CONTROL you are aiming for is on a linear feature at right angles to your line of approach such as a track or stream.

This will mean that the CONTROL may be difficult to find if you aim straight for it since if you miss it, you will not know for sure whether it is, for instance, to the North or South.

This problem can be overcome simply by aiming off to one side of the

ORIENTEERING

CONTROL, say the North, then when you reach the stream/track you will know that the CONTROL is to the South.

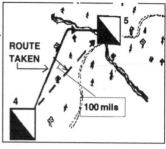

This will cut down the time that you spend searching for the CONTROL.

Orienteering is an exciting sport with the added benefits of practicing and improving your Map Reading and sharpening your wits, at the same time keeping you physically fit.

Many units enter teams for the annual Army Orienteering Championships.

TERMS USED IN MAP READING

BEARING The angle, measured clockwise, that a line makes with a fixed zero line. It may be a True Bearing, measured from True North - a Magnetic Bearing measured with a compass from Magnetic North, or a Grid Bearing measured from Grid North.

COL (SADDLE): See also SADDLE for description.

CONTOUR: An imaginary line on the surface of the ground at the same height above mean sea level throughout its length. Contour lines are drawn a map to show the shape of the ground.

CREST: The highest part of a hill or range of hills. That line on a range of hills or mountains from which the ground slopes down in opposite directions.

DATUM or DATUM LEVEL: The level from which altitudes are measured; generally mean sea-level.

DETAIL: All the topographical information on a map.

DIVIDE: The line along a range of hills from which the water flows in opposite directions, e.g., the continental divide.

ESCARPMENT: The steep hillside formed by a drop in land level, usually at the edge of a plateau.

FIXED POINT: Used in making a map to denote a point that has been fixed on the paper by survey methods.

MAP READING

GORGE: A narrow stream passage between steep rocky hills; a ravine with precipitous sides.

GRADIENT: A slope described by a percentage, mostly used on roads to indicate the rise and fall in a road; e.g., a steep hill.

GRATICULE: Lines of longitude and latitude drawn on a map as the basis for a system of map references.

GRID: Lines drawn on the map forming squares as a basis for a system of map references.

GRID NORTH: Except through the origin, grid lines do not lie true north and south or east and west. Grid North is the direction of the north-south grid lines on a map.

HACHURES: A conventional method of showing hill features by shading in short lines drawn in the direction of the slope. thicker at the top of the slope than at the bottom.

HORIZONTAL EQUIVALENT (HE): The horizontal distance on the ground between two adjacent contours.

ISOGONAL: A line drawn on a map through places having the same magnetic variation.

KNOLL: A small knoblike hill.

LEFT or RIGHT BANK: The appropriate bank of a stream or river when facing DOWN stream.

LOCAL MAGNETIC ATTRACTION: Attraction of the compass needle due to presence of metal or magnetic iron ore. NOT to be confused with Magnetic Variation.

LUBBER LINE: Sometimes referred to as the HAIR LINE running through the glass lid of the Prismatic Compass, used for sighting on an object when taking a bearing.

MAGNETIC VARIATION or DECLINATION: The angle between True North and Magnetic North.

MAGNETIC NORTH: The point in far north of Canada, to which a compass needle points.

MERIDIAN: A true north and south line.

ORIENTING a MAP: Placing it so that its True North line points True North (or Magnetic or Grid North line points to Magnetic or Grid North). This is also called "Setting the Map".

MAP READING

PLATEAU: A table land: A raised plain, usually quite flat, above a level of the land.

PLOTTING: Transferring to a map bearings and other measurements.

RAY: A line drawn from the position of an observer to fix the direction of an object.

RAVINE: A long deep valley worn by a stream

RE-ENTRANT: A shallow valley or ravine, usually between two spurs, running inwards towards the hill or mountain top. Usually found where a stream runs off a hillside.

RIDGE: The line along a hill or range of hills or mountains from which water flows in opposite directions; a divide; sometimes the crest of a line of hills as it appears along the horizon.

RESECTION: The process of finding a position by taking bearings on two identifiable points and plotting them on a map, also by fixing a position by observation of at least two previously identified points.

SADDLE: A depression between adjacent hill or mountain tops: also called a col.

SECTION: A line drawn to represent the shape of the surface of the ground along a line between two points.

SPOT HEIGHT: A point on a map whose height has been found by survey methods, identified by a dot with figure against it.

SLOPES (Concave and Convex): Convex "bulges out", Concave "caves in".

SPUR: A hill feature or low ridge, running out from a hill or high ground, often found between two re-entrants.

TRIG POINT: A concrete pillar with a brass mounting used by Ordnance Survey for their survey work. The correct name is a Triangulation Point. Marked on a map by a small triangle with the height above sea level shown next to it.

TRUE NORTH: The direction of the North pole from that point.

VERTICAL INTERVAL (V.I.): The difference in level between two adjacent contours on a map.

WATERSHED: The line, usually mountain range where waters divide to flow into different river systems; the edge of a river basin.

FIELDCRAFT

The subject of Fieldcraft in this section is dealt with only at individual and infantry section level.

In recent times the introduction of the SA80 and LSW, plus the LAW (Light Anti-Tank) weapons have had an effect on infantry tactics and training.

The other dramatic changes have been the introduction of the Warrior Armoured Personnel Carrier and the Saxon (wheeled APC) as a result of which the Armoured Infantry Battalions are now well established. Changes in tactics and training of personnel throughout the various levels in the battalions has been taken 'on board'. The consequences of having 'armour' in the units requires the back up services to be expanded and facilities made available.

The reference made to *tactics* needs some explanation. It could be defined as making the best use of the resources you have at your disposal, taking into account your own and the enemy's strength and situation. The likely action the enemy will take. Immediate and past experience, and to some extent the knowledge required to make a calculated risk in committing the available resources with the least risk to those valuable resources

INTRODUCTION

You will have been instructed in this subject during your initial training, although that will have concentrated on the Individual Fieldcraft skills. Later you will have become accustomed to more advanced aspects of the subject, by being trained as a member of a Section at the same time using other skills, weapon training, battle drills etc.

As a soldier - irrespective of your Regiment or Corps you will always have to retain these basic skills and may be called upon to use them when least expecting to do so.

Like so many skills as a soldier, unless you are constantly practicing them you will *lose your edge*, you don't need to be told, but the standards of skill you maintain in Fieldcraft could mean the difference in the length of your life span. Your ability to react, to use cover

FIELDCRAFT

correctly, make the right decision on when and where to move,
"sus out" and make an appreciation of the situation; are all down to
practice in the application of your personal Fieldcraft skills.
Provided you train yourself to use your eyes - powers of observation
can teach you a great deal of fieldcraft.
You will be aware that the wild life "get a living" off the land by being
experts in the use of their skills of stealth, speed, patience, fitness,
stamina, planning and cunning, and by having natural ability in the art
of camouflage and concealment.
Fieldcraft is their prime skill in catching their food and in many ways
to be good at Fieldcraft you could do no better than to study the
actions of wildlife at every opportunity.
Observe how a cat stalks its quarry, how the Sparrow Hawk, hovers
patiently, observing the right moment to drop in on the Field Mouse,
the Fox, using the hedgerows to move from one field to another, see
how well a Rabbit is camouflaged against the ground.
All of these examples are types of Individual Fieldcraft skills
exercised for the purpose of either "defence" or "attack".
Once you have an understanding of the need to imitate those skills
that wild life practice to survive in the field, then you will be on the
way to attaining an acceptable standard of Individual Fieldcraft.

Section Organisation

The Infantry Section is the smallest 'unit' within the Battalion. There
are several different organisations which are adopted within the
Section, depending upon the role they are carrying out and or the
circumstances under which they are operating.
With the introduction of the SA80 Rifle and the LSW Light Support
Weapon, the LAW LIght Anti-Tank Weapon has changed how some
of the minor tactics are now performed.
The Section will often be organised in two equal groups, when they
may have to work as half-section patrols or double sentries etc.
The normal fighting strength of a Section in the Regular Army (650
strength Battalion) is two NCO's and six men, but it can operate with
one NCO and five men.
In the diagram on the next page the Section organisation is shown
with 2 LSW's and 6 Rifles.
The new groups are called *Fire Teams* as a sub-unit of the Infantry
Section which usually consists of an NCO and 3 soldiers.
The fire team structure is essentially flexible and any combination of

the resources within the Section can be called a Fire Team.
The introduction of the Warrior Armoured Personnel Carrier has also
had a marked affect upon the conduct of operations within the
Infantry Battalions.
Armoured Infantry Battalions have carried out extensive training in
the tactical deployment of infantry from the Warrior. The vehicle has
undergone rigorous use under severe conditions and gained the
respect of those who operate and use it.
The diagram below of a Battalion is not hard and fast, as elements
of other arms are always attached to a Battalion depending upon its
theatre of operations and the role it is tasked to carry out.

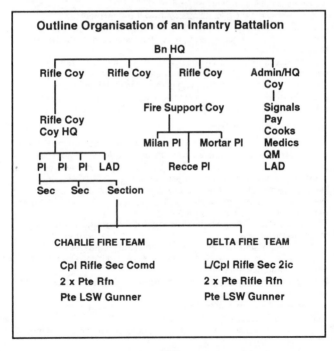

Outline Organisation of an Infantry Battalion

Bn HQ

Rifle Coy — Rifle Coy — Rifle Coy — Admin/HQ Coy

Rifle Coy Coy HQ

Fire Support Coy

Signals
Pay
Cooks
Medics
QM
LAD

Milan Pl — Mortar Pl

Recce Pl

PI — PI — PI — LAD

Sec — Sec — Section

CHARLIE FIRE TEAM

Cpl Rifle Sec Comd
2 x Pte Rfn
Pte LSW Gunner

DELTA FIRE TEAM

L/Cpl Rifle Sec 2ic
2 x Pte Rifle Rfn
Pte LSW Gunner

FIELDCRAFT

INDIVIDUAL FIELDCRAFT

As a soldier no matter which Regiment or Corps you are serving in, your first line of responsibility is to be an efficient Soldier. You are required to be proficient in the use of your particular PW (Personal Weapon). The same level of efficiency is required in your fitness and your ability to perform as an effective member of a team/section. The application of individual Fieldcraft Skills in tandem with Skill at Arms is essential for your survival, therefore this section of the Pocket Book is NOT JUST FOR THE INFANTRY.

You will need a lot of practice and patience to develop the natural ability to react in defence of your survival. This is applicable both as an individual and a member of a team.

Be good at fieldcraft and survive - you seldom get a second chance.

FIELDCRAFT SKILLS

METHODS OF JUDGING DISTANCE

Why judge distance; if you can judge distance you will know the approximate area in which to look when given an order. If your sights are not correctly adjusted, your shot will probably miss the target.

USE A UNIT OF MEASURE

100 metres is a good unit, The Range is marked out at 100 metre intervals. A Full Size Football pitch is about 100 metres long.

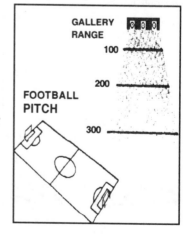

DO NOT USE THE UNIT OF MEASURE METHOD OVER 400 METRES IF YOU CAN'T SEE ALL THE GROUND BETWEEN YOU AND THE TARGET.

FIELDCRAFT

AIDS TO JUDGING DISTANCE

When you know what a 100metres looks like, practice fitting your Unit of Measure between you and your target.

APPEARANCE METHOD
By noting what a person looks like at a set distance, you can then use the Appearance Method

Common objects may also be used for this method.

FIELDCRAFT

Things seem closer

Further away

REMEMBER

Things seem closer .. In bright light, if they are bigger than their surroundings, if there is dead ground between you and them, if they are higher up than you.

Further away ... With sun in your eyes, in bad light. When smaller than surroundings. Looking across a valley, down a street or along a path in a wood, if you are lying down.

KEY RANGES
If the range to one object is known, estimate the distance from it to the target.

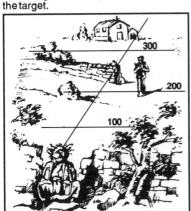

BRACKETING

Calculate mid-distance between nearest possible and furthest possible distance of target.
Nearest - 100
Farthest - 300.
Mid-distance - 200.

HALVING

Estimate the distance halfway to the target then double it:
$100 \times 2 = 200$

FIELDCRAFT

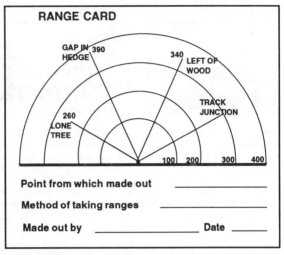

RANGE CARD

GAP IN HEDGE 390

340 LEFT OF WOOD

TRACK JUNCTION

260 LONE TREE

100   200   300   400

Point from which made out _____

Method of taking ranges _____

Made out by _____ Date _____

THE SMALL ARMS RANGE CARD

Range Cards are to be prepared whenever a position is occupied for 30 mins or more.

Section and platoon commanders are responsible for ensuring the range card is made out and that it is accurate.

A range card must be made out for every separate position i.e. trench and should be passed to the next occupant who must check its accuracy.

A pre-printed range card is available on the 24-hr ration packs, these should be retained and used when necessary.

By practicing at making out Range Cards you will be applying all the skills of Judging Distance and as a result improve your accuracy.

FIELDCRAFT

PERSONAL CAMOUFLAGE AND CONCEALMENT

The enemy is looking for you so - don't make it easy. Merge with your surroundings

TOO MUCH   JUST RIGHT   TOO LITTLE

LOSE YOUR SHAPE
Make sure nothing shines.
Blend in with your surroundings - if they vary, so must you.

AVOID THE SKYLINE

STAND BACK FROM WINDOWS

merge into the shadows - don't lean out - you will be seen

FIELDCRAFT

Don't use isolated cover - it stands out.

SOMETHING IS SEEN BECAUSE ITS:-

Shape
Shadow } **IS FAMILIAR OR STANDS OUT**
Shadow

Surface
Spacing } **IS DIFFERENT FROM ITS SURROUNDINGS**
Movement

SEEING IS .... Noticing details.

EASY TO SEE   **DIFFICULT TO FIND**
SHAPE...... Disguise your shape -
including equipment and weapons

FIELDCRAFT

SHADOW .... Keep in the shadows

SILHOUETTE

Don't Skyline

SURFACE..... Don't differ from your surroundings.

133

FIELDCRAFT

SPACING... Keep spread out - but not equally spaced.

MOVEMENT .... Move carefully - slowly when concealed - sudden movement will attract attention.

Look through cover - if possible - not round it .
You MUST SEE without being SEEN.

FIELDCRAFT

TARGET RECOGNITION
 The correct target must be located and fired at

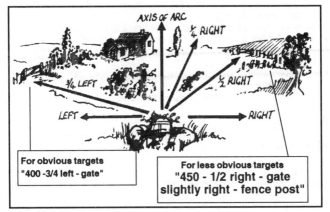

For obvious targets
"400 -3/4 left - gate"

For less obvious targets
"450 - 1/2 right - gate
slightly right - fence post"

For difficult targets use the Clock Ray Method -

"350 half left - house,
right 3 o'clock -
small bush"

"350 - half left - house,
8 o'clock, hedge"

FIELDCRAFT

FIRE CONTROL ORDERS.

When the Section comes under fire the Section Commander will give the order 'TAKE COVER'.

The drills for this are covered later, however there will come a time when the Section Commander will need to take control of the fire power of the Section to concentrate it on the enemy, this is achieved using a **Fire Control Order.**

You must learn how to do this instinctively so that you can:

a. React to the Fire Control Order correctly.

b. Give an order yourself if no one else can see the target.

To give a correct Fire Control Order you have to follow a set sequence, it will help you if you remember it by the "Key Word" **GRIT**, as follows:-

G =	WHICH **GROUP** IS TO FIRE (*"No 2 SECTION"*).
R =	**RANGE** IN METRES (*"450"*)
I =	**INDICATION** WHERE TO LOOK (*"HALF RIGHT GAP IN WALL"*)
T =	**TYPE** OF FIRE (*"RAPID FIRE"*)

When giving this type or order remember it is an order therefore to give it: -

C	=	**Clearly**
L	=	**Loudly**
A	=	**As an order**
P	=	**With Pauses**

136

FIELDCRAFT

TYPES OF FIRE CONTROL ORDER

The details of the Fire Control Order you get depends on the Type of Target to be engaged.

BRIEF Orders -

"Section - quarter right rapid fire".

FULL Orders - *" Charlie Fire Team - 450 left-house*

doorway - fire".

DELAYED Orders.

"Delta Fire Team -300-quarter right-small wood -

when enemy appears - rapid - await my order.

(When enemy appears) - fire".

INDIVIDUAL Orders

"No 1 and 2 riflemen - slightly left - small bush -enemy

in that area - watch and shoot"

When a section comes under effective fire the Section Commander will give the order to *'TAKE COVER'.* The drills for this are set out later, however there will come a time when he will need to take control of the fire power of the Section to concentrate it on the enemy. This is achieved by using a FIRE CONTROL ORDER. You must learn how to automaticall respond to this instinctively.

MOVEMENT IN THE FIELD

When close to the enemy you do not want your movements to be seen-therefore use cover. Remember to: Use the hedges and walls for cover.

Leopard Crawl Crawl on the inside of your knees and your elbows. Useful for moving behind very low cover. Move by using alternate elbows and knees, rolling your body a little as you bend your knees. Keep your heels, head and body down, you must observe at all times.

FIELDCRAFT

**Leopard Crawl —
with a rifle.**
Hold your Rifle with
the right hand on the
Pistol Grip and the
left hand on the Hand
Guard.

The Monkey Run
This is the normal 'hands and knees'
crawl. Useful to move behind low
cover.
You can move quite fast, but it does
make a noise.
Moving slower and to prevent twigs
cracking as you move, put your knees
on the spot where your hands have
been.
Keep your 'rear-end' and head down,
but continue to observe.
With a rifle hold it at the point of
balance, make sure that no dirt gets
into the muzzle.

The Walk
The Rifle is held in the ALERT position,
ready for instant action.
You must adopt a positive and alert attitude,
observing in all directions.
Don't walk on the flat sole of your boots, use
the edge to walk quietly.
It helps to keep your balance if you slightly
bend your knees as you move.

FIELDCRAFT

The Roll
The quickest way of getting off a skyline
or crest of a hill.
Protect your Rifle, hold closely into your
side. Keep feet together and your body
straight.

MOVEMENT AT NIGHT
Always move quietly.
Movements used during daylight are not
suitable at night- they have to be adapted.
The Ghost Walk
Lift legs high, sweeping them slowly outwards.
Feel gently with toes for safe place for each
foot, put weight down gently. Keep knees bent.
Use the left hand to feel the air in front of you
from head height down to the ground checking
for obstructions, trip wires, booby traps or
alarms etc

The Cat Walk
Crawl on hands and knees. Search ground
ahead for twigs, move knee to where hand
has searched.

The Kitten Crawl
It is quiet-but slow. *It is very tiring.*
Lie on your front, search ahead for twigs,
move them to one side.
Lift your body on your forearms and
toes, press forward and
lower yourself on
to the ground.

FIELDCRAFT

NIGHT NOISES

At night you hear more than you see.
Stop and listen.
Keep close to the ground, turn your
head slowly and use a cupped hand
behind the ear. Freeze if you hear a
noise.

MOVING AT NIGHT - REMEMBER

Keep quiet .... have no loose equipment.

Move carefully ... use the ghost walk, cat walk or kitten crawl.

Clear your route ... dry vegetation will make a noise.

Use available cover ... flares, thermal imaging and night observation
devices will turn night into day.

Keep to the low ground ... you split your party at night at your peril.

TREAD CAREFULLY

ON SOFT OR SANDY GROUND

ON 'STONEY' GROUND OR IN WOODS

WALKING ON GRASS

LISTENING AT NIGHT

Use your ears - trurn them towards any
sound.

If the enemy is about - keep an ear close to
the ground

The closer you are to the ground, the more
chance you have of seeing the enemy on
'skyline'.

FIELDCRAFT

NIGHT VISION

We can see in the dark - but REMEMBER our eyes take 30 minutes to get used to the dark.

We see less than in daylight. We see shapes - not detail.

We see skylines and silhouettes. We may see movement.

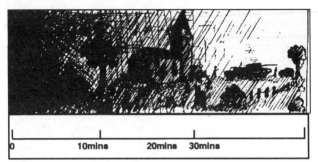

0	10mins	20mins	30mins	

YOUR EYESIGHT

Your eyes have two sets of cells, one set for daylight (CONES) in the centre of your eyes, the other set for darkness (RODS), which are around the CONES.

The night cells work when the day cells are affected by falling darkness.

With constant practice night observation can be improved. If you have a cold, headache or are tired it can reduce your night vision.

You will find that there is a limit to the time you can concentrate effectively on any given point or your vision becomes blurred.

Most units use Thermal Imaging (night sights) that "turn darkness into daylight" in as much that they pick out an object giving out heat (body heat),

The SUSAT sights on the SA80 Rifle (an optical sight) has advantages similar to that of binoculars for night observation.

BRIGHT LIGHT RUINS YOUR NIGHT VISION

If caught in the light of flares take cover at once in open ground. If in a wood - FREEZE. If you see a flare, quickly close one eye to protect your night vision, use the other eye to look about you taking advantage of the light, but do not move suddenly as this will give you away.

DUTIES OF A SENTRY

Sentries are the eyes and ears of the unit. If the job is done well, the unit will be safe and secure.

When you are a Sentry make sure:-

That you know and understand your orders.

That you know what to do if your post is approached by a person or vehicle.

That you ask questions if you do not understand anything.

What ground to watch.

Direction of the enemy.

Signal for defensive fire.

Names of prominent landmarks.

Where neighbouring posts are.

About patrols that maybe in the area, or coming through your post.

Equipment to carry

Torch. Whistle. Range Card. Duties list. Notebook and pencil.

142

FIELDCRAFT

SENTRIES AT NIGHT IN THE FIELD

At night sentries work in pairs.

Sentries must know:-

What to do if anyone approaches their post.

What ground to watch.

The Password.

Sentries close to the enemy must know :-

Direction of the enemy.

Name of forward land marks.

Where neighbouring posts are.

Signal for them to fire defensive fire.

About patrols that may come in or out through their posts or near them.

FIELDCRAFT

HOW TO CHALLENGE.

When you see movements which you think may not be your own troops - alert your Section Commander, cover him/ them with your weapon - SAY - **'HALT' HANDS UP. 'Advance one'. "Halt".** **Give the challenge half of the password - quietly, so that only the first man can hear it.** **ACTION** - Password correct Allow friendly troops through, **know how many and count them through - one at a time.** **If password is incorrectly given - Section opens fire at enemy troops.** NOTE: Be aware of a common trick which is for the enemy to approach a sentry, listen and learn the first half of a PASS WORD then fade away.

An **inexperienced sentry** may allow this to happen. The same enemy then approaches another sentry and challenges them before they can challenge them. Again the inexperienced sentry might then give the reply then allow the enemy into the position. So be careful, never allow anyone into your position unless you can positively identify them, **when in doubt call for help.**

USE YOUR SENSES

How can they help in Fieldcraft? On a Patrol or on duty as a sentry, you will use your EYES, EARS and your TOUCH when feeling your way through difficult cover.

Your sense of TASTE may not be used often, but your sense of SMELL - depending upon the smell - may remind you of TASTE.

SMELL - Body smell or the smell of cooking or anything else that drifts on the air can give your and the enemies presence away.

FIELDCRAFT

ATTACK

Principles of Attack are;
1. Surprise, by the speed carried out and from where it came.
2. The volume of fire from different weapons.
3. The ease and simplicity in which is was carried out.

Attacks can take place by day or night, on foot, from the air or APC's. They may be carried out quickly as you 'bump' the enemy on the initiative of your Platoon Commander or carefully planned, rehearsed and carried out with all available support. All Attacks have five distinct stages, they are;
1. Planning and Prep.
2. Winning the Fire Fight and bringing the maximum fire onto the enemy position.
3. The final Assault.
4. Fighting through the objective.
5. Reorganization.

At the Platoon and Section level these five stages are set out in the following pages as Battle Drills. They are *'drills'* in the sense of being a framework to ensure that no point is overlooked in the planning of an attack, also to give the individual commander on the spot the opportunity to make his own appreciation and plans as the Attack progresses.

Fire and Movement

All attacks are based on fire and movement. The term Fire and Movement and the principles behind it are important to learn and adopt. In reality it means that while one FIRE TEAM is up and moving, the other(s) are down in a fire position giving covering fire to those on the move. Remember it by thinking of *"keeping one foot on the ground"*.

At a Section level Fire and Movement is not too complicated, but if it is part of an overall plan on a much larger scale then it can be very important to keep to the plan in detail. The use of supporting arms, artillery, Anti-Tank Guided Weapons, mortars, aircraft could all be used during a final assault - timing and good communications would be needed!

Weapons

The Platoon and Section commanders will have to consider the correct use of available weapons depending upon their Range, mobility and rate of fire, ability to hit the target, the shape of the ground or any obstacles, the advantages of one weapon against another.

Movement

Only with practice will your skill be acquired to suit the ground and the tactical situation. The effective appreciation and use of ground will enable a Section to close effectively with the enemy.
A Section comprises six riflemen and two LSW gunners, usually divided into two fire teams. Their weapons will to a great extent depend upon the threat of armour and the tasks they are to carry out. Likewise the Section can be brken down into diferent groups or teams as required acording to their role etc.

Control of the Platoon

Control is exercised by the Platoon Commander at all times byusing radio, whistle, voice, flares or field signals or by a member of the Section acting as Runner.

SECTION BATTLE DRILLS

These notes are for a Section organised with a **Fire Support Team** and **an Assault Fire Team.**
The following "Mnemonic" will help you to remember all the detailks to be covered in your BATTLE PREPARATION:-
P Protection, sentries, cover, camouflage, NBC, alarms.
A Ammunition, supply, reserves.
W Weapons, scales, distribution, checking and preparation.
P Personal: camouflage, hygiene, food and water.
E Equipment, scales required, distribution.
R Radio - communications, rehearsals.
S Specialist equipment for tasks, cutting, climbing.
O Orders, 'O' Group timings

SECTION BATTLE DRILL No 1. BATTLE PREPARATION.

a. Personal camouflage. Break up outline, use scrim net and local foliage typical of area.
b. Check weapons. Clean, servicable, sights set at 300.
c. Check ammo. Magazines and Grenades (HE and Smoke) distributed.
d. Check all radio links are working.

FIELDCRAFT

Section Commanders Orders
a. **Ground** ref points.
b. **Situation** Enemy and Friendly forces. Pl fmn and Task.
c. Attachments and detachments.
d. **Mission** - the section mission.
e. **Execution** Fire Team group (if altered). Route. Sec Fmn.
f. LSW and LAW tasks.
g. Service support - Info from Pl Commanders orders.
h. Command & Signals; info from Pl Commander orders.

REFERENCE POINTS & ANTICIPATORY ORDERS.
In the 'Advance to Contact' the Section Commander will look out for :-
1. Positions giving cover in anticipation of effective en fire.
2. Reference points for Fire Control Orders

SECTION BATTLE DRILL No 2 - REACTION TO EFFECTIVE FIRE.

The drill to be adopted is: On the order of the section commander -
"TAKE COVER", DASH - DOWN - CRAWL - OBSERVE - SIGHTS - FIRE.
Get off the area immediately. Move to nearest cover as indicated.
Take cover, crawl into chosen position to observe. Return fire use
tracer to indicate enemy position.

SECTION BATTLE DRILL No 3 - LOCATION OF THE ENEMY

Location of the enemy is usually difficult, failure means casualties and
losing the initiative as result. Three stages in this drill:
a. Observation - look in area from which thump came from. Use
binoculars or SUSAT sight. Look for movement, smoke etc.
b. Fire - fire order to couple of riflemen or LSW to fire at likely target -
remainder of Section observe.
c. Movement - Section commander orders rifleman to move while
remainder of section observe.
Note: The terms "CRACK and THUMP". THUMP relates to the time/
speed of the sound that the firing of a weapon takes to reach you.
The CRACK is the sound of the round hopefully passing over you in
its flight.
In locating the enemy it is an aid to establish the direction from which
a shot is fired. Sound tarvels at approx 600 metres per second, a
bullet much faster.

FIELDCRAFT

SECTION BATTLE DRILL No 4 WINNING THE FIRE FIGHT

As soon as the Section Commander knows the enemies position, a fire order must be given to bring sufficient weight of fire on the enemy to neutralize them and or make them keep their heads down. It is important that the Section Commander takes control of the Fire Fight at the earliest, otherwise the large amount of ammunition that could be used might jeopardise the operation.

SECTION BATTLE DRILL No 5 - THE ATTACK BATTLE ORDERS

When a Section Commander reaches the forward enemy position they look for any defended positions. If they are any part of the objective they will issue snap orders so that they can carry out an assault. This is always divided into three stages;

The Approach - including Quick Battle Orders (QBO's)

The Fight Through

The Attack will always be one of the following depending on the number of stages in the attack. They will be as brief as possible.

Orders for a **one stage attack,** that is when the Assault Fire Team goes straight into the assault

1. Fire and Movement to close with en, L or R flanking.
2. Asslt Fire Team prep to move. *Fire Sup Team fires.*
3. *Assault Fire Team move.*

Orders for a **two stage attack,** that if when the fire support team move to another position before the assault fire team assaults.

1. Direction of assault, L or R flanking.
2. Fire Support Team moves first. *prepare to move*
3. Assault fire team fire. *Fire Support Team move*

Orders for a **three stage attack** in which the fire team moves first, then fire support team moves and finally the assault fire team assaults.

1. Direction of the assault, possibly L or R flanking.
2. Assault Fire Team moves first to ...Prep to move *Fire Support Team fires.*
3. Fire Support Team move. *Assault Fire Team fires*
4. Assault Fire Team prep to assault. *Fire Support Team fire and switch.*
5. Assault Fire Team moves. *Fire Support Team fires*

Fire Suppoprt Team should fire or move automatically on the previous order to the Assult Fire Team.

FIELDCRAFT

The Assault and Fighting through the Objective

All movement by either fire team must be covered by fire from the other. An angle of 1600 mils between the two Fire Teams allows the most effective fire support for the assault. As the assult is made the Fire Suppoprt Team should fire across the objective for as long as possible, then switches it's fire across the objective onto enemy in depth positions.

Watch out for enemy interference from flanks. Section Cmdr make continuous appreciation during the fight through.

DRILL No 6 REORGANISATION

When objective cleared of enemy the Section Commander must regain close control over men and position, ready to beat off counter attack.

Reorganisation must be swift and efficient, if not all that was gained will be lost.

The Section Commander will:

1 Allot fire tasks to each member of section.
2. Post sentries.
3. Check on casualties.
4. Check ammunition, arrange redistribution of ammo.
5. Supervise re-digging of shell scrapes.
6. Send prisoners and captured kit to rear.
7. Report to Pl Cmdr for orders.

The Fire Support Team will;

1. On prearranged signal, rejoin the Assault Fire Team once Section in in control of the objective.
2. Check LSW and redistribute ammo.

Riflemen should;

1. Check weapons and equipment.
2. Check ammunition and grenades.
3. Recharge all magazines.

NOTE: While the 'fight-through' is in progress the capture of the objective is the first priority. As soon as the position is cleared, then casualties take high priority.

"MAKE EVERY SHOT COUNT -
AMMUNITION STILL HAS TO BE CARRIED"

FIELDCRAFT

SECTION AND PLATOON FIELD SIGNALS

Field Signals are a silent means of communication between members of the platoon. They should be used whenever possible and be constantly practised, even when going about normal duties it is as well to use them, so they become second nature to everyone.

Very often there is a need to attract the attention of those who are to receive the signal, especially if the Section Commander wants to tell several members of his section at the same time. This does not absolve you as a member of the section from watching out for signals, there may be times when an audible signal is not practical. There are four recognised methods of attracting attention:-

EXPLANATION AND KEY TO FIELD SIGNALS

1. A SINGLE whistle blast - during fire contact only.

2. Snapping forefinger and thumb.

3. Knocking butt of weapon with knuckles.

4. Silent whistle.

Whistle BLASTS are often used to indicate situations, they are as follows:-

1. SHORT BLASTS - ALARM - air attack, NBC attack, etc.

2. LONG BLASTS indicate "STAND DOWN".

KEY TO FIELD SIGNAL ILLUSTRATIONS
(See illustrations on following pages)

1. READY TO MOVE. Move hands as if cranking handle.

2. DEPLOY. Arm extended below shoulder level, waved slowly from side to side, hand open. If deployment to either flank is wanted, commander points to flank, after completing signal.

3. ADVANCE or FOLLOW ME. Arm swung from rear to front below shoulder.

4. HALT or REST. Arm raised until the hand is level with shoulder. Indicate length of halt by number of fingers. Point to 'rest area'.

5. GO BACK or TURN ABOUT. Hand circled at hip height.

6. CLOSE or JOIN ME. Hand placed on top of head, elbow square to the right or left, according to which hand is used. Point to RV area.

FIELDCRAFT

7. DOUBLE. Clenched hand moved up/down between thigh/shoulder.

8. SLOW DOWN (APC). Arm extended to the side below shoulder, palm downwards, moved slowly up and down, wrist loose.

9. LIE DOWN or DISMOUNT (APC). Two or three slight movements with the open hand towards the ground (palm downwards).

10. AS YOU WERE or SWITCH OFF (APC). Forearm extended downwards, hand open, waved across body parallel to ground.

11. ENEMY SEEN or SUSPECTED. Thumb pointed towards ground from clenched fist.

12. NO ENEMY IN SIGHT or ALL CLEAR. Thumb pointed upwards from clenched fist.

13. GUN GROUP. Clenched fist raised to shoulder height.

14. SCOUT GROUP. Clenched fist with forefinger upright.

15. RIFLE GROUP. 'Victory' sign - fist and second finger extended and open in 'V' remainder of fist clenched.

16. LIGHT MORTAR. Weapon held vertical. Imitate loading mortar rounds.

17. LAW/MAW. Weapon placed on shoulder and held like a LAW/MAW.

18. SECTION CMDR. Two opened fingers held against arm to indicate Corporal's Stripes.

19. PLATOON CMDR. Two opened fingers held on shoulder to indicate a Lieutenant's stars.

20. GIVE COVERING FIRE. Weapon brought into aim.

21. OBSTACLES. CROSSING. TRACK JUNCTION.
Arms crossed. For water obstacle make waves.

22. HOUSE or HUT. Hands folded in inverted 'V'; to indicate shape of roof.

23. RECONNAISSANCE. Hand held to eye, as though using eye glass.

24. ATTACK. A chopping movement with edge of hand in direction attack is required.

25. MOVE UP. Fingers spread, arms swung slowly in direction movement is required.

26. FORM AMBUSH. Hand placed over face, followed by pointing to place of ambush.

27. FREEZE AND LISTEN. Hand cupped to ear.

28. 'O' GROUP. Fingers together, moved in conjunction with thumb to indicate person talking.

29 RIGHT or LEFT FLANKING. A curved sweeping movement of the arm in direction concerned.

30. FIRE & MANOEUVRE. One hand used in a rolling forward action in front of the body.

31. SPACE OUT. Palm of hands held against weapon and moved away several times.

32. SINGLE FILE. One arm fully extended above head.

33. STAGGERED FILE. Both arms fully extended above head.

34. ARROWHEAD. Both arms forced backwards or forwards at a angle of 800 mils, depending whether arrow is to the back or forward.

SPEARHEAD. As for arrowhead plus indicating Gun Group to move in at rear.

35. DIAMOND. Arms raised above the head with arms slightly bent so that hands touch to form diamond shape.

36. EXTENDED LINE. Arms raised to the side level with the ground, indicate flank and which group is to go.

FIELDCRAFT

FIELDCRAFT

*THE BEST WAY TO LEARN FIELD SIGNALS
IS TO USE AND PRACTICE THEM ON
EVERY POSSIBLE OCCASION*

SECTION FORMATIONS.

As a member of a rifle section you move as part of your Section. How you move depends on six factors.

The country you are crossing.

The likely direction of enemy fire.

How far you can see.

How the Section can best be controlled.

Need to produce maximum fire effect.

Who controls the air space.

YOU MAY MOVE IN;-

SINGLE FILE

This is good for - moving along hedges or at the edges of woods. Good control - especially at night. Makes a good target for enemy. Firing to the front is restricted.

FIELDCRAFT

FILE

This is good for -
control of
movement,,movement
at night,
But - Makes a good
target for enemy fire.

ARROWHEAD

This is good for - Moving across open country. Producing effective
fire against enemy frontal attack. But - difficult to control particularly
when engaged by flanking fire.

DIAMOND

Formation only used when
crossing open country at
night. Easy to control, has all
round observation and
protection, each person can
see next, the Section
Commander can be at the
front or in the middle.

FIELDCRAFT

EXTENDED LINE

EXTENDED LINE
- this is good formation for -
an assault on enemy positions,
but difficult to control movement.

REMEMBER

When moving in Section Formation:-

Watch your section commander for hand signals.

**Keep in contact with members of the section on each side of you
- but not too close.**

Keep quiet and listen for commands and anticipatory orders.

Keep in correct position for formation.

Be observant.

Be ready to change to new section formation.

DO YOU KNOW *ALL* YOUR FIELD SIGNALS ?

FIELDCRAFT

CHOOSING A ROUTE.

If you are to move across country check in advance exactly where to make for - a given map reference. Check the map and any other information you can find out, then decide on the best route, taking the following into consideration.

PLANNING -You must plan your route in advance, using maps, air photos, sketches and information from previous patrols or recces. Consider alternative routes or diversions that may have to be made..

You must move in 'bounds', 'legs' or 'stages' (all meaning the same thing) from one observation point to another. Check and re-check your direction and navigation all the time.

Use and trust your compass.

Keep in cover, you must see but not be seen.

If you have to take a chance choose a route which offers the risks early in your approach rather than later on, since you will have less chance of being seen.

The best route will have good OP's with a covered line of approach.

Don't go blindly on towards the enemy.

Look out for likely ambush sites.

Look for good fire positions and cover from view - you may need them.

Not to have impassible obstacles en route, such as marsh land, open ground or ravines to cross.

Record the route on a Route Cards, each leg - distances, bearings, reference points for outward and reverse journey.

FIELDCRAFT

PACING

Pacing is necessary because you must always know how exactly far you have gone when counting a number of your own 'paces'.

You should know your 'Pacing Scale', over different types of ground conditions, IE tarmac roads or tracks, grasslands, woodlands etc.

To find your PACING SCALE, put two markers out 100m apart. Walk the distance between them as you would on a patrol, counting the paces as you go.

If it has taken you 120 paces to cover the 100m, then that is your PACING SCALE.

It follows, to use this scale if you were on a patrol and had to go a distance of 300m, you would have to count out 360 paces.

Under some conditions you can use a specific length of string, tying knots at every 120 paces. Having used the length of string, un-tie the knots and repeat the process on the next 'leg' of your route.

It is always advisable to have a CHECK PACER, remembering to check that your PACING SCALE is the same by day and night.

NAVIGATION

This is the art of moving from one place to another and consists of three important stages that MUST be carried out if you are to be successful, they are as follows:-

1. PLANNING.
2. KEEPING DIRECTION.
3. GOOD PACING.

PLANNING - Cannot over emphasised - you must plan your route in advance, using maps, air photos, sketches and information from previous patrols or recces.

KEEPING DIRECTION - Always take several compasses and as many 'pacers'. Ensure that someone else checks your navigation, at both the planning stage and while you are executing the movement. It is often hard to keep direction, especially at night, in fog or in close country.

When it is necessary to make a detour to avoid an obstacle or seek cover, it is easy for those leading to miss the correct lines of advance. Check ALL your compasses for their I.C.E.

FIELDCRAFT

AIDS TO KEEPING DIRECTION.

Some of the aids to keeping direction are:-

a. The compass, map and air photographs.
b. A rough sketch copied from a map or air photograph.
c. Keeping two prominent objects in view.
d. Using a series of easily recognisable landmarks, each visible from the previous one.
e. The stars and also the sun and moon if their natural movement in the sky is understood.
f. Memorizing the route from a map or air photograph. Helpful details are the direction of streams, distances between recognisable features coupled with pacing, and the course of contours.
g. Trees in exposed country tend to grow away from the direction of the prevailing wind. Moss may grow on the leeward side of tree trunks.
h. Remembering the back view, patrols and others who may have to find their way back should look behind them from time to time and pick up landmarks to remember for the return journey.
j. Leaving directions marks on the outward journey, these may be pegs, small heaps of stones.
k. If the route is being walked by day by those who are to guide along it by night, they must take note of skylines and objects or features which they will be able to recognize in the dark.

SELECTING LINES OF ADVANCE.

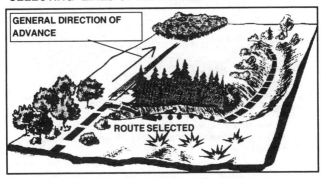

FIELDCRAFT

Remember the key word - G R O U N D

G   Ground from the map. Open/close., Rolling/flat.

R   Ridges, water courses and watersheds(highest) mark on map or talc.

O   Observation good view points.

U   Undergrowth - study woods, scrub, trees, villages.

N   Non Passable obstacles, rivers, ravines, marshland.

D   Defilade covered lines of advance and areas which offer cover can now be selected.

OBSERVATION — SEARCHING GROUND

The skill of searching ground is based upon learning to "scan" an area using an accepted system.

It will test your concentration and exercise your knowledge of "why things are seen" and the principles of Camouflage and Concealment. In the diagram on the next page, we have - for the purpose of illustrating to you — drawn lines across the landscape.

In practice you would choose prominent features, landmarks, roads etc., and draw your imaginary lines across the landscape through these reference points.

FIELDCRAFT

Scanning.
In the diagram on the previous page, the landscape is divided into
FOREGROUND, MIDDLE DISTANCE and **DISTANCE**. You can
further divide this by indicating a centre line (again based on
reference points), calling left of the line **"LEFT OF ARC"**, and right of
the line **"RIGHT OF ARC"** as shown in the illustration.
Having divided the landscape, the correct method is to scan each
area horizontally (left to right or right to left).
View the area in short overlapping movements in a very precise
manner, especially any features that are at an angle from your
position.
Searching
While scanning you may see something move or that requires further
investigation. There may be an area where you may come under
observation from, it would be as well to check that out early.
Weather conditions can give you a clue when searching, frost on
bushes, foot marks will show up clearly, if the weather is hot
camouflaged positions can be given away when leaves or grass dry
off changing colour.
Search across hedges and rows of trees , NOT along them. At all
times consider WHY THINGS ARE SEEN.

FIELDCRAFT

PATROLS

There are three reasons for patrolling:
1. To obtain up-to-date and accurate information.
2. To dominate the ground between a commanders own unit and that of the enemy.
3. To destroy and disrupt enemy forces.

Successful patrolling calls for a high standard of individual training, good team work, initiative and determination on the part of the patrol leader. Patrolling enables the defence to be conducted in an aggressive manner.

The foundation of successful patrolling is through preparation.

TYPES OF PATROL.

All Patrols fall into one of three types as set out in the following pages.

Reconnaissance Patrols

Patrols of minimum strength for task, usually a Patrol Commander and three to five soldiers, who gain information by observation and operate by stealth.

They avoid combat except for self-protection or to take advantage of unusual opportunities.

The roles in which a reconnaissance patrol may be employed include:-
1. Collecting topographical information on features, tracks and state of ground.
2. Obtaining details of minefields and the extent of enemy positions.
3. Locating enemy machine gun and defensive fire (DF) areas, where fire is immediately directed on call in case of emergency.
4. Investigating noises made by the enemy, habits, equipment, movement and patrol routes.
5. Checking own wire and/or minefields at first or last light.
6. Acting as listening posts, to give early warning of enemy approach and with the ability to call down fire.
7. Carrying out surveys for radioactive or chemical contamination by fallout or chemical attack in the area.

"TIME SPENT IN RECONNAISSANCE IS SELDOM WASTED"

FIELDCRAFT

Standing Patrols

Minimum strength 1 NCO and 3 men, to gain information of enemy movement, to prevent or disrupt enemy infiltration.

They move into position quietly - try to remain hidden - gain information until required to withdraw or if discovered, fight their way out. They must have good communications to enable them to call for supporting fire from mortars, artillery etc.

Equipment should include LSW's and LAW.

Their main tasks are to:-

1. Watch and listen on likely enemy approaches.
2. Watch over dead ground in front of and between friendly areas.
3. Watch over mine fields and obstacles, for which they should have good communications, so that they can inform the main body.
4. Prevent infiltration into unoccupied hides or positions.
5. Secure and mark up the Forming Up Point and Start Lines for a night attack.

Fighting Patrols

These are patrols organised for a particular task with sufficient strength and backup to achieve the mission. Their role is to harass, ambush, attack or to create a diversion. The strength can vary according to the task to be performed and the expected combat level:

1. Denying enemy patrols freedom of action in No Man's Land.
2. Driving in enemy protective patrols.
3. Interfering with enemy working parties.
4. Distracting enemy attention from other activities.
5. Carrying out raids.
6. Capturing prisoners for identification purposes.
7. Tank hunting.
8. Laying ambushes.
9. Protecting reconnaissance and working parties of other arms.
10. Escorting stretcher parties.

FIELDCRAFT

SEQUENCE OF ACTION TO MOUNT CARRY OUT AND DEBRIEF A PATROL.

The success of a patrol depends on good planning beforehand as well as good action during the actual patrol. Compliance with the following by the Patrol Commander ensures that nothing is forgotten.

PATROL COMMANDER

Issues a warning order to include brief outline of patrol task, members of patrol including second-in-command, time and place for briefing and any special administrative arrangements including weapons and equipment.

Normally dress and equipment should be as light as possible but must include water and emergency rations in case the patrol is cut off and has to lie up for a period before returning to base.

Studies Air Photos, Maps, previous Patrol Reports and sketches.

Selects observation posts for his recce.

RECCE

Carries out recce from OP's during which they look for:

1. Routes to and from objective (to be different).
2. Obstacles on route out and back.
3. Landmarks.
4. Enemy OP's, listening posts and surveillance devices.
5. Dead ground and covered lines of approach.
6. Likely places for ambush - by us or by enemy.
7. Enemy positions, DF areas and fixed lines of fire.
8. Consider light, time, weather conditions, moon, etc.

Makes his Appreciation and Plan, keeping them as simple as possible.

DRAWS A FIELD SKETCH showing distances (in paces), bearings and timings of bounds. RV's and FRV. Nicknames and Code Words

PREPARES MODEL of the area for briefing the patrol.

Prepares Patrol Orders and plans Rehearsal.

FIELDCRAFT

BRIEFS THE PATROL

By showing members the ground from an OP (individually if necessary) and points out minefield lanes, gaps in wire etc.,
Gives out his orders:
With aid of a cloth/sand model of ground, under following headings:-

1. GROUND.

Describes, incl. landmarks, obstacles, and "going". Use OP's, maps, air photos, models, etc.

2. SITUATION

a. Enemy Forces. FEBA, ptl activity, routine, sentries, DF, FPF, minefields, wire, trip flares, fixed lines.
b. Friendly Forces. Own positions, other ptls, fire support available, minefields, wire, trip flares, fixed lines. DF, FPF, stand by ptl.

3. MISSION.

To Recce, Fighting - definite task.

4. EXECUTION Phase 1. General Outline.

a. Number of phases - route, action on objective, return.
b. Who taking part - appointments and position in the patrol.
c. Prep Moves - Drop Off Point. Time leaving rehearsal/base area. Method of move. Loading Plan. Route to and ref of DOP. Arcs of obsn/fire. Order of March (OOM).
d. Action if Ambushed. Action at DOP. Time out. Confirmation or orders/detail.

Phase 2. Route Out, to final RV (FRV).

Fmn. Obs drills/action on mines/trip wires/booby traps. Actions on: PW. Cas. If separated from ptl. If lost.
Confirm FRV ref.

FROM/TO	Bearing	Distance	Fmn	Ground	RV
(1) Leg 1					
(2) Leg 2					
(3) Leg 3					

Phase 3. Action in final RV.

On arrival:
(1) Occupation. Move in. Secure. Fmns, position of grps, sig for FRV.
(2) Recce Group - Composition, Tasks. Route. OOM, fmns, arcs. Action on ambush, sig to open fire. Action if FRV gp loc by en.
(3) Remainder - Composition, Tasks, Arcs, Actions - on en pre-seen

FIELDCRAFT

or ambush, sig to open fire, if recce gp loc by en, on return of recce gp or if fails to return. Confirmation or orders/info.

Phase 4. Action on Objective

(1) Cover/Fire Gp. Composition, Fmn, posn, routes, tasks, arcs, action if en act first, duration on SP's, Sigs for opening fire. Action if separated from group.

(2) Recce/Assist/Snatch. Composition, fmn, task, posn, routes, action on recce/asslt/snatch, sigs for sp fire. Action if surprised, sig net, wire, illumination.

Phase 5. Withdrawal and action in final RV.

Sig to wdr. OOM sequence of gp wdr, arcs, fmns. Action and posns in FRV -pack kit etc. Head check and sig to move out. Actions: if in contact, PW's, if gp fails to return, if FRV gp has moved, if surprised in FRV. Pass on info sketches etc. Confirmation of orders/info.

Phase 6. Route Back

Route. Fmns. RV's. Obs. Actions; en pre-seen, ambush, sig to open fire, cas, if lost, if separated. Action on arr at pick up point (PUP). Time in. Confirm orders/info.

Coordinating Instructions

Timings. Meals, rest, rehearsals (day/ni), weapons test, inspections, time in/out constraints. Debrief. Action on halts, lights. Fireplan. Rehearsals loc and details. Deception and security.

Summary of execution.

1) Summary of Timings - Rehearsals, prep of eqpt, inspection, rest, meals test wpns, night rehearsals, final check time out, time in. RV's and refs.
(2) Action on white Lts
(3) Action on Halts - for obsn/protection.
(4) Action to take on Meeting En if:- Pre-seen or Ambushed
    On the Route Out .... On the Route In ....
(5) Action on Cas
    On Route Out........ On obj......... On the Route In........
(6) Action on crossing Obs
(7) Action with PW
(8) Rehearsals
(9) Lost procedure
(10) Action on Mines
(11) Distr on Ni Vis Aids

FIELDCRAFT

5. SERVICE SUPPORT

Ammo. Feeding. Dress and Eqpt. Special Eqpt - Toggle ropes, wire cutters, IWS/Suit, radio spares, etc. Wpns type and distribution. Rats, meals before during and after, water. Med, Fd dressings, stretcher, med pack, morphine, casevac method. PW handing on/after capture. Tpt to DOP/from PUP. Confirm orders/info.

6. COMMAND AND SIGNAL

Chain of command 1i/c, 2i/c and 3i/c and conditions for taking over cmd. Location of ptl comd. Sigs, radio, radio checks, other sigs. Password. Use of Radio and restrictions. De-briefing location, who doing. Patrol report. Special instrs on reporting Info.

Rehearsals

Carries out daylight or night rehearsals which must include:

a. **Moving out** and returning through own FEBAS.

   Patrol Commander goes forward to contact the sentry. Normal challenging procedure follows.

b. **Formations** and drill for changing formations.

   One or more of the three formations = single file, file or diamond - is adopted during a patrol depending on ground and visibility.

c. **Use of Scouts.** Move by bounds ahead and are followed by the Command Group (Patrol Commander, Radio Operator and his protector).

d. **Movement.** Every member is allotted his specific task, movement must be silent, frequent halts to observe and listen, when approaching the enemy position and also at night. When halted sink down to the ground level, avoiding a jerky movement, and make use of the skyline. Make use of the previously prepared signal to move - a silent "touch" signal - to ensure that no-one is left behind.

e. **Action on objective.** Nearby RV. This is an RV to which the patrol goes after completing the task, it must be easy to find and indicated to all members of the patrol during the approach to the objective.

f. **Firm Base.** If a patrol has to move a long way it may leave a party between its own and the enemy position, this forms a "firm base" from which remainder of patrol carries out main task and to return afterwards. On arriving near the objective, the Patrol Commander will:-

FIELDCRAFT

(1) Search the area, especially the RV or Firm Base for unexpected enemy.

(2) Make a brief Recce, Appreciation and Plan, brief the patrol members concerned

g. **Action on Lights.** If time allows get away - otherwise, freeze, close one eye to preserve night vision. If a trip flare move from area quickly as possible, get down and observe.

h. **Encounter drill.**

Action will depend on the task and circumstances. It may be desirable to avoid action and move away as quickly as possible. If this is impossible an immediate assault is the alternative.

If ambushed, scatter and move individually to previously arranged RV.

j. **Crossing Obstacles**

(1) On encountering an obstacle, Commander goes forward to recce it, decides whether to cross or go round.

(2) Requirements of obstacle crossing drill are:-

(a) Silent movement.

(b) Posting a man to guide others over.

(c) At all times at least one man ready to fire his weapon or throw a grenade if the patrol is surprised.

k. **Casualty Evacuation**

(1) All casualties must be brought back.

(2) Improvise a stretcher.

(3) If on the way out, the patrol may have to pick up the casualty on its return or summon help.

Prisoners

(1) If a fighting patrol takes a prisoner they must be brought back alive whether or not this was the task of the patrol. - prisoners are valuable sources of information.

(2) If a prisoner cannot be taken with the patrol, they may be put under guard and collected later either by the same patrol or by another one detailed or summoned by radio for this purpose.

Carries out Final Inspection

a. Dress and equipment light as possible, but include emergency rations and water.

b. Dress and equipment to be properly fitted and silent. Jumping up and down will show whether it is satisfactory.

c. No documents will be taken which can afford useful information to the enemy if captured.

FIELDCRAFT

LEADS PATROL OUT THROUGH FEBA.

a. **Navigation**. Previous study of air photos and maps etc. use of
   landmarks. By compass bearing and counting paces -especially at
   night. "Legs" to be measured to the nearest 50 paces from map. If
   the patrol becomes dispersed, RV at the end of the previous leg.
   Avoid prominent cover, e.g. edges of woods, tracks, hedges,
   defiles - likely places for enemy ambushes or standing patrols.
b. **Fire Support.** Pre arranged or called for by radio -
(1) To distract enemy.
(2) For support on objective.
(3) To help the patrol extricate itself in emergency.

DEBRIEFED ON RETURN.

Verbal report followed by a written report.
On the next page is shown the layout of a Patrol Report.
This is produced as guidelines for you to use when preparing a
report, and includes many of the factors that should be taken into
consideration.
This serves as a reminder of the vast amount of valuable
information and activities that a Patrol Commander is expected to
deal with.
This is a standard format use as a Patrol Report and you would be
well advised to study it in readiness for when you have to do a
report.

AMBUSHES

INTRODUCTION

Ambushes are usually carried out as a part of patrolling activity. It
requires close team work, skill, intelligence, fitness, cunning and
discipline.
An ambush is a surprise attack, by a force lying in wait, upon a moving
or temporarily halted enemy. It is usually a brief encounter, conducted
at comparatively close quarters.
When well prepared and executed it can cause heavy causalities
and serious loss of morale amongst the enemy; however poor
planning, preparation and execution may result in failure, and
serious losses to the ambush party.

FIELDCRAFT

PATROL REPORT

Date _____ Destination of Patrol _____

Aim _____

Maps _____

Size and composition of Patrol _____

Task _____

Time of Departure _____ Time of Return _____

Routes (Out and Back) _____

Terrain - (Description of the terrain - dry, swampy, jungle, thickly wooded, high brush, rocky.Depth/width of ravines, rivers/streams/canals.Width/ depth and condition of bridges as to type, size and strength, effect on armour and wheeled vehicles.)

Enemy - (Strength, disposition, condition of defences, equipment, weapons, attitude, morale, exact location, movements and any shift in dispositions. Time activity was observed, coordinates where activity occurred.)

Conditions of Patrol - (including disposition of any casualties)

Conclusions and Recommendations - (including to what extent the mission was accomplished and recommendations as to patrol equipment and tactics)

Date _____ Time _____ hrs

Signature of Patrol Commander

ADDITIONAL REMARKS BY INTERROGATOR

Date   Time   hrs   Signature.

FIELDCRAFT

TYPES OF AMBUSH

a. **DELIBERATE** - with time to plan in advance, may be on a large scale.
b. **IMMEDIATE** - In response to 'hot' information, to 'contact' the enemy, with no time for recce.

AMBUSH SITES

The best places for an ambush site include:-
a. Known enemy routes.
b. Known admin/supply/water points, food or ammo dumps, approaches to villages.
c. Where the terrain changes - edge of woods or forest, where a valley has steep sides. Where a river crossing is shallow etc.
d. Approaches to own bases or positions, also on route out of your own positions - if enemy follows you back.
e. Possible routes of enemy withdrawal after an attack.

PRINCIPLES OF AMBUSH

a. **Good intelligence** to ensure contact and success. Surveillance devices
b. **Thorough planning** and preparation, planned Recce, ambush well rehearsed.
c. **Security** - careful Recce - not to betray ambush site. Be prepared for an attack on yourselves.
d. **Concealment** - good track discipline, no signs of your whereabouts, good camouflage and concealment.
e. **Good control** and communications - all know the plan in detail, signals, plan for springing ambush. Must be kept simple, and thoroughly rehearsed.
f. **Battle Discipline** -ambush only successful if everyone alert, no noise, restricted movement, fast reaction to signals, weapons always ready to fire.
g. **Fire Power** - maximum use of all available fire power,. Hit en outside the killing area. Disrupt any counter attack. Harass the en in flight. Assist ambush party to withdraw.
h. **Safety** - all weapons in "made safe" state while on the move. No firing at individuals - even when minimum distance of 50 metres between muzzle and the enemy.

FIELDCRAFT

THE DELIBERATE AMBUSH

The ambush parties are subdivided into smaller groups, each with their own leaders. Normally the groups are as follows:-

a. **THE AMBUSH GROUP** - covers the chosen place for the ambush and springs the ambush. Group contains Ambush Commander and the Fire Team(s). Four men to ambush a section. A Section and Platoon HQ to ambush a Platoon.

b. **CUTOFF/STOP GROUPS** - serve to give warning of enemy approach, cut off their lines of retreat or help to take care of a counter attack from a flank. For a section ambush the group would consist of two men. A platoon ambush would be a section strength.

PLANNING - prior to occupying an ambush position the following sequence of planning events must be carried out:-

Recce. Issue preliminary orders in the base camp. Preparation and rehearsals in the base camp.

Move to the ambush area.

Final Recce by Amb Cmdr and Cut Off Grp Cmdr's.

Amb Cmdr issues final orders if required.

Occupy ambush position.

RECCE - Amb Cmdr should - if possible - carry out recce of amb site before giving orders. He may be limited to air photographs, maps, patrol reports or sketches made. Must try to put himself in enemy position/point of view, he must select/confirm:-

a. Ambush area, positions of the Ambush Group and cut off Groups, detailed siting of FIRE TEAM(s), booby traps, trip flares etc.

b. Check positions for each group for: concealment, approach routes, good fields of view and fire and of the enemy approach route.

c. The withdrawal routes for all groups.

d. The final RV, and routes to and from it.

ORDERS, PREPARATION, REHEARSALS & MOVE OUT.

ORDERS - Like all Patrols the information given and the quality of the orders must be very thorough and detailed, using a model of the area and leaving sufficient time for preparation and rehearsals.
The orders for an ambush follow the same sequence and detail as Patrol Orders, but need to have extra details under the 'EXECUTION' phase, as follow:-

FIELDCRAFT

ACTION ON ARRIVAL AT FINAL RV/FIRM BASE

Entry order of march. Positions and arcs of fire - describe these, also cover in rehearsals. Sentries if necessary. Action if surprised. Action if recce party does not return within.... minutes. Confirmation of orders, timing, refs, RV's etc.

ACTION IN AMBUSH AREA

Order of march. Method of entry. Positions. Laying of communication cord. Arcs to be covered.

Sig for 'Ambush Set'. Time ambush to be set by ..... hrs.

ACTION ON APPROACH OF ENEMY -

Warning signal from Cut Off Groups. Signal to stop. Search party if required.

WITHDRAWAL TO RV/FIRM BASE - Signal for withdrawal. Order of march. Action at final RV/Firm Base - reorg, check numbers, weapons, redistribute ammo, prepare to move out.

Thorough preparation is essential for success and should include the following:-

Cleaning and testing of all weapons. Testing and checking special equipment, ropes, night viewing aids, boats or rafts, safety and medics. Radios and spare batteries. Camouflage of clothing and equipment.

REHEARSAL - If for a night ambush, then rehearsals should be held in the daytime and also at night. They must:—

Show where each group and those who are within them are in relation to each other. Test signals/communications. Cover alerting, and springing of the ambush.

Practice withdrawal to Firm Base/Final RV.

MOVE TO AMBUSH AREA - Ambush party move to the Final RV/Firm Base and take up defensive position and wait for the Amb Cmdr and the Cut Off Grp Cmdrs to do their final recce.

FINAL ORDERS Only need for confirmation or last minute changes that need to be made as a result of the final recce. This could be more likely and important by night than day and could include:-

a. Description of the ambush area, enemy approaches and counter attack routes.

b. Individual tasks if they vary from rehearsals.

OCCUPATION SEQUENCE

Having completed his recce and returned from any Final Orders briefing, Ambush Cmdr will remain on the position, sending Cut Off

FIELDCRAFT

Group Cmdrs back for remainder of party. If a platoon operation, sentries would be taken forward, posted and remain in position throughout the move to the ambush area.

Cut Off Group followed by Killing Group move into position, Ambush Cmdr places himself in central position for control and near to the FIRE TEAM(s)

SETTING UP AMBUSH - Once all groups in position, Cut Off Group start laying communications cord/cable to Ambush Cmdr. Set up trip flares, booby traps etc.

AMBUSH SET - When Ambush Cmdr receives signal from all groups that everyone in position, gives the 'Ambush Set' signal. After this signal no one leaves their position, Care taken to make no movement or noise. Get into a comfortable position for the time you are waiting for the ambush to be sprung.

SPRINGING THE AMBUSH - On sighting the enemy, Cut Off Group alerts Ambush Cmdr of their approach and direction using communication cord, alerts remainder of the force. All prepare for ambush, carefully moving into aim .

Ambush Cmdr waits until as many as possible of enemy are in ambush area. Gives signal for springing ambush.

This signal usually a burst of fire from the FIRE TEAM(s), a shot from commanders weapon or setting off a trip flare.

It is NEVER the commander shouting 'FIRE'.

AFTER SPRINGING AMBUSH THE FIRE FIGHT - short and sharp. Cmdr gives 'STOP' or 'CEASE FIRE'. Pause while all check for: movement of enemy survivors. Enemy counter attack. Enemy moving back to collect casualties, thinking ambush has withdrawn.

WITHDRAWAL - On receiving withdrawal signal, all groups withdraw to Final RV, in order as rehearsed. Minimum time spent there, check all present, check no enemy follow up, recall sentries and move off by return route.

SCOUTS

When a Platoon is on the move each member must always be on the alert ready to react to enemy action. Fast reaction under these circumstances will prevent casualties.

When moving in an area where the enemy has not been located it may be advisable to use 'scouts' to move ahead and on the flanks. Their use does slow down progress and if speed is essential then they may not be used , instead every member of the Platoon is responsible for their allotted arc of observation.

AIM OF SCOUTS

To detect the enemy well in advance of their platoon or sub unit. They must remain unseen by stealth, by drawing fire either deliberately or as a deception.

They may often find gaps in enemy positions for their platoon or sub unit to pass hostile positions.

Scouts work in pairs and move in 'bounds'. A bound is deemed to be from one selected point to another, which should have a good view of the view ahead and from which the scout can signal his section.

As each place for the next bound is selected, one of the scouts selects the route and moves rapidly towards it, while the other observes and covers him.

When the first scout reaches the bound, the other one is signalled forward. The process is them repeated.

The reason for this 'drill' is:

1. The second scout is available to cover the advance of the first and help them if surprised by the enemy.
2. If the leading scout gets into trouble, the other can inform the section early enough for action to be taken.

The control of scouts and their ability to communicate with the section will depend upon the nature of the ground/country. They should not move too far ahead and as a result lose contact.

The success of scouts is the good measure of early warning they are able to give their section commander of the enemy's presence and reliable information about them.

"Scouts move in bounds - always keeping one foot on the ground"

EMERGENCY ALARMS

When operating on an exercise IT IS more than likely you will be subjected to a surprise attack of one type or another. Units have their Emergency Alarms set up and practice them in order to cope with these situations. Some examples of these are given below:-

ALARM SIGNALS

1. GROUND ATTACK

a. Visual. Personal weapon raised above the head at the full extent of the arm pointing toward the enemy OR a clenched fist, with the thumb down and the arm pointing toward the enemy.

b. Sound. Shout STAND TO

2. AIR ATTACK

a. Visual. Rapid crossing of the arms above the head.

b. Sound.

1. Long blasts of whistle/horn. 12 secs.

2. Shout "AIR ATTACK"

3. NBC ATTACK

a. Visual. Putting on of respirators and drawing attention to this.

b. Sound.

1. Banging two metal objects together.

2. Short horn blasts of 3 secs.

3. Shouting. GAS GAS GAS (with respirator on).

Your unit will have their own **Standard Operational Procedures SOP's** that will cover these and many other procedures and no doubt practice you in their use and application

PASSWORDS and CHALLENGING.

Passwords consist of a challenge bigram and an answer bigram eg AW ~ DE and are changed daily at 1200 hrs. If it is suspected that the Password has been compromised the local commander must be informed immediately.

You should remember that passwords are only an indication of identity. Other methods of confirming identity are;

RECOGNITION. ID CARDS. QUESTIONING. CHALLENGING PROCEDURES

EMERGENCY ALARMS

Challenging must be done early enough to be effective, firmly and if possible quietly.
The sentries actions are:
a. Alert Local Commander.
b. **"HALT HANDS UP"** Given as quietly as possible but do not let unknown man get too close.
c. **"ADVANCE ONE"** If faced with a group.
d. **"HALT"**
e. **CHALLENGE** Quietly and ONLY if person is not recognised.
f. **"ADVANCE (one)"** First man gives number of men in group. Then call fwd remainder, all at once or one by one.

ROUTINE IN THE FIELD.

INTRODUCTION

It is easily forgotten that in times of war and on exercise that a number of activities still need to be attended to each day. These are routines which must be carried out no matter where or when a unit is in the field. Routines apply to all parts of a unit whether in defence, in hides or in patrol bases. They must be followed and should become a drill.
Not all aspects will always apply, but those that do should be strictly adhered to.
The routine **MUST** happen, though **WHEN** is not important, as this will be determined by operational requirements. A unit will normally be divided into half-sections for this purpose. The following notes are typical examples of **Routine in the Field.**

MORNING

Reveille - Usually at least half an hour before first light. Strike shelters, if erected. Pack sleeping bags. Renew camm or alter for day use.
Stand-to: Usually lasts about half an hour.
1. All personnel present, alert and correctly equipped.
2. All occupy fire positions and man weapons.
3. Ammo to scale and available.
4. Pl Comd/Sgt check on range cards/arcs of fire/passwords/loc of obs known/ptatrol activity known, etc.
5. GPMG (SF) fixed lines and tasks.
6. Communications checked.

ROUTINES IN THE FIELD

7. Surveillance devices checked.

8. Camouflage.

9. Dress and Equipment, including state of NBC kit.

There must be NO undue movement above ground in the area during 'stand-to'.

Stand Down silently on order; Clearing patrols sent out. GPMGs manned by sentries. 2i/c posts single sentry(ies). Change to day routine. Position and pers cam renewed/adjusted. Track discipline maintained. Sick report. Clearing patrols report in to CP.

Weapons and Ammo cleaned; Cleaning staggered for security. Inspections of weapons and ammo by Pl Sgt. Defects and deficiencies reported.

Personal Hygiene: Shaving and washing. Cleaning boots. Skin and foot inspection by Pl Comd. Clean teeth. Comb hair. Visit latrine. Treatment of cuts etc. Re-apply cam.

Water Discipline: Fill water bottles with filtered water. Sterilize all water. Breakfast; May be cooked centrally and delivered to posns. Cooked under section arrangements. Cooked by the individual. Utensils cleaned & stored.

Digging: Improve trenches, shelters, hides, communication routes, latrines etc. Improve general defences.

Check clothing and equipment: All necessary eqpt laid out for instant use. Clothes mended. Boots inspected. Defects in eqpt reported. **ORDERS :** Briefing on days activity. Patrol requirements. Rehearsals Recce. Rosters duties. Rest and work roster org. Midday meal. **Further activities: Patrols. Recces. Rehearsals.** Concurrent activities; Improvements to fire trenches, cam, wiring, fields of fire etc. Rest, particularly for patrol members.

AFTERNOON: Re-clean weapons. Check equipment:- Patrol equipment. Radio webbing carriers. Batteries. Ammo. Evening meal.

Night preparation: Shelters erected, if permissible. Re-supply of water. Renew or alter cam for night. Night orders issued; Check everyone knows arcs of fire. Defensive fire details Position of listening posts. Returning patrol details Check everyone knows the **STAP** (Surveillance and Target Acquisition Plan).

Listening Posts Posted. Stand-To:

All members wear eqpt and man fire positions. Clearing patrols sent out. Clearing patrols report in. Change from day to night routine.

NIGHT: Stand-down silently on order. Double sentries posted in the GPMG pit. No movement within perimeter except; Patrols. Routine post changes. When sleeping is possible; Troops must be fully clothed. Equipment should be handy. **Weapons must be secure and handy.** Sleeping bags should be under cover.

EQUIPMENT PACKED: AT ALL TIMES equipment not in use must be packed READY TO MOVE in an emergency, to prevent it being lost **or left behind . .**

ARTILLERY AND MORTAR INDICATION

INTRODUCTION

FOOs and MFCs (Forward Observation Officer (Artillery) and Mortar Fire Controllers) may not always be attached to those units which require artillery support. Platoon and Section Commanders should be able to call for, and direct, their own fire missions.

Communications with Guns and Mortars

There are various methods of communicating with the guns and mortars. If frequencies of nets are known then the following will often be available for use in an emergency.

Company net. Artillery net. Mortar net. Battalion Command net .

INITIAL ORDERS & SEQUENCE OF ORDERS

The Cardinal Rule is:-

"ALWAYS WRITE DOWN A FIRE ORDER BEFORE SENDING IT"
NEVER THINK ON THE AIR" .

PROCEDURE

1. **"Fire Mission"** (this is a warning order and sent as a separate transmission). The net is normally kept open by using "Over" and not "Out" at the end of their acknowledgement. This is followed by:
2. **Where it is.** A GRID reference e.g., "Grid 456789. Reference can be given to previous target.
3. **The direction of the target** from your position "Direction 1589" (specify GRID or Magnetic) given in mils, it should be accurate to the nearest 10 mils taken with a compass.
4. **What it is and a description:** "Mortar now firing from north side of track junction".

ARTILLERY AND MORTAR INDICATION

5. **What is to be done:** "Smoke" or "Neutralize" Remember to destroy
   a target a lot of time and ammunition may be required - you may not
   have much of either.
6. **For how long and at what time:** "Now", "For "X" minutes" or "For
   'X' minutes at 'Y' hours".

The OP officer will acknowledge your order and will give "Wait Out"
and will attempt to identify the target. If report confirms identity you
have no further part to play. If the target is not identified shot will be
fired for *adjustment of fire*.

ADJUSTING FIRE

a. First, correct for *target direction line* as soon as possible, this is
   important, as until the line is approximately correct bracketing for
   range cannot start. Corrections are ordered as "LEFT or RIGHT X
   metres. (All corrections should be to the nearest 25m).
b. Second, *bracketing for range*, this means establishing two salvos,
   one short (minus) and the other beyond (plus) the target. When you
   are certain that the salvo is plus or minus of the target, correct by
   ordering ADD or DROP. If a round is observed during bracketing to
   hit the target order "On Target" without delay.

FIRE FOR EFFECT

The "On Target", means 'Produce the type of fire requested in the
initial orders'.

END OF MISSION

Always report the mission complete and its results to the guns/mortars
with, for example, "END of MISSION target destroyed" .
A Word of Warning - unless you have specified RECORD in your
order the guns at the "End of Mission" will not be able to re-engage the
target without ranging again. Recorded targets can quickly be engaged
without adjustment of fire.

HINTS ON SHOOTING

Direction. Measure bearings as accurately as you can with a
compass. If in a position for some time know the grid bearings to
several reference points, measure distances to likely targets.
Use of binoculars. Do not use binoculars until you see the first salvo.
A salvo as little as 60 mils off the target my go unobserved if you do.
Measuring Line Corrections. If a large correction is required,

FIELD ARTILLERY SAFETY

measure it with your hand. An average hand held at arms length with fingers spread measures 350 mils from tip of thumb to tip of little finger.
Zone of Gun. Guns like machine guns have a 'beaten zone'. If guns are firing from a flank, you may see half of the zone. Therefore, for line corrections, imagine the *target direction line* more as a lane.
Double Corrections. Normally avoid combined line and range corrections. However, if you are experienced in shooting or if you are quite certain that a salvo is plus (or minus) as well as off for line, then use double corrections, for example "Right 100. Add 400".
If you have **unobserved rounds** do one of the following:
1. Order "Repeat".

FIELDCRAFT ARTILLERY SAFETY

Operational Safety. In time of war artillery and mortars are used to provide fire support for attacking units. Often this fire will need to be fired in close support as troops are advancing. If this is the case there will come a time when fire needs to be halted for the safety of our own troops. The final responsibility for this operational safety lays firmly on the shoulders of the officer in command while his unit is in the assault. Both the FOO and the MFCs attached to the coy will work out safety limits and deal with operational safety in the normal course of their duties.

ARTILLERY AND MORTAR MINIMUM SAFETY DISTANCES

Weapon	Effective frontage of one HE shell	Safe distance for tps in the open	
		Observed	Predicted
105mm SP	35m	250m	500m
155mm SP	50m	350m	500m
FH 70	45m	350m	500m
8" SP	60m	700m	800m
81mm Mor	40m	250m Ch1-4	
		300m Ch5-8	

TANK TARGET INDICATION

INTRODUCTION

It is a fact that the best antitank weapon is another tank and that tank fire can be used to great effect and accuracy by the infantry to destroy enemy positions. To do this however you must be able to indicate the enemy position to the tank crew .

The essence of tank target indication is to get the tank commander looking in the right direction and give him a good and accurate target indication.

SEQUENCE FOR TARGET INDICATION

a. Attract the tank commanders attention.

b. Get him looking in the right direction.

c. Give the range from tank to target.

d. Describe the target.

e. Order, destroy, neutralize, etc.

f. Correct fire until the tank commander sees the target.

METHODS OF INDICATION

a. Reference Points hasty or prearranged.

b. Gun Barrel of tank (quickest method).

c. Shot for reference from other tank or infantry weapon.

      1. left/right = 3200 mils.

      2. 1/2 left/right = 1600 mils.

      3. 1/4 left right = 800 mils.

Communications with Tank Commander

a. Personal contact.

b. Tank telephone (rear left of hull, ensure he knows you are going to use it if not you might get run over).

c. Radio.

It is essential to develop a close liaison when working with Tanks on exercise to become accustomed to these procedures. Each method has advantages in different circumstances. The best is personal contact, but it will often be impractical and either of the other two must be used.

TANK TARGET INDICATION

Procedure: Whatever method of Target Indication is used it must follow a sequence:-

1. **Attract attention** of the tank commander - radio - personal contact - tank telephone.
2. Direct tank commanders **attention to target area**. There are three ways of doing this:

a. **By Reference Points.** If possible prearrange. They must be limited to clearly defined features which allow no confusion, to direct tank commanders eyes by clockface method or along physical landmarks on the ground.

b. **By using the Tank Gun Barrel.** If reference points cannot be used, the gun barrel can be used as a 'datum' line from which a switch in direction can be made. The terms "quarter right", or "half left" used to indicate direction of switch. Even if you cannot see the barrel, you can estimate the direction of it from the position of the tank turret.

c. **A Shot for Reference.** If it is not possible to use either of the methods described above, the burst of a shell or the strike and line indicated by tracer can be used as a datum point from which corrections can be made. You must tell the tank commander which approximate area to watch, likewise the tank commander if firing a reference shot must tell the supporting infantry and to say when he is about to fire.

d. **Range and Description.** A good estimate of the range given first helps the tank commander to narrow the area he must search, followed by an accurate description, especially if it is not an easily identified target than those that are prominent.

e. **Executive Orders.** How target is to be dealt with: "to destroy" or "to neutralize". If to neutralise, you should indicate for how long or for what purpose, e.g., "neutralize five minutes", or "Neutralize and cease on my order - am moving to right flank". Order usually given by radio, but sometimes a light or visual signal may be pre-arranged.

Correction of Tank Fire

If the Tank Commander fails to engage target you give him a correction from the fall of the shot or another description. Corrections given are from the position of the tank - as "Left" or "Right" and "add" or "drop", leaving it to him to make adjustment for his different viewpoint and any variation in the ground. The aim must always be to direct the tank commander's eyes on to the target - speedily and effectively.

2. Order a correction that should bring the rounds into the open..
3. Ask for smoke.
4. Order "Lost". Then the OP officer will;
a. Fire another salvo at the same place, or
b. Give a correction to produce a visible salvo, or
c. Fire Smoke.

Smoke. Use the drifting of HE smoke. It may indicate whether a salvo off for line is plus or minus when it drifts past the target.

WORKING WITH HELICOPTERS

DUTIES OF THE CHALK COMMANDER

Whenever you use helicopters you will be placed into what is known as a *CHALK*. Safety is always very important and there will usually be an NCO in charge of each chalk.

The list of things which the Chalk Commander should check:
a. Webbing is worn over epaulettes.
b. Headdress off or secured by strap under chin.
c. Chalk forms up at the 2 o'clock position and numbers off.
d. Weapons are in the outside hand.
e. Radios, packs or other equipment are in the inside hand.
f. Radio antennae are safely folded and securely stowed.

On the thumbs up signal from the pilot or crewman he should:-
a. Lead chalk to door and assist in emplaning, quickly.
b. Hand crewman loading card showing,
1. GRID of destination.
2. Direction that the DOOR is to face on landing.
c. Check chalk for thumbs up.
d. Put on intercom if available.

On deplaning;
a. Assist chalk out of helicopter.
b. Check that no kit remains inside.
c. Indicate to pilot or crewman that the helicopter may lift off.

HELICOPTER MARSHALLING SIGNALS

Hand signals used for the marshalling of Helicopters are illustrated on the following pages. They are the signals required by marshallers for everyday use in the field.

Marshallers wear tightly fitting headgear for obvious reasons - they would get it blown off by the downwash from the rotor.

When their tactical situation permits they would wear a fluorescent panel tied around their waist or fluorescent sleeves.

Marshallers should stand with their backs to the wind.

If required to identify a Landing Place a fluorescent panel is displayed and if a vehicle is available - secured across the windscreen.

A smoke grenade can be used to indicate a location, but only thrown on the request of the pilot who would advise the colour to confirm his sighting.

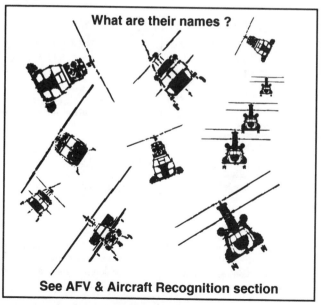

What are their names ?

See AFV & Aircraft Recognition section

WORKING WITH HELICOPTERS
MARSHALLING SIGNALS

THIS WAY.

Arms overhead in vertical
position with palms
facing inward.

**PROCEED TO THE
NEXT MARSHALLER**

HOVER.

Arms extended horizontally
sideways, palms downwards
(signal to airborne helicopter
when required to
hold present position).

LAND.

Arms crossed and
extended downwards in
front of the body

**RELEASE
LOAD.**

Left arm extended forward
horizontally, fist clenched, right
hand horizontal slicing
movement below left fist,
palm downwards.

**LOAD HAS
NOT
RELEASED.**

Left arm outstretched,
horizontally across chest;
open right hand pointing
up vertically to centre of
left hand.

WORKING WITH HELICOPTERS
MARSHALLING SIGNALS

CUT ENGINE(S). Right hand, palm down, is moved from right to left across the body with arm extended.	**AFFIRMATIVE.** Hand raised, thumb up.
MOVE AHEAD Arms a little aside, palms facing backwards and repeatedly moved upward-backward from shoulder height	**MOVE BACK.** Arms by sides, palms facing forward and swept forward and upward repeatedly to shoulder height.
MOVE TO PORT (LEFT) Right arm extended horizontally sideways in direction of movement and other arm swung above head in same direction, in a repeating movement	**MOVE TO STARBOARD (RIGHT)** Left arm extended horizontally sideways in direction of movement, other arm swung above head in same direction, in a repeating movement

WORKING WITH HELICOPTERS
MARSHALLING SIGNALS

MOVE DOWNWARDS

Arms extended horizontally sideways beckoning downwards, with palm turned down. Speed of movement indicates rate of descent.

MOVE UPWARDS

Arms extended horizontally sideways beckoning upwards with palms turned up. Speed of movement indicates rate of ascent. NOTE. This signal also used to raise helicopter from ground to the hover

NEGATIVE

Hand held out to one side below waist level, thumb (wand) turned downwards.

READY FOR TAKEOFF

Pilot using right arm gives 'thumbs-up' signal.

HOOK - UP TEAM APPROACHING AIRCRAFT

Marshaller raises left arm above head with palm towards aircraft. Right arm is extended at shoulder height, palm downwards

WAVE OFF/OVERSHOOT (MANDATORY)
Marshaller waves out-stretched arms from waist level to crossing overhead.

PRISONERS OF WAR

INTRODUCTION

There will come a time on exercise when you will capture prisoners. It is very important to handle them correctly not only to follow the rules of war regarding prisoners, but also to ensure that any information, documents or maps etc, are passed back quickly. Always carry out the following procedures.

IMMEDIATE ACTION WITH PRISONERS OF WAR

a. Disarm of all visible weapons.
b. PW to lay face down, hands on head.
c. Complete a body search, remove all hidden weapons, military equipment, documents except for ID and protective equipment.
d. CASEVAC wounded through normal means and inform commander of this.
e. Separate into groups by sex, rank, svc and those carrying maps or mil docs.
f. Allow NO communication between the PW or between PW and own troops.
g. Do not allow PW to observe activities in the area. Keep face down or blindfolded.

DISPOSAL

a. PW are the Pl/Tp Sgts responsibility, he will arrange for them to be escorted back to the CSM/SSM/BSM with any Captured equipment and/or documents.
b. He will then be responsible for the back loading of PW to the IO at Bn/Regt HQ.
c. All documents and equipment must be sent back by the same channels.
d. PW should carry any sleeping bags, food etc with them.

SIGNALS

INTRODUCTION

Communications for a modern army are as important as bullets and petrol. Without good communications things can very quickly go wrong. The following notes are intended to help you with some basic background information which you may find useful. We do not go into the details of the current equipment nor speculate on the future methods of communications, save the fact that with the advances in methods and the advanced technology being experimented with, there is no doubt that you will be using different types of equipment for communication throughout your service. However we make no apologies for including some of the 'old' methods of sending and receiving messages, but do not include 'smoke signals'.

SECURITY

Specific procedures are used to communicate between radio users.They are designed to ensure that:
1.Security — every word can be heard by the enemy.
2. Accuracy and brevity — interference causes misunderstanding.
3. Discipline — to prevent more than one speaking at a time
Obey the following rules
1. Keep your message as short as possible.
2. Speak clearly without over emphasis
3. If possible make a note or rehearse what you are going to say, DO NOT think on net.
3. If it is a long message split it into bits.
5. Encode those bits of the message which might give information to the enemy, grid references for instance.
6. If you cannot get through to other stations, move, and try a different position for your antenna before increasing power.

PHONETIC ALPHABET

If communications are difficult you may need to spell a message, in this case you should use the phonetic alphabet. Always precede the spelling with the words " I SPELL " to give the signaller at the other end warning that he will need to write down the letters.
You will need to constantly practice using the Phonetic Alphabet for it to become an automatic response, we suggest the you practice when passing car number plates, you will soon learn.

SIGNALS

PHONETIC ALPHABET

A - Alpha	B - Bravo	C - Charlie	D - Delta
E - Echo	F - Foxtrot	G - Golf	H - Hotel
I - India	J - Juliette	K - Kilo	L - Lima
M - Mike	N - November	O - Oscar	P - Papa
Q - Quebec	R - Romeo	S - Sierra	T - Tango
U - Uniform	V - Victor	W - Whiskey	X - XRay
Y - Yankee	Z - Zulu		

e.g., The town name "York" would be sent as:

" I SPELL Yankee Oscar Romeo Kilo"

Numbers/Figures can also be sent digit by digit in bad conditions.
e.g. "Twenty three fifty nine hours" would be sent as

" FIGURES - two, three, five, nine, hours"

CODES

The usual method of ensuring that the enemy does not find out what you are doing is through the use of codes. The most secure of these are known as a 'one time code' that is, a code which is used only once and then discarded. The British army now uses a code of this type called BATCO, short for Battalion Code. It is easy to use for simple Grid References or long messages. See your Signals NCO for more details.

APPOINTMENT   TITLES

Appointment titles were once used for all key personnel in a unit, however they now have been replaced by call signs except for the appointment title SUNRAY who is any Commander. e.g. Bde, Regt, Bn, Coy, Pl, Tp or Section.
In addition the second in command is known as SUNRAY-MINOR. This is useful since you and the person you are talking to will know who you are talking about, but others will not.

CALLSIGNS

All radio stations on a military net have a callsign. This identifies the user to other users without the need to give away unit names. Always find out which callsign you are before you use a radio.

SIGNALS

SIMPLE VOICE PROCEDURE

Why is Voice Procedure Necessary?
1. Because every spoken word on a radio set can be heard by the enemy as well as our own troops.
2. Because even the best radio communications may suffer, at times, from interference, therefore messages may be misunderstood.
3. Because most radio systems are designed for one person to speak at a time, if more speak, at the same time , chaos will result.

AIDS TO ACCURACY

The following are at our disposal to ensure correct reception of messages, orders etc.
1. Phonetic Alphabet.
2. Prowords.
Both of these are dealt with later in this section.
It should also be remembered that when transmitting a message the following should be observed;
Rhythm: keep a natural rhythm. Divide the message into sensible phrases.
Speed: slightly slower than normal conversation, to allow it to be written down.
Volume: as for normal speech. There is no need to shout.
Pitch: the voice should be pitched higher than usual, but discomfort should be avoided.

RULES FOR ABBREVIATIONS

Abbreviations are primarily designed to save time in writing, but can also save time in talking and a large number are part of every day speech.
e.g. MT, DR, NAAFI, NATO, NCO etc.
1. In Good Conditions: Common abbreviations are spoken as if normal conversations.
DR as DR instead of Delta Romeo.
MT as MT instead of Mike Tango.
HQ as HQ instead of Hotel Quebec.
hrs as hours.
recce as recce, ... and so on.
2. In Bad Conditions: Abbreviations should only be used when they save time, it may be better to use the correct full words.
Despatch Rider - this is shorter than "*I spell Delta Romeo*".

SIGNALS

Headquarters - shorter than *"I spell Hotel Quebec"*.
Reconnaissance - is better than *"I spell Romeo Echo Charlie Charlie Echo"*.

OPERATOR DISCIPLINE

The Control Operator, irrespective of their rank, is in charge of the net and is responsible for its efficient operation.

Only one station may speak at one time, therefore, to prevent confusion, the following rules must be obeyed:

1. Listen out before speaking, to ensure the frequency is clear, and don't cut-in on other transmissions.
2. Leave a short pause at the end of a conversation.
3. Answer all calls immediately, and in the correct order.

A RADIO NET

This can be defined as a group of stations working together for the purpose of communicating with each other. There are two types of station.

a. Control
b. Substation.

Note: The control station has a call sign - 0.
The substations callsigns' are A10, B10, B20, and B30, the callsigns are a combination of letters and figures which identify a communications station, organisation or individual on a radio net.

SIGNALS

SEQUENCE OF ANSWERING

Calls are to be answered in Alphabetical Sequence first, then numerically throughout the net, but control always answers first if included in the call.

TYPES OF CALL

The main types are:

1. Single Call from one station to another

> e.g. *"Hello B10 this is B20"*
>
> or *"Hello A10 this is 0"*

2. Multiple Call - from one station to two or more stations, but not the whole of the net;

> e.g. *"Hello 0, B10 and A10 this is B30"*
>
> or *"Hello 0, A10 and B10 this is B20"*

3. All Stations Call - from one station to all stations.

> e.g. *"Hello all stations this is 0"*
>
> or *"Hello all stations this is B10"*

4. Collective Call - a call to 2 or more selected stations on a net identified by a predesignated call:

> e.g. *"Hello Charlie Charlie 1 this is 0"*

OFFERS

An offer is a short transmission made to warn the station(s) concerned that a message follows, an offer is made when:

1. The sender suspects that the receiver may be too involved for operational or other reasons, to receive a message at all.

e.g. Callsign B10 has a message for callsign B20 that does not need to be written down, but is not sure if they are in a position to receive - in fact they are able to do so:

> *"Hello B20 this is B10 over"*
>
> *"B20 send over"*
>
> *"B10 move when ready over/out"*
>
> *"B20 roger out"*

2. The receiver has to take notes, this depends entirely on the length and contents of the message.

The sender must use their common sense and experience as to when they make an offer.

> e.g. *"Hello 0 and B20 this is B10 message over"*
>
> *"0 send over"*

SIGNALS

"B20 send over"
"B10 no movement seen at grid 6ATCRWD or grid BMPDUS or grid BTRRAC my forward units now returned, over"
"0 roger out"
"B20 roger out"

CORRECTIONS and REPETITIONS

A sender may make a mistake during transmission and have to correct it, this is done by the use of the proword WRONG and going back to the last correct word transmitted.

e.g. *"Hello A10 this is 0 Tanks reported grid 331762 WRONG"*
"reported grid 331752"
"A10 roger out"

Sometimes it may be required to emphasize a particular part of the message, this is done by use of the proword "I SAY AGAIN", This procedure is time consuming and should only be use sparingly.

e.g. *"Hello B10 this is B20 0A left my location now on way to C/S 0".*
"I SAY AGAIN C/S 0 then to your location, over"
"B10 roger out"

If it was required to emphasize the whole of the message you would use *"I SAY AGAIN"* at the end of the message and send the whole message again.

During the reception of a message the receiver, for many reasons, may miss part or parts of the message. They can obtain the missing parts by referring to a part already received (known as 'catchwords' or 'catchphrases') and saying what they want repeated, by using one of the following PROWORDS:

SAY AGAIN. WORD BEFORE. WORD AFTER. ALL BEFORE.
ALL AFTER. FROM .... TO ....

If they require the whole message they would use SAY AGAIN.

e.g. *"Hello B20 this is A10 send rations before 1800 hrs over"*
"B20 say again over"
"A10 send rations before 1800 hrs over"
"B20 roger out"

It is unlikely that they didn't receive part of the message, therefore it would be wasting valuable transmission time
to get the whole of the message repeated, so the correct way is to

195

ask for the part missed.

> e.g. *"Hello all Stations this is 0 my Sunray will be at HQ
> until 1730 hrs Sunray will return with C/S B23 and B21 and
> call sign A10 then call sign B10 on way back Sunray
> callsign B20 and B30 are requested to be here by*
> > *2045 hrs over"*
> > > *"A10 say again WORD BEFORE will return over"*
> > > "B10 say again ALL AFTER Sunray callsign B20 over"
> > > "0 Sunray callsign B20 and B30 are requested to be here
> > > > by 2045hrs over"
> > > "B10 roger out"
> > > "B20 say again WORD BEFORE until (pause) WORD AFTER
> > > > C/S B23 and, over"
> > > "0 HQ until (pause) B23 and B21 over"
> > > "B20 roger out"
> > > "B30 say again FROM B21 to callsign B10 over"
> > > "0 B21 and call at callsign A10 then callsign B10 over"
> > > "B20 roger out"

Note: Stations are dealt with individually, using the correct sequence of answering, until "roger" is obtained.

The sending station does not use; *I SAY AGAIN* in reply to a request for a repetition.

The CATCH WORD or CATCHPHRASE must be easy to identify, it is wrong to use a word that appears more than once as this causes confusion.

Although not shown in these examples the PROWORD "OUT" should be used whenever possible in good working conditions.

On single calls, C/S may be dropped after the initial exchange.

LIMITED RESPONSE

When it is known that all called stations are in communication, use should be made of limited response in order to improve security since the callsigns responding to CHARLIE CHARLIE (Collective Call) and ALL STATIONS calls are of value to an enemy. The procedure is to nominate one or two stations only to acknowledge as shown in the examples below and over page.

Example 1.

> "Hello All Stations this is 0, Text, A10 Acknowledge over"
> "A10 roger out"

SIGNALS

Example 2.
> "Hello CHARLIE CHARLIE 3 this is 0, Text, A10 and B30
> Acknowledge over"
> "A10 roger out"
> "B30 roger out"

PROWORDS

"I SPELL" — I am going to spell out a word, as letter group, letter by letter.

e.g. *"Bolton I spell Bravo Oscar Lima Tango Oscar November"*

"FIGURES" — I am going to send a number figure by figure.

e.g. *" figures One Two Seven Zero Zero One"* (127001)

These PROWORDS can be combined if required:

e.g. "figures Two Three I spell Whiskey Golf Figures Three

Three (23 WG 33).

"HELLO" — used as an introduction in an initial call.

"SEND" — go ahead with your transmission.

"MESSAGE" — offer of an unregistered message (notes are required).

"OVER" — this is the end of my transmission, a reply is required. Go ahead and transmit.

"OUT" — this is the end of my transmission. No reply is expected.

"WAIT OUT" — your transmission is received; a further transmission on the same subject will follow later.

"ROGER" — Message received satisfactorily, or I have received your last transmission satisfactorily.

"WRONG" — what had been said is wrong, the correct version is ....

SIGNALS

MORSE CODE

A	·—	N	—·	1 ·————
B	—···	O	———	2 ··———
C	—·—·	P	·——·	3 ···——
D	—··	Q	——·—	4 ····—
E	·	R	·—·	5 ·····
F	··—·	S	···	6 —····
G	——·	T	—	7 ——···
H	····	U	··—	8 ———··
I	··	V	···—	9 ————·
J	·———	W	·——	0 —————
K	—·—	X	—··—	
L	·—··	Y	—·——	
M	——	Z	——··	

You may never need to resort to using the Morse Code for any of
your communications. But, as we said at the beginning of this section,
if at any time your 'high-tech' equipment malfunctions - then you
may not have any option, the Morse Code could be the answer if you
have knowledge of it.

Some Technical advice from a Yeoman of Signals -
                                    "never *pee* on an earth spike".

MINES

In this section there is no intention to instruct you on becoming an expert on mines, nor give you information other than how to recognise different types in common usage, at the same time to have a healthy respect for those Sappers who are trained to handle them.

Having said that, it is invariably the soldiers first contact with the enemy when mines are discovered - hopefully before they find you. It is one of those instances when no amount of training will help you, unless you are observant and alert at all times.

Many countries produce a variety of mines, but the majority are "clones" of those produced by the Soviet Union.

There essentially two categories we have shown, they are:-

1. ANTI-PERSONNEL.

2. ANTI-TANK.

The mines illustrated in the following pages are those in common use that you should be conversant with:-

FOREIGN MINES

MINE ANTI-TANK METALLIC MODEL TM-46. (USSR)

Description: (Illustrated on the next page). This metallic mine may be placed under water in a stream or river beds and be distributed mechanically. It uses an MV-5 fuse, but has no means of external arming for mechanical laying.

The TM-46 has a secondary fuse 'WELL' in the side underneath the carrying handle. The mine has a pressed steel body and is painted dark Green.

The version with 'anti-life' fuse looks identical, but is known as the TMN-46.

Use: The TM-46 is laid in Anti-Tank minefields or as above.

Functioning: The mine is armed by withdrawing the Safety Pin. It is operated by pressure forcing the pressure cap down on the head of the fuse, depressing it and releasing the striker to detonate the mine.

MINE, ANTI-TANK TMN-46 ANTI-LIFT (USSR)

Description: The mine body is made of sheet steel and the mine is assumed to be waterproof. The pressure plate is integral with the mine case.

MINES

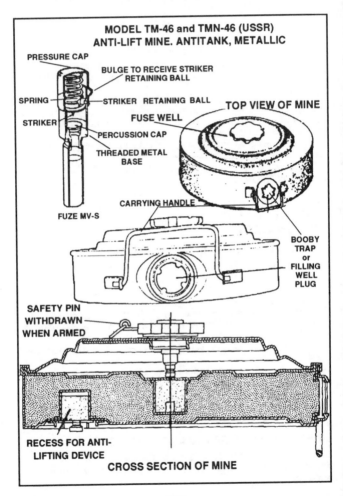

MODEL TM-46 and TMN-46 (USSR)
ANTI-LIFT MINE. ANTITANK, METALLIC

PRESSURE CAP

BULGE TO RECEIVE STRIKER
RETAINING BALL

SPRING

STRIKER RETAINING BALL

TOP VIEW OF MINE

STRIKER

FUSE WELL

PERCUSSION CAP

THREADED METAL
BASE

FUZE MV-S

CARRYING HANDLE

BOOBY
TRAP
or
FILLING
WELL
PLUG

SAFETY PIN
WITHDRAWN
WHEN ARMED

RECESS FOR ANTI-
LIFTING DEVICE

CROSS SECTION OF MINE

MINES

The mine has a centrally located fuse 'WELL' on top and a filling hole directly beneath the handle.

A second fuse 'WELL' is located on the bottom, presumably for a booby trap device.

Use: The TMN-46 is laid in anti-tank minefields, in streams or river beds.

Functioning: The mine is set off by pressure shearing pressure plate with respect to the mine case. When the required load is applied on the pressure plate, it actuates the fuse, setting off the main charge.

MINE ANTI-PERSONNEL PMN, NONMETALLIC (USSR)

Description: (Illustrated on the next page). The PMN is a delay-armed, pressure fired mine. The major external components are a plastic case, a rubber covered pressure plate, and a firing assembly adaptor plug. It therefore has a very low metallic content. It is mid-green in colour. It is quite a large mine as far as Anti-Personnel mines go and will inflict severe casualties.

Use: The PMN is designed for use against personnel.

Functioning: Delay arming, When the safety pin is withdrawn, the firing pin spring moves forward under pressure of its spring until a wire attached to the firing pin spindle is caught on a lead strip in the arming delay assembly.

After approximately 15-20 minutes, the wire cuts through the lead strip, releases the firing pin to move forward into a cavity of the cylinder, where it is held by a step in the cylinder. The firing pin remains in this position until the mine is fired.

Firing: When a pressure (approx half a pound) is applied to the pressure plate, the pressure plate is forced downwards against the cylinder, compressing the cylinder spring, and causing the cylinder step to be moved downwards in relation to the firing pin.

The firing pin spring forces the firing pin through the cylinder cavity, firing the initiator which, in turn, detonates the main charge.

Precautions: In this mine the initiator assembly has a booster charge and a percussion-fired primer-detonator. The mine contains a cocked firing pin.

MINES

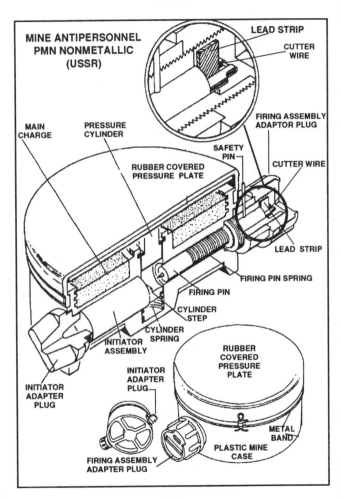

MINE ANTIPERSONNEL
PMN NONMETALLIC
(USSR)

LEAD STRIP

CUTTER WIRE

MAIN CHARGE

PRESSURE CYLINDER

RUBBER COVERED PRESSURE PLATE

SAFETY PIN

FIRING ASSEMBLY ADAPTOR PLUG

CUTTER WIRE

LEAD STRIP

FIRING PIN SPRING

FIRING PIN

CYLINDER STEP

CYLINDER SPRING

INITIATOR ASSEMBLY

INITIATOR ADAPTER PLUG

FIRING ASSEMBLY ADAPTER PLUG

INITIATOR ADAPTER PLUG

RUBBER COVERED PRESSURE PLATE

METAL BAND

PLASTIC MINE CASE

MINES

MINE ANTIPERSONNEL, METALLIC POMZ-2 (USSR)

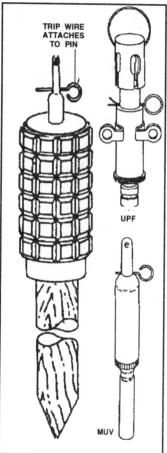

TRIP WIRE ATTACHES TO PIN

UPF

MUV

Description: This has been one of the most commonly used metal-cased antipersonnel mines. The mine consists of a wooden stake, a cast iron body and a cylinder of cast TNT. Originally the fuse 'WELL' was not threaded and a grove was cut in the stake to allow water to drain from the mine.
A later model, the POMZ-2M has a threaded fuse 'WELL'. This mine has been widely copied and is olive green in colour.
It employs the MUV or VPF fuse.

Use: POM-Z2 mines are mounted on stakes at a height of about 25.5 cms above the ground in high grass, bushes or woods. They are sometimes interspersed in Anti-Tank minefields.

Functioning: With either types of fuse - see diagram - a pull on the trip wire removes the striker retaining pin or pull-ring, releasing the spring-driven striker against the percussion cap.

MINES

BRITISH MINES **ANTITANK HE BLAST** **L98A1 (BARMINE)**	**C3A1 (ELSIE)** **ANTIPERSONNEL** **(REMOVABLE** **DETECTOR RING)**
LIGHT NON-METALIC **L3A1 ANTI-TANK**	**RANGER ANTI-PERSONNEL**
Mk 7 ANTI-TANK	**M18A1** **(CLAYMORE)** **ANTI-PERSONNEL** **(DIRECTIONAL** **FRAGMENTATION)** FRONT TOWARD ENEMY
OFF ROUTE L14A1 **(DIRECTIONAL ANTI-VEHICLE)**	**TRIP FLARE**

MINES

MINEFIELDS

Well sited and carefully concealed mine fields, which are covered by fire are an effective obstacle to troops and all types of vehicles. There are four types of minefields

1. **Tactical.** Planned as an obstacle to delay, divert, or break up an advance.
2. **Protective** Used to defend a position, often as a part of a planned defensive area.
3. **Nuisance** Laid to disrupt and disorganise the enemy, to affect their will to carry out patrols in your area., to demoralize them.
4. **Phoney** or 'make-believe'. To simulate the appearance of a minefield with the aim of deceiving the enemy.

Mines may be found close to enemy defensive positions and will be covered by a small arms capability. You may encounter mines in small numbers which have been laid to create a nuisance delaying you 'getting on'. They may not be marked and more than likely will be booby trapped.

Should minefields be encountered they are normally dealt with by one of the methods described below.

Cleared by explosives.

1. Bangalore Torpedo is a tube filled with an explosive charge which when set off clears a path through anti-personnel mines about half a metre wide for the length of the tube.
2. Giant Viper is a hose 228 metres long containing explosives which is projected across a minefield by rocket motors. It blasts a path up to 8 metres wide and 180 metres long through an anti-tank minefield.

Cleared by mechanical means.

This is done by mounting a plough on the front of certain armoured vehicles, normally carried out by Royal Engineers.

By Hand Clearance

If it is necessary to clear mines to gain advantage of a tactical surprise, then hand clearing would be the only way. This is a very slow method and could take several days/nights to carry out

"DON'T TAKE A CHANCE - LEAVE IT TO THE EXPERTS"

MT DRIVER

INTRODUCTION

These notes are provided to remind you of your obligations as a
driver of an MOD vehicle on the road in the UK. If abroad then Road
Traffic laws of that country apply, but at the same time you must
realise that instructions as set out in the MOD Driver's Handbook
apply to you no matter where you are driving, although they may be
varied at times to conform with prevailing conditions in any theatre
of operations.

The Motor Vehicles (Construction and Use) Regulations and the
various Road Traffic Acts in force as the Law provides for every
contingency that you are likely to be involved in while in charge of a
vehicle. The scope of these laws cover over three hundred offences
and therefore as a driver it is very easy to fall foul of one or more of
them - no doubt you may have already had that experience.

We do not intend to give you chapter and verse on all the laws, but
would start by reminding you that as soon as you take charge of a
vehicle you are responsible for the following :

Maintenance and use of a vehicle so as not to be a danger

1. While on the road: the vehicle and it's trailer and any part of the
   vehicle must be in such a condition that it causes no danger to
   passengers or other road users.

   The way passengers are carried /seated, the correct weight and
   distribution of any load, the packing and adjustment of the load
   shall ensure that no danger is caused or likely to be caused to any
   person in or on the vehicle or trailer or on a road.
2. The load carried must be secure, it must not be a danger nor a
   nuisance to any person or property, by any part of it falling or being
   blown from vehicle or trailer, or by movement of the load.
3. No vehicle or trailer is to be used for a purpose which it is
   unsuitable and causes or is likely to cause danger to any person in
   or on the vehicle or trailer or on a road.

A summary of the above is that as the driver you are:
1. **Responsible to see that the vehicle is roadworthy.**
2. **That the load is secure and not over weight.**
3. **That you are responsible for the safety of the "load" you are
   carrying.**

DRIVERS STANDING ORDERS

You will have a copy of Standing Orders for Drivers, which are there for your guidance and to a great extent follow the lines of the Highway Code, of which you no doubt have an up to date copy.

Traffic Accident Procedure

If you have an accident do the following:

1. STOP YOUR VEHICLE in a safe place and if required render First Aid.
2. KEEP CALM and do the following -
3. DON'T LOSE YOUR TEMPER nor argue with other people involved.
4. GET YOUR FACTS only from friendly witnesses who volunteer a statement - you cannot demand one. Get their names and addresses, complete your Form MT 3-2, give the tear off slip to the police or third party involved in accident. Report the accident to your unit.
5. DO NOT, IN ANY WAY, ADMIT LIABILITY.

If a Police officer asks you to make a statement, you may do so if you wish. The statement must only be made to the officer and not in the hearing of any other witness or witnesses.

Immediate Action:

a. Warn other Traffic. Switch off engines carry out Fire precautions.
b. Check emergency services have been called.
c. Get injured to place of safety.
d. Stay at scene until Emergency Services have arrived.

Should any vehicles involved be carrying dangerous substances:

a. Ensure that detailed information is passed to Emergency Services.
c. Keep people away, beware of any spilled liquids, dust or vapour being blown about.

EMERGENCY FIRST AID

This is fully covered in the First Aid Section of this Pocket Book. Only render First Aid if you have had training in the subject, if not and provided others are present who have, it is better left to those with experience.

MT DRIVER

PARKING AND SAFEGUARDING YOUR VEHICLE

1. You are responsible for safe custody of your vehicle and its load.
2. Normally park on MOD property.
3. Do not park illegally. Ask the Police for a suitable parking place .
4. Make sure vehicle is secure. If parked on a hill, leave it in gear.
5. A bulk fuel vehicle or cargo vehicle with packed petrol or
   explosives must have an attendant with it at all times.

"SERVICE VEHICLES ARE NOT EXEMPT FROM CIVILIAN PARKING REGULATIONS"

VEHICLE LOADING

You should know what the permitted maximum and axle loads of your vehicle and to ensure that the permitted loads are not exceeded.
Do not drive your vehicle when it has been overloaded. Request the loading unit to offload before proceeding on your detail.
You are responsible for the restraint of your load to prevent any movement.
If you load overhangs by more than 1.83 metres to the front and 1.07 metres to the rear or 305 mm to the side, you should seek advice about load markers.
If you drive a bulk petroleum vehicle you are responsible for ensuring only the permitted fuel for your vehicle is loaded and the correct recording and accounting for the fuel.
You are responsible for all ancillary equipment or machinery connected with your vehicle, its correct and safe operation and that it is properly stowed when not in use.
You are responsible for checking and recording the quantity of goods off-loaded from your vehicle. This is for your own benefit so that you have evidence of delivery should any item(s) be mislaid or misappropriated.
If you find that your load has been tampered with report it to the Police.
You are not permitted to drive a vehicle loaded with hazardous material until briefed on the safety precautions and emergency action in the event of an accident.
You are responsible to ensure that load restraints are not fastened to sheeting hooks.

TABLE OF TYPICAL BRAKING DISTANCES
(distance in feet and metres)

Miles and Km per Hour		DISTANCE					
		Thinking		Braking		Overall Stopping	
		ft	m	ft	m	ft	m
20 mph	a	20	6.97	20	6.97	**40**	**13.94**
32 Km	b	20	6.97	25	7.62	**45**	**14.59**
30 mph	a	30	9.14	45	13.71	**75**	**22.85**
48 Km	b	30	9.14	50	15.24	**80**	**24.68**
40 mph	a	40	12.19	80	24.39	**120**	**36.58**
64 Km	b	40	12.19	90	27.43	**130**	**39.62**
50 mph	a	50	15.24	125	38.11	**175**	**53.35**
80 Km	b	50	15.24	140	42.68	**190**	**57.92**
60 mph	a	60	18.29	180	54.87	**240**	**73.16**
96 Km	b	60	18.29	200	60.97	**260**	**79.26**
70 mph 112Km	a	70	21.34	245	74.69	**315**	**96.03**

a = Saloon Car   **b = Bedford MK (laden)**

NOTE: 20mph x 2 = 40ft to stop.   30mph x 2 1/2 =75ft to stop
     40mph x 3 = 120ft to stop.   50mph x 3 1/2=175ft to stop
     60mph x 4 = 240ft to stop.   70mph x 4 1/2 = 315ft to stop

You must appreciate that the figures given in the table above are approximate and are given on the assumption that the vehicles are:
On dry roads, with an average surface, in good state of repair.
The vehicle has a good set of tyres.
That the driver is an alert experienced driver.
Under those circumstances a vehicle has a reasonable chance of stopping in the distances shown. However, remember these are the **shortest stopping distances.**
Stopping distances will increase considerably with wet and slippery roads, poor brakes and tyres, and a tired driver.

CARE ON THE ROAD

Driving an Army vehicle you are immediately recognised by all other road users. They will know you have been trained as a competent driver and apart from the same laws that apply to them, will be aware that Army drivers have other rules and disciplines that you will be required to conform with.

Regretfully there is a large proportion of civilian drivers who have not had the benefit of the driving instruction that you have had. Nor will they have been "brought up" in an environment where they are expected to set a good example of road manners, personal courtesy, patience and strict compliance with the laws of the road. Whenever you are on the road, your driving will be seen by other road users as the current standard of driving for the Army. They expect you to set a good example, that is the reputation the Army has, and you should be mindful of this at all times.

If you drive badly or are discourteous, not only will it reflect on you personally, but bring discredit to both you, your unit and the Army.

Drive with Care - pay attention to the road - avoid distractions.

Drive with discretion - don't take risks.

Drive defensively - be prepared for the unexpected.

Drive thoughtfully - make allowances for others.

REMEMBER:

SPEED - limit it to prevailing conditions, drive at a moderate , even and safe speed.

ACCELERATOR - a light foot, use your gears keeping the 'revs' down, save wear and fuel.

GEARS - Use the right gears for the speed, use all the gears, use them for slowing down.

BRAKES - Use them with care in conjunction with gears, anticipate hazards. Check them daily.

SAFE DISTANCE - Keep more than the Braking Distance away from the vehicle in front of you.

OVERTAKING - Only if there is room and you can get well past before pulling over. If you're not sure - DON'T.

OBSTRUCTION - If driving a slow vehicle - have good road manners - pull over for traffic to pass.

PEDESTRIANS - They have priority on official crossings and side streets, if you are turning into it off a main road.

MT DRIVER

LIGHTS - For you to see and be seen. Parking lights are for parking. Poor visibility you must use your headlights.
DRIVER FATIGUE - Don't drive if you are tired. Turn off the road, park safely/securely, stretch your legs, have a rest.

HAZARDOUS DRIVING CONDITIONS

Watch out, as without warning you may run into any one or more of these conditions. Your driving pattern will have to be adjusted to take the conditions into account.

1. **Rain and surface water.** 2. **Fog and mist.** 3. **Strong winds.**

4. **Mud and leaves on the road.** 5. **Snow and ice.** 6. **Sun glare or**

misted windows. 7. **Road repairs and diversions.**

You are the driver, you would be well advised to check the route - especially if no one else has done so - should the weather or other conditions cast any doubt in your mind as to the driving conditions you might encounter. How will it affect the timing of the journey. Where are locations for stops etc.

NATIONAL SPEED LIMITS	* Built-up Areas	Elsewhere		Motorways
		Single Carriageways	Dual Carriageways	
TYPE OF VEHICLE	M.P.H.	M.P.H.	M.P.H.	M.P.H.
Cars incl vans & m/c's	30	60	70	70
Cars towing Caravans or Trailers	30	50	60	60
Buses & Coaches not over 12m long	30	50	60	70
Goods Vehicles not over 7.5 tonnes	30	50	60	70
HGV's exceeding 7.5 tonnes (M.L.W)	30	40	50	60

The above limits apply to all roads, unless signs show otherwise.
* The 30 mph limit applies to all traffic on roads with street lighting unless signs show otherwise

MT DRIVER

HAND SIGNALS FOR USE WITH TANKS, APC's AND 'B' VEHICLES

Hand signals are used when vehicles are near enough and are within sight of each other in daylight. At night a torch can be used, naturally NOT in a battle/tactical situation.

Hand signals should be used to confirm orders and to pass on simple orders for movement.

Using hand signals reduces the radio traffic leaving the air to more important transmissions for the conduct of a battle, passing information, detailed orders, etc. Hand signals come into their own if a radio silence is imposed or when there is jamming or if there is a radio breakdown. The figures are not 'martians', so do not be put off by them, their messages are important

ADVANCE
Arm fully extended above head - swung from rear to front.

SPEED UP
As for advance but given on the move

HALT
Arm raised to full extent above the head

SLOW DOWN
Two or three movements with open hand towards the ground

MT DRIVER

DISMOUNT
Two or three movements with
the open hand towards the
ground (two hands)

**SUB UNIT COMMANDERS
TO ME**
The hand placed on
top of the head

ALL COMMANDERS TO ME
Both hands on top of head

START UP
Circular movement of
the hand as if turning
a starting handle

MOUNT
Two or three movements
upwards with the open hand,
palm uppermost

**TAKE UP POSITION OF
OBSERVATION**
Palm open and back of hand
placed against forehead

MT DRIVER

SWITCH OFF
One arm extended parallel to the ground with hand open and moved across the body

LINE AHEAD OR 'ONE UP'
Arm extended above the head and swung from side to side. Arm pointed at tank or APC required to lead

'TWO - UP'
Both hands extended above the head and swung from side to side. Point at the tanks or APC's required to lead

LINE
Both arms extended sideways parallel to the shoulders

TURN ABOUT
Large circular movement of the arm above head

DO NOT CONFORM
Both hands extended parallel to the ground with palms open, moved across body.

MT DRIVER

TAKE UP A FIRE POSITION
Clenched fist shaken in
direction of position to
be taken up

RALLY
Both arms swung across
each other above the head

FOLLOW ME
Signal for 'line ahead'
followed by commander
pointing at his own tank or
APC

OPEN OUT
Both arms move sideways
from chest in a breast
stroke manner

ACKNOWLEDGMENT OF SIGNALS
Both hands clasped above
the head and shaken

MOVEMENT IN TRANSPORT

Bad movement discipline on the part of drivers in a column may cause chaos, delays and congestion. In an operational situation this would make the whole column a sitting target for air and artillery attack. Normally vehicles move in *'packets'* of four to eight vehicles depending upon the size of the units involved in the move. Each packet has a senior rank appointed as the commander and in each vehicle an individual is detailed as the commander - the packet commander and vehicle commander could be one and the same person.

Drivers will be given orders for the speed they are to travel and the interval distance between each vehicle.

ROAD DISCIPLINE

1. **Packet Commander**: Will have a copy of movement order and will have been briefed by the convoy commander. A radio link would normally be established for reporting progress along the route.
2. **Vehicle Commander:** Will be the senior rank in the vehicle responsible for the conduct of the driver and passengers. They must travel in a position to observe all round the vehicle. If unable to see to the rear, to appoint an individual in back of vehicle to do so. Must have a copy of the route card and a map which must be followed. At unexpected halts must not leave the vehicle unless told to do so by the packet commander.
3. **Traffic Density:** This is the average number of vehicles that take up a kilometre of road space and is expressed as vehicle/ kilometres. The density of a convoy is laid down to avoid congestion and taking up too much road space.
4. **Speed**: This is laid down according to the type of vehicles, road conditions whether it is day or night. Some individual vehicles may be authorised to move quicker.
5. **Overtaking and Double Banking:** Overtaking and double banking are not allowed, except on the orders of those controlling traffic. Vehicles that have dropped behind wait until the packet has stopped before moving back to their position.

MT DRIVER

6. Halts: The times and duration will have been laid down in the movement orders. In an operational situation naturally the halts would be made at prearranged locations to give cover off the road and camouflage the vehicles.

NOTE: Should a packet come under attack the space between vehicles opens up to 400 metres and drivers increase their speed.

7. Breakdown: Park vehicle at side of road, show a yellow flag by day and a red triangle by night - this action obviously not in an operational situation. If breakdown is temporary, post a sentry on opposite side of road to direct traffic. If breakdown is beyond immediate repair, and vehicle is obstructing road, push it clear even at risk of more damage being caused.

Usually the last vehicle in the column or packet is the breakdown vehicle and carries a blue flag. The breakdown vehicle may be capable of short distance tow using a ridged bar, or be able to call up REME Recovery.

Today road conditions preclude the use of steel wire tow ropes for towing over long distances. They can be used with extreme care for towing in 'off-road' conditions, provided the casualty can be driven to assist in its rescue.

The need for caution and care using steel wire ropes cannot be over emphasised, as if they break under load the 'whiplash' is lethal.

8. Movement Orders: Are issued for all moves, to include route, speed, vehicle density, number of vehicles in a packet, action on halts and details of support services.

All details in the movement order should be made known to those taking part in the move.

"Don't drive with your thumbs inside the spokes of your steering wheel"

"If you drive with care today - you'll live to drive another day"

SECURITY

INTRODUCTION

In this section we are bringing to your attention the constant need to be vigilant, to be observant, to be alert, for both you and your 'buddy' to stay alive.

At the Hillsborough Disaster enquiry conducted by Lord Lane said "Complacency is the enemy of safety".

You are personally responsible for your own and others security and safety in your unit.

In the 'military context' we are dealing with terrorist attacks, which can be combated, provided you are CONSTANTLY AWARE that it is a PERSONAL RESPONSIBILITY to be SECURITY CONSCIOUS at ALL TIMES of the DAY and NIGHT.

No doubt there will be times when you will be confronted by someone that you will have to challenge and search, or you may be involved in the searching of property or a vehicle.

There are basic rules and procedures to follow, we outline them in the following paragraphs, but you must bear in mind that these rules can be varied according to the security situation in the theatre of operations where you are involved.

These variations will of course be made known to you through your unit SOP's, and you will have been trained and tasked to meet these threats.

You will have been told many times and we make no apologies for telling you again, that should you be confronted by a suspect device or a situation arises giving concern that an incident is imminent, then don't 'go it alone', raise the alarm, clear the area of personnel, and let those who are trained to handle explosives do their job.

It is of great assistance to the ATO when he arrives on the scene, to have everything under control and to be given a full, clear and concise report on the situation.

SEARCHING - THE REASONS

The requirement of well conducted searches is to find terrorist supplies of munitions, this must be your goal.

To achieve this it is necessary to:-

1. Catch them and have sufficient of the right evidence for them to be brought to court and be dealt with according to the laws of the land.

SECURITY

2. To starve the terrorist of his munitions, thus restricting their activities.
3. To obtain intelligence material of all types, to enable the planning of action.
4. To disrupt the terrorists plans and movement, exposing them to added surveillance activity.

SEARCHING - WHAT TO LOOK FOR

When carrying out a search you must be on the lookout for a wide variety of items of munitions and anything that could possibly be used in the production of any device connected with the pursuit of terrorism, such as:-

1. Weapons of any kind, home made, stripped down and carried or hidden in single pieces by any number of different people.
2. Ammunition of any kind, it all carries an explosive charge.
3. Explosives of both civilian or military natures.
4. Anything to do with demolition materials or accessories, detonators, fuses, tapes etc.
5. Small transistor radios, transmitters, switches, relays, batteries, micro switches, wire and connectors.
6. Unusually large quantities of items such as batteries, lengths of wire, nails, empty bottles, sugar or petrol.
7. Chemicals, fertilizers, weed killers, flour and silver paint, all potential items for the construction of home made explosives.
8. Books, diagrams and documents which may be of intelligence interest.
9. Individuals who are on the 'wanted' list.

PERSONAL SEARCHES

When it comes to personally searching an individual, there are two types of body search, as follows:-
1. A quick body search.
2. Detailed body search.

THE QUICK BODY SEARCH

This is normally carried out when:-

1. Having to carry out a search of a large number of people where it is not possible to stop them and carry out a detailed body search of

them all. In this situation it is normal for a random sample to be taken of individuals to be searched.

An example of this would be during a road check or a large arrest operation.

2. An initial search, prior to a detailed body search when dealing with a specific suspect. This is to disarm the individual and for you secure any item that may be destroyed or be disposed of before a detailed search is made.

SEARCHING A DANGEROUS OR VIOLENT SUSPECT.

1. Searchers work in pairs, one searching the other covering him. When searching, NEVER work between the suspect and your covering buddy's line of fire.

2. Stand suspect away from, but facing wall or vehicle, with legs apart, hands on wall - leaning forward. This position has suspect at disadvantage, cannot move without falling over and is easily knocked over. If no wall/vehicle, make suspect stand with feet wide apart, arms spread wide above head, when in this position carry out search from behind suspect.

3. Search from TOP to TOE, covering all parts of the body. Check that fists are not clenched concealing anything.

4. When searching the suspect keep your hands in contact with the suspects body, never part contact with them, but use a stroking movement. Searching limbs use both hands, with your thumbs and index fingers touching when possible.

5. The degree of thoroughness will depend upon the importance of the suspect and the time available. If the suspect has to remove their clothes, close supervision is required.

6. Any personal belongings, coats, bags, etc., must be carefully searched.

Detailed Body Search

This requires special facilities, a room set aside and properly adapted for this to be conducted. A special team must be organised consisting of a Commander and not less that Two searchers.

If women or children are to be body searched the team must include female searchers, or a suitably chaperoned medical officer.

The search procedure should be carried out in the following sequence:-

SECURITY

1. Establish the identity of the suspect.
2. Establish their ownership of any articles they are in possession of.
3. Invite them to empty their pockets, handbags, and produce any documents or articles they are carrying.
4. Ask them to remove all their clothing, to include wrist watches and jewellery.
5. The suspects body will be inspected from head to the soles of their feet, with special attention to their hair, ears, mouth, artificial teeth, body orifices, crevices and between their toes.
6. Careful examination of their clothes, their pockets, linings, seams, buttons, belts or braces. Female clothing where padding is present, especially the Bra and the wire sometimes use in the manufacture of foundation garments. The noting of information provided by garment labels, name tags and cleaners ID labels can provide intelligence information that can be very helpful in subsequent interrogation of the suspect.
7. Examination of any baggage or other associated items such as a walking stick, personal stereo, camera etc.

SEARCHING VEHICLES

The searching of a vehicle is a highly skilled exercise, requiring great powers of observation and considerable patience, apart from constant training and practice.

There is an ever increasing number of motor vehicles on the road, a vast number of different makes, models and sizes to contend with. The ability of the terrorist to adapt parts of a vehicle to conceal munitions makes it one of their most used lethal weapons against our society.

Techniques used for searching

This can be divide into three categories, as follows:-

The Initial Check.

This form part if the selection process carried out on vehicles at Vehicle Check Points (VCP) or Road Blocks. It is of limited duration, usually two or three minutes and carried out by three soldiers.

The Primary Search

This is carried out at the roadside on vehicles selected for a more detailed search by the Vehicle Check Point (VCP) commander or it may fall into one of the following categories:-

SECURITY

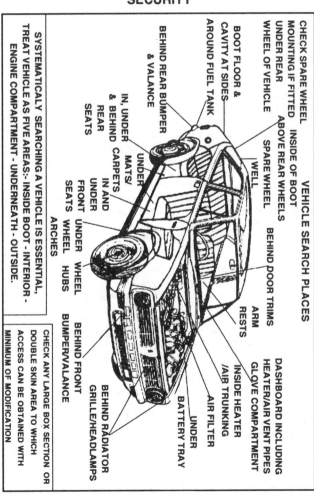

VEHICLE SEARCH PLACES

CHECK SPARE WHEEL
MOUNTING IF FITTED
UNDER REAR
WHEEL OF VEHICLE

INSIDE OF BOOT
ABOVE REAR WHEELS
SPARE WHEEL
WELL

BOOT FLOOR &
CAVITY AT SIDES

AROUND FUEL TANK

BEHIND REAR BUMPER
& VALANCE

IN, UNDER
& BEHIND
REAR
SEATS

UNDER
MATS/
CARPETS

IN AND
UNDER
FRONT
SEATS

UNDER WHEEL
WHEEL HUBS
ARCHES

BEHIND DOOR TRIMS

ARM
RESTS

INSIDE HEATER
/AIR TRUNKING

AIR FILTER

UNDER
BATTERY TRAY

DASHBOARD INCLUDING
HEATER/AIR VENT PIPES
GLOVE COMPARTMENT

BEHIND FRONT
BUMPER/VALANCE

BEHIND RADIATOR
GRILLE/HEADLAMPS

SYSTEMATICALLY SEARCHING A VEHICLE IS ESSENTIAL,
TREAT VEHICLE AS FIVE AREAS:- INSIDE BOOT - INTERIOR -
ENGINE COMPARTMENT - UNDERNEATH - OUTSIDE.

CHECK ANY LARGE BOX SECTION OR
DOUBLE SKIN AREA TO WHICH
ACCESS CAN BE OBTAINED WITH
MINIMUM OF MODIFICATION

SECURITY

1. It may be a vehicle on the WANTED list, requires checking as such.
2. There is a request from Intelligence.
3. There are suspicious circumstances, about the vehicle or
   passengers.
4. By an intelligent guess/selection by the VCP commander.

The PRIMARY SEARCH of a commercial vehicle is not an easy task,
and this type of search is better carried out by a specialist team at a
designated centre, where the load can be properly examined.

Secondary Search

When a decision has been made to carry out a Secondary Search of
a vehicle, it has to be taken to a secure place, where the REME will
be involved in the removing body panels and other mechanical parts.

SEARCHING A VEHICLE

When carrying out a search on a vehicle your first consideration must
be for the passengers who will be treated courteously and without
making remarks that will immediately offend them. The search must
be conducted thoroughly and with speed and efficiency. Do not cause
any damage to the vehicle.

As the search is progressing bear in mind previous searches of
similar vehicles and look for similarities of points that were of
intelligence interest. Ask yourself - is there anything that looks
unusual or out of place?

Physical Inspection

The vehicle can be divided into five sections for the purpose of
carrying out a systematic search. Within each of these sections there
are many likely area that explosives can be located and will need you
to pay attention to detail if you are to find them.

1. Underneath the vehicle

Bottom of the radiator, engine sump, exhaust silencer, fuel tank and
whole chassis framework and sills - look for signs of modification.
New or unusual welding or brazing. New soldered cables or paint that
could reveal a false bottom fitted.

2. Outside the vehicle.

Check behind the lights - this may be easier from under the bonnet.
Check under the wings/mudguards. Remove petrol filler cap, look for
item suspended in filler tank pipe.

3. Inside Boot

Examine the hollow reinforcing ribs on the under side of the boot lid.

SECURITY

Check under rear window shelf. Check spare tyre for air or explosives - let some air out into a detector. Tail light assemblies - very often have space. Recess for spare wheel - is it a spare wheel?.

4. Inside the vehicle

1. Back seat: Remove it, check if there has been any new stitching done to the fabric. Check the area occupied by the seat, both above and below.
2. Heating System: Check the inside of the heating and air ducts.
3. Ashtrays: Remove the container, check the contents and the recess for the tray.
4. Front seats: Look up underneath the seat and check that the back rest has not been re-stitched or tampered with.
5. Check the gear stick and hand brake housing - space to pack some SEMTEX.
6. Remove carpets and rubber floor covering. Look for any signs of the floor being cut out and re-welded.
7. Dash board/facia: Look up underneath, any newly soldered joints, or unusual fittings. The radio; is it for real or is the recess packed with you know what.
8. Windows and door panels: Wind down the windows, do they all wind down equally?, is there any obstruction. Check the door panels, any signs of them having been removed and refitted?
9. Inside the roof: The fabric lining in the roof usually has a space over much of the roof. Look for any signs that it is sagging or has been tampered with.

Engine Compartment

1. Oil Filter:- Has it been recently changed or modified - they can be modified to bypass the engine oil, leaving the filter bowl available for explosives.
2. Radiator: If engine still hot, CAREFULLY REMOVE both radiator filler cap and or cooling system cap, check that no objects are suspended therein.
3. Engine Compartment: Check spaces in chassis beneath engine mounts. Has anything been added to engine that looks suspicious?. Look for any spaces where the body is mounted on the chassis. Check the hollow reinforcing ribs on the underside of the bonnet.

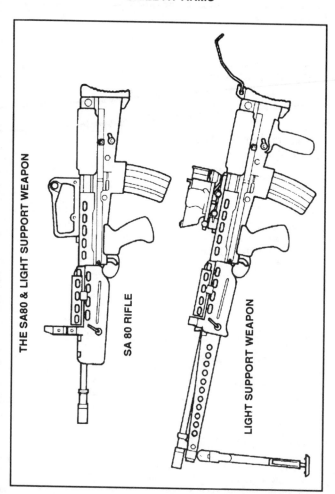

THE SA80 & LIGHT SUPPORT WEAPON

SA 80 RIFLE

LIGHT SUPPORT WEAPON

225

TECHNICAL DATA

AMMUNITION	SA80	LSW
Calibre (mm)	5.56 mm	
Types	Both weapons	
	Ball, Tracer, Blank.	
Weight of Round (g)	12 g.	
MECHANICAL FEATURES		
Firing Modes	Single Shot & Automatic	
Methods of Operation	Gas and Spring	
Locking	Rotary Bolt, Forward Locking	
Feed	Magazine (30 rounds)	
FIRING CHARACTERISTICS		
Muzzle Velocity (m/s)	940 m/s	970 m/s
Recoil (joules)	4 j	
Number of Barrel Grooves	4	
Pitch of Rifling (mm)	1 Turn in 175	
Twist of Rifling	Right Hand	
SIGHTING		
Optical Sight (SUSAT)	Sight Unit Small Arms Trilux	
Magnification	x 4	
Field of View (mils)	177 mils	
Eye Relief (mm)	24 mm	
Range Setting (metres)	300 to 800	
Iron Sight		
Foresight	Post	
Backsight	Twin Apertures	
Sight Radius (mm)	290 to 320 mm	
Range (metres)	Up to 300	
WEIGHTS (kg)		
With SUSAT and Full Magazine	5.08 kg	6.88 kg
Weapon only	3.8 kg	5.6 kg
Magazine with 30 Rounds	0.48	
Magazine empty	0.12	
SUSAT	0.8	
Iron Sight	0.3	
Bayonet and Scabbard	0.3	
LENGHTS (mm)		
Weapon	780 mm	900 mm
Bayonet	300 mm	
SA80 with Bayonet Fixed	980 mm	

SKILL AT ARMS

INTRODUCTION

The 5.56 SA 80 Rifle and the Light Support Weapon have the same
basic components and therefore most parts are interchangeable. In
view of this fact and when ever possible we refer to it as the 'weapon'
The LSW differs from the SA80 in having a LONGER BARREL, an
OUTRIGGER with a BIPOD, a smaller front HAND GUARD, a small
rear HAND GRIP on the BUTT and a SHOULDER STRAP. As
illustrated on the previous page.

Both weapons use a short stroke gas operated system and a rotary
forward-locking breech mechanism to give either single shot or
automatic operation from a 30 round MAGAZINE. The weapon is
designed to be fired from the RIGHT shoulder only.

On the SA80 Rifle, the 22mm diameter FLASH ELIMINATOR enables
the firing of rifle grenades, using a GRENADE LAUNCHER. The Rifle
is your personal weapon, with it you must become highly skilled to
handle every situation in which a you may find yourself. Above all, you
must handle the weapons safely at all times.

The tactical advantage of the weapon and its capability of firing single
rounds or bursts, is in producing :-

a. Quick, accurate fire at short range opportunity targets.

b. A high rate of accurate controlled fire at longer ranges.

c. Effective section fire power at ranges up to 600 metres.

There are two sighting systems for the weapons, the fully optical
SUSAT (Sight Unit Small Arms Trilux) or an IRON SIGHT, comprising
a FORESIGHT and a BACK SIGHT incorporated in the carrying
handle. The basic weapon can be stripped down into seven major
groups as shown on the next page.

Further stripping of some groups is possible and in some may be
required for cleaning or replacing damaged or worn parts.

Safety Precaution Drills are dealt with in later pages, but before
handling the weapon your instructor will carry out the Normal Safety
Precautions.

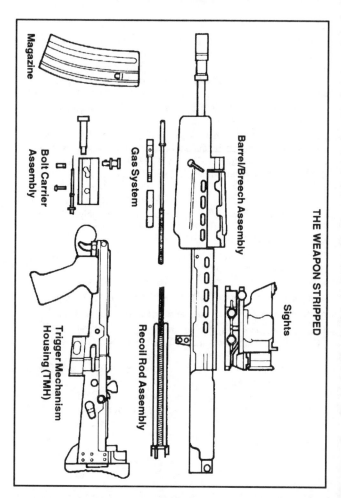

Magazine

Bolt Carrier Assembly

Gas System

Barrel/Breech Assembly

THE WEAPON STRIPPED

Sights

Trigger Mechanism Housing (TMH)

Recoil Rod Assembly

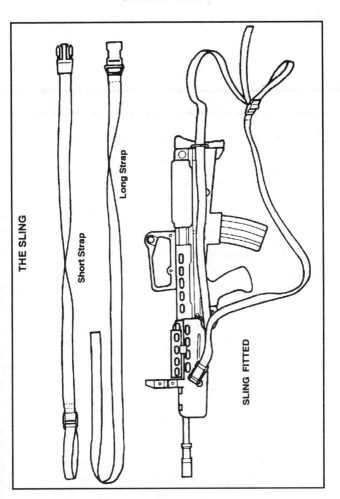

THE SLING

Short Strap

Long Strap

SLING FITTED

SKILL AT ARMS

ACCESSORIES & SPARES

Additional items, listed below, are not necessarily essential to fire the
weapon, but their use and application are explained in the following
paragraphs:-

The Sling. The Bayonet & Scabbard.
The Blank Firing Attachment. The Tool Roll & Spare Parts.

The SLING - see the illustration on previous page - is made of two
lengths of webbing type material, which link together with a special
quick release BUCKLE CLIP.

The first longer piece has, at one end, a female part of the clip and a
flat plastic loop attached, the other end of the strap is clear.

The second shorter piece has the male part of the clip at one end, and
the quick release buckle and loop at the other.

Fitting the Sling see illustrations 1 to 6 over page.

1. Take the longer strap and lay it flat along the weapon, with the
   FEMALE CLIP end towards the MUZZLE and the flat plastic loop
   pointing outwards. Feed the clear end through the FRONT SLING
   LOOP and then through the FLAT PLASTIC LOOP on th e strap.
   Pull tight.
2. Take the SHORTER strap and, holding it parallel with the first strap
   and with the MALE clip end pointing outwards, feed the clear end
   of the LONGER strap through and over the RIDGED EDGE of the
   gate in the base of the male clip on the SHORT strap, connect the
   male and female parts of the clip together.
3. Ensure that the LONGER strap remains untwisted, then feed the
   CLEAR end through the REAR SLING LOOP on the weapon.
4. Check that the SHORTER strap is not twisted, then feed the clear
   end of the LONGER strap outwards through the main gate of the
   BUCKLE BAR.
5. Finally, thread the CLEAR END of the LONGER strap through the
gate in the BUCKLE. TO REMOVE the SLING, reverse the fitting
procedure as above.

USES OF THE SLING - see illustrations on next page

Essentially the SLING can be used in two ways, although other
variations may be possible.

FRONT SLUNG POSITION. Separate the two straps and
insert your head, right arm and shoulder through the loop so

SKILL AT ARMS

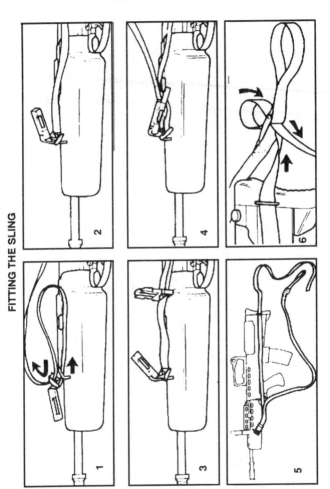

FITTING THE SLING

formed. The weapon will now be suspended from your left
shoulder across your chest. Adjust the position of the
weapon by pulling down on the CLEAR end of the LONGER
strap. Pulling the QUICK RELEASE loop or releasing the
CLIP will allow the weapon to be brought into the aim.

BACK SLUNG POSITION Separate the SLING to form TWO loops.
Put an arm through each loop to position the weapon, MUZZLE down,
in the centre of your back, COCKING HANDLE uppermost.

FRONT SLUNG

BACK SLUNG

ONE VARIATION

The BAYONET

The BAYONET is shaped to provide good thrust penetration. It has a cutting edge, blade channels and a ribbed portion for rope cutting. A slot at the forward end is for use with the scabbard when used as a wire cutter. The handle is shaped to enable the bayonet to be used as a fighting knife: at the

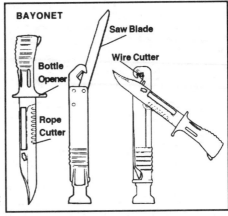

rear of the handle is a release catch which secures it onto the Muzzle of the rifle. The blade end of the handle can be used as a bottle opener. The SCABBARD is normally carried on your belt, attached by

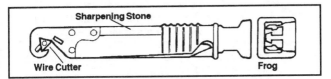

THE SCABBARD

a frog or to a side of an ammunition pouch. Quick release catches are fitted.

As well as providing stowage for your BAYONET, the SCABBARD has other uses Vis:- As a SAW BLADE which unfolds from one edge of the SCABBARD and is for use on WOOD - NOT METAL.
A SHARPENING STONE integral with the opposite side of the SCABBARD. Use with light oil.
As WIRE CUTTERS by engaging the LUG of the SCABBARD with the

slot in the BAYONET, ensuring that the sharp edge of the BAYONET faces away from the HOOK END of the SCABBARD.
The wedge shape on the back of the BLADE together with a corresponding hardened insert of the SCABBARD HOOK forms an effective wire-cutting device.

BLANK FIRING ATTACHMENT (BFA)

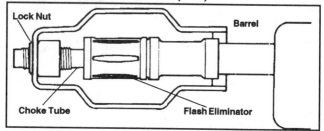

This will normally be fitted when you are using your weapon on training exercises when BLANK ammunition is issued. No other accessories are required for firing BLANK ammunition.

FITTING THE ATTACHMENT.

1. Unscrew the CHOKE TUBE as far out as necessary to allow the attachment body to be fitted over the FLASH ELIMINATOR. The rear of the ATTACHMENT BODY sits on the BARREL immediately behind the FLASH ELIMINATOR.
2. Screw in the CHOKE TUBE by hand until it butts up to the MUZZLE. Using the COMBINATION TOOL inserted into the slot of the CHOKE TUBE, rotate the TUBE a further half turn, then tighten the LOCK NUT.

NOTE:

The reason for the HALF TURN when tightening the CHOKE TUBE, is to stretch the ATTACHMENT BODY to ensure that sufficient force is applied to the CHOKE TUBE/MUZZLE INTERFACE to prevent gas leakage. IF there IS a gas leakage, then the weapon will suffer short recoils. However, NO safety hazard will be associated with incorrect fitting.

SAFETY PRECAUTIONS
RULES FOR HANDLING WEAPONS OF
ANY TYPE AT ALL TIMES

1. Whenever you pick up a weapon, or have a weapon personally handed to you or when you take over a weapon, ALWAYS carry out the NORMAL SAFETY PRECAUTIONS (NSP). Whether it is your own or someone else's weapon, ALWAYS examine it to ensure that it is NOT loaded.

2. NEVER point a weapon at anyone - even in fun.

3. ALWAYS handle a weapon so that it points in such a direction that there is NO DANGER if a round is accidentally fired.

4. NEVER rest the muzzle of a loaded weapon, or a weapon 'made safe' on your foot or against your body. Similarly, do not hold a weapon with your hand or hands placed over the muzzle.

5. Weapons will NEVER be carried in VEHICLES either loaded or in a 'made safe' state. Operational conditions excepted.

6. YOU will NOT fire any weapon until such time as you have been fully trained, exercised and tested to be capable of safely handling the weapon.

7. When handing over a weapon to someone else, SHOW/PROVE to them first that it is in a SAFE and in an UNLOADED state.

8. When anyone hands a weapon to you - NO MATTER WHO THEY ARE - *INSIST* THAT THEY SHOW/PROVE IT TO YOU.

9. NO weapon will be tampered with to make modifications etc., severe action will be taken against anyone doing this.

"IT'S BETTER TO BE SAFE THAN SORRY"

SKILL AT ARMS

OPERATIONAL SAFETY

When circumstances dictate in an 'operational situation' the following SAFETY RULES must be followed:-

SAFE HANDLING WITH A MAGAZINE FITTED

1. Once an order has been given to "LOAD", you keep your weapon in that state until ordered to "UNLOAD". At all times you are responsible for the SAFE HANDLING of your Weapon.
2. The SAFETY CATCH is always at 'S' unless the situation demands otherwise, the FINGER is OFF the TRIGGER and the MUZZLE is pointed in a SAFE direction.
3. If a LOADED weapon is to be CARRIED IN A VEHICLE or on an AIRCRAFT it should be correctly slung or secured in the rack provided.
4. The weapon is UNLOADED on command OR when no longer able to ensure its SAFETY, such as when handing it over to, or leaving it under guard of another soldier.
5. If a LOADED weapon MUST be handed over, the SAFETY CATCH will be applied, the recipient WILL BE TOLD OF THE STATE OF THE WEAPON, i.e., "LOADED" or "READY". The recipient WILL repeat back the STATE. If they are CORRECT, the weapon will be handed over - ensuring that the MUZZLE is kept pointing in a SAFE direction.
6. **If it is necessary to pick up a weapon WITH a MAGAZINE FITTED - UNLOAD the weapon as taught.**

RISK TO HEARING. Small Arms FULL BORE.

Ear Defenders or other suitable hearing protection must be worn by those firing and firing point staff during all full bore firing.
SA BLANK.
Hearing protection is not required for SA 80 BLANK firing PROVIDED that the following limits ARE applied:-
a. Blank Firing Attachment is ALWAYS fitted.
b. You are exposed to a LIMIT of up to 90 rounds per day.
c. That there are NO reflecting surfaces in the vicinity.
Those NOT firing are NOT to be closer than TWO metres to the flank of the weapon.

"BE SAFETY CONSCIOUS AT ALL TIMES "

SKILL AT ARMS

CARRYING OUT SAFETY PRECAUTIONS.

As with all SKILL at ARMS training the first thing you must learn is the drill to carry out the NORMAL SAFETY PRECAUTIONS. (NSP). Safety Precautions will always be carried out at the beginning and end of every lesson, practice or range period, and immediately on returning from a patrol or exercise or duty, and when handing the weapon over to anyone.

LOW
PORT
POSITION

To carry out the SAFETY PRECAUTIONS with a weapon adopt the LOW PORT POSITION as shown in the illustration on the left.

1. Hold by PISTOL GRIP with the RIGHT hand, forefinger outside the TRIGGER GUARD. Point MUZZLE upwards and rest the butt on waist belt or right pouch. Tilt weapon to the right.

THIS IS THE POSITION ADOPTED TO CARRY OUT THE FULL ROUTINE OF SAFETY PRECAUTIONS.

2. Make sure that the SAFETY CATCH is at SAFE **(S)** and the CHANGE LEVER to Repetition **(R)**.

3. Cock the WEAPON. To do this, tilt it slightly to the left and, using the left hand over the top of the weapon, weapon, gripping the COCKING HANDLE with thumb and forefinger and pull FULLY to the rear.

4. Hold the COCKING HANDLE back with the forefinger - depress the HOLDING OPEN CATCH with the thumb, ease the COCKING HANDLE forward until the CATCH stops the forward movement of the CARRIER. When done, place LEFT hand underneath HAND GUARD.

5. For the weapon to be inspected, push it away from your body, horizontal to the ground and tilting to the left, so as the breech can be inspected. After it has been inspected adopt the LOW PORT POSITION.

SKILL AT ARMS

6. On the command 'EASE SPRINGS':-
(a) Operate the BOLT RELEASE CATCH with your left hand, letting the working part go forward.
(b) Put SAFETY CATCH to FIRE (F) with RIGHT forefinger.
(c) Operate the TRIGGER.
(d) Put the SAFETY CATCH to (S) using your LEFT thumb.
(e) Close the DUST COVER with RIGHT hand, folding up and back in its slot.
(f) Ground Arms ensuring that the weapon is laid on its left side - COCKING HANDLE uppermost.
(g) Undo pouches, remove MAGAZINES, and contents for inspection. When the inspection has been completed, you put the MAGAZINES back in your POUCHES, FASTEN YOUR POUCHES, pick up yourweapon and adopt LOW PORT position.
THESE SAFETY PRECAUTIONS MUST BE CARRIED OUT BY EVERYONE IN THE SQUAD TAKING PART IN THE TRAINING OR WHEN WEAPONS ARE BEING HANDLED - THIS INCLUDES ALL INSTRUCTORS AND ALL RANKS PRESENT.

BASIC MECHANISM OPERATION
The operation of the basic mechanism is the same for both the SA80 and the LSW.
Mechanism - how the weapon works.
1. When the safety catch is at `S' the TRIGGER cannot be fully operated.
2. When the safety catch is at `F' and the TRIGGER is pressed, the HAMMER is released and hits the rear of the FIRING PIN, driving it forward on to the CAP in the BASE of the ROUND. The ROUND is fired and GASSES are produced which drive the BULLET up the BARREL.
3. Some of this GAS enters the GAS BLOCK and is diverted by the GAS PLUG into the GAS CYLINDER, pushing the PISTON to the rear and at the same time compressing the PISTON SPRING.
4. The rear of the PISTON strikes the CARRIER, forcing it backwards. The compressed PISTON SPRING re-asserts itself and forces the PISTON forwards again.
5. The BOLT is unlocked by the rearward movement of the CARRIER forcing the CAM STUD down the CAM STUD SLOT.

BASIC MECHANISM OPERATION

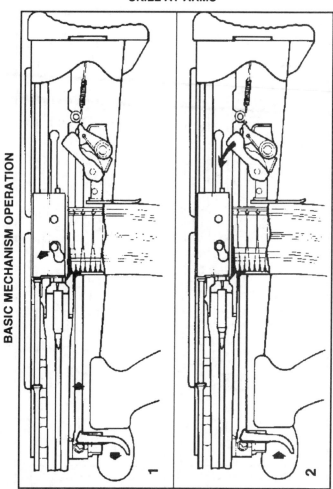

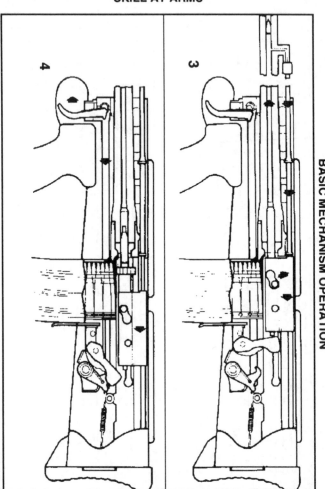

BASIC MECHANISM OPERATION

6. The CARRIER and BOLT go back together, cocking the HAMMER as they go. The EMPTY CASE is withdrawn from the CHAMBER by the EXTRACTOR and ejected out of the weapon to the right, through the EJECTION OPENING.
   The RETURN SPRING on the GUIDE ROD is also compressed at this stage. Rearward movement of the CARRIER and BOLT ceases when the rear of the CARRIER strikes the BUFFER.

7. The RETURN SPRING re-asserts itself and aided by the BUFFER drives the CARRIER and BOLT. As it does so the BOLT feeds the next ROUND out of the MAGAZINE and into the CHAMBER. The EXTRACTOR grips the ROUND and the EJECTOR is compressed. The BOLT is rotated to lock into the BARREL EXTENSION by the continuing forward movement of the CARRIER, CARRIER, forcing the CAM STUD to slide up the CAM STUD SLOT. It is only when the parts are fully forward and locked that the SAFETY SEAR can operate to free the HAMMER into its ready position. A distinct CLICK will be heard.

8. The weapon is now ready to fire again. This action will continue each time the TRIGGER is operated until the last ROUND has been fired and the rearward action takes place. The working parts will then be held to the rear by the HOLDING OPEN CATCH being lifted up by the MAGAZINE PLATFORM.

BASIC MECHANISM

With the change lever at AUTOMATIC (`A'). The operation of the mechanism as previously explained applies equally to the AUTOMATIC role.

The difference being that the weapon will continue to fire as long as the TRIGGER is kept pressed and there are are ROUNDS left in the MAGAZINE.

The SAFETY SEAR allows one shot only per TRIGGER operation with the CHANGE LEVER at `R'.

When the CHANGE LEVER is at `A' the SAFETY SEAR is held out of its working position and AUTOMATIC fire results.

SKILL AT ARMS

SIGHTS

The Weapon may be fitted with two types of day SIGHT, either the **Sight Unit Small Arms Trilux (SUSAT)** or an **IRON SIGHT**.

SUSAT SIGHT

The SUSAT consists of an OPTICAL BODY fixed to a MOUNTING BRACKET. On top of the SIGHT BODY is the EMERGENCY BATTLE SIGHT (EBS). Each sight has its own unique number, stamped on the underneath left side of the OPTICAL BODY. **You would be well advised to remember this number.**

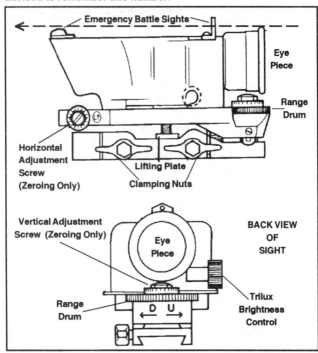

SKILL AT ARMS

SIGHT SETTING

The SUSAT sight as illustrated on the previous page.

The RANGE DRUM is graduated in units of 100 from 300 to 800 metres. Sights are set at a BATTLE RANGE of 300 metres, and should be used for normal infantry work. To set a RANGE, turn the DRUM until the required figure is facing straight to the rear.

The OPTICAL BODY contains the OPTICAL SYSTEM which has a magnification factor of x 4 and a field of view of 177 mils.

The BODY comprises :-

The EYEPIECE which is made of rubber and is glued to the rear of the optics. It is designed to protect the LENS from water and of a length to ensure correct positioning of the eye.

The POINTER within the OPTICS is seen in your field of view. In daylight the POINTER appears as a dark pillar with a clear centre. At night POINTER tip can be illuminated by the TRILUX lamp. The light from the lamp is reflected up into the pointer and is seen as a reddish glow.

A BRIGHTNESS CONTROL is located at the RIGHT REAR of the BODY and can be rotated to change the light intensity from zero to full brightness.

The OBJECTIVE LENS HOOD is part of the BODY which is shaped to overhang the OBJECTIVE LENS, so reducing reflections and also protecting the LENS from rain.

EMERGENCY BATTLE SIGHT (EBS)

The EBS consists of a BLADE FORESIGHT and an APERTURE BACKSIGHT. It is matched to the OPTICAL CENTRE of the SUSAT lenses during manufacture and therefore no zeroing adjustment is provided. It is for use in an emergency should the SUSAT become damaged, until such time that the IRON SIGHT can be fitted in its place.

SIGHT MOUNTING BRACKET consists of:-

The MOUNTING SHOE and SIGHT MOUNT. The MOUNTING SHOE is dovetailed to match the SIGHT BASE on the weapon.

A LOCATING PLUNGER protrudes through the SHOE to engage in one of the three holes in the SIGHT BASE.

Two CLAMPING UNITS secure the SHOE to the SIGHT BASE.

A lifting plate for the PLUNGER protrudes on the RIGHT side of the BRACKET.

This enables the fore/aft position of the SIGHT to be adjusted to give you the most comfortable SIGHT PICTURE, you can then mark the position for your own use.

The SIGHT MOUNT links the MOUNTING SHOE with the OPTICAL BODY.

For zeroing purposes, the MOUNT is fitted at the FRONT with a HORIZONTAL adjustment screw, at the REAR is a VERTICAL adjustment screw and immediately below the EYE PIECE is a RANGE DRUM which is marked from 3 to 8 in increments of 100 metres.

FITTING THE SUSAT - see illustration below.

1. Check sight serial number is correct one for your particular weapon.
2. Rotate RANGE DRUM so that the 300 metre setting is faces directly to the rear. Release the SIGHT CLAMPING NUTS and open the weapon TOP COVER.
3. Hold the weapon with the RIGHT hand and grip SUSAT with the LEFT hand.
4. Using your forefinger to raise the LIFTING PLATE and withdraw LOCATING PLUNGER, align the rear of the MOUNTING SHOE with the front of the SIGHT BASE, then slide the SIGHT towards the rear of the weapon until the required position is reached, then release the LIFTING PLATE.
5. Check that LOCATING PLUNGER has engaged in correct recess on SIGHT BASE. Test by attempting to move the SIGHT forwards or backwards. Tighten CLAMPING NUTS - DO NOT OVER TIGHTEN. Close the weapon TOP COVER.
6. FOR SIGHT ADJUSTMENTS, see SETTING & ADJUSTMENTS.

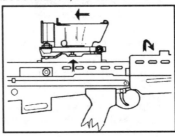

SKILL AT ARMS

REMOVING THE SUSAT

1. Note exact position of LIFTING PLATE in relation to SIGHT BASE. (For use to accurately refit the SIGHT).
2. Hold the weapon by the PISTOL GRIP with the right hand so that it is horizontal and upright. Open TOP COVER and undo the SIGHT CLAMPING NUTS.
3. Grip the SUSAT with the left hand, use the forefinger to raise the LIFTING PLATE and disengage the LOCATING LUG from the SIGHT BASE, then slide SUSAT forward and off the SIGHT BASE. Close the TOP COVER of the weapon.
4. Check and make a note of the SERIAL NUMBER of the SUSAT.

The IRON SIGHT

The IRON SIGHT consists of a FORESIGHT BLOCK and a CARRYING HANDLE, which incorporates a dual leaf APERTURE BACKSIGHT.
THE FORESIGHT consists of a BLADE mounted in a FORESIGHT BLOCK, the base of which contains a female dovetail which fits into its matching male dovetail on top of the weapon GAS BLOCK.
The two are held together by a RETAINING SCREW. The FORESIGHT BLADE is protected by extensions of the BLOCK and the rear of the BLADE houses a TRILUX element which emits light through a small hole.
A vertical adjustment screw, retained by a LOCKING PLUNGER, provides for ZEROING adjustment.

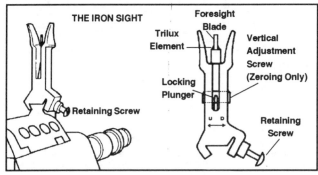

245

SKILL AT ARMS

Fitting the IRON SIGHT

1. Loosen the FORESIGHT RETAINING SCREW fully, using the COMBINATION TOOL.
2. Ensure the TRILUX element is facing to the rear, mate the dovetail joints, check that the sight is flush front and rear then tighten the RETAINING SCREW - DO NOT OVER TIGHTEN.
3. Using the COMBINATION TOOL, loosen the CARRYING HANDLE RETAINING SCREWS and release the LOCATING SCREW sufficiently for the handle to slide easily along the SIGHT BASE dovetail.
4. Open the weapon TOP COVER and slide the HANDLE rear-wards on to the SIGHT BASE to the required position, ensuring the LOCATING SCREW aligns with one of the three holes in the SIGHT BASE.
   Tighten the LOCATING SCREW and RETAINING SCREWS - DO NOT OVER TIGHTEN. Close the weapon TOP COVER.

NOTE: When an IRON SIGHT has been fitted as a replacement for the SUSAT sight, then the weapon must be zeroed - Refer to SETTING and ADJUSTMENTS.

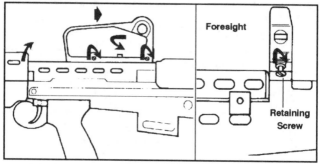

Removing the IRON SIGHT

1. Fully release the FORESIGHT BLOCK RETAINING SCREW and slide the BLOCK off the dovetail. Tighten the RETAINING SCREW.
2. Open the weapon TOP COVER, loosen the RETAINING SCREWS

and the LOCATING SCREW on the CARRYING HANDLE, then slide the HANDLE forwards clear of the SIGHT BASE. Close the weapon TOP COVER.

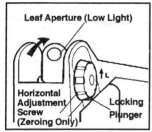

THE IRON SIGHT

Backsight and Carrying Handle

The BACKSIGHT and CARRYING HANDLE is fitted to the SIGHT BASE by means of matching dovetails.

The handle is positioned by a LOCATING SCREW which engages in one of three holes in the SIGHT BASE, and is secured by two RETAINING SCREWS.

The BACKSIGHT has two LEAF APERTURES, a small one for ranges up to 200m and a larger one for use - in conjunction with the TRILUX element -in conditions of low light or darkness.

To change the APERTURE, push the LEAF forwards or backwards. Extensions on the HANDLE protect the apertures.

A horizontal adjusting screw on the right side, retained by a locking plunger, is used for zeroing.

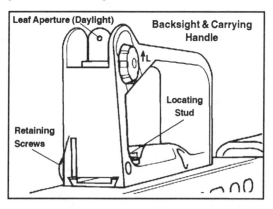

SKILL AT ARMS

HANDLING
WEAPON CONTROLS - see below..
This illustrates the position of the weapon controls.

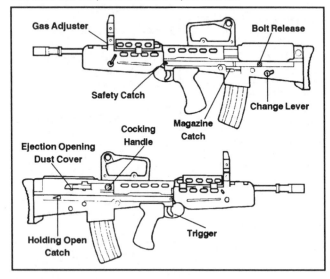

FILLING MAGAZINES

Each MAGAZINE will hold 30 ROUNDS of 5.56 rimless ammunition.
There are two methods of filling MAGAZINES, one using a
CHARGER and the other by hand.
The Charger can only be used if the AMMUNITION is issued in
CLIPS.
Before filling your MAGAZINE ensure that it is not damaged
particularly in the area of the MAGAZINE GUIDE LIPS.
On operations always fill your MAGAZINE with 30 ROUNDS.
During training different numbers of ROUNDS may be ordered.

SKILL AT ARMS

FILLING A MAGAZINE - USING THE CHARGER

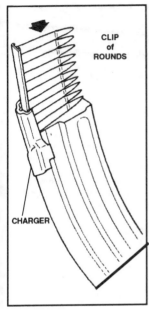

CLIP
of
ROUNDS

CHARGER

1. Having inspected the MAGAZINE, grip it in LEFT hand, support on a firm surface, ensure the back of MAGAZINE is facing away from the BODY.

2. Fit the wide end of CHARGER onto the back of MAGAZINE, ensure that it is fully seated.

3. Put CLIP of 10 ROUNDS into the Charger.

4. Using your RIGHT thumb, push down on the top ROUND, until all ROUNDS are fed into MAGAZINE. Remove the CLIP.

5. Each time clip is fed into MAGAZINE ensure that BASE of last ROUND is firm against the rear wall of the MAGAZINE. When the MAGAZINE is full remove the CHARGER and retain in pouch for further use.

FILLING WITH LOOSE ROUNDS

1. Hold MAGAZINE as when using CHARGER.

2. Push ROUNDS into MAGAZINE, depressing the PLATFORM, BULLETS towards the narrow wall of the MAGAZINE, one at a time, making narrow wall of the MAGAZINE, one at a time, making sure that the BASE of each ROUND is firm against the MAGAZINE REAR WALL.

SHOULD YOU DROP A ROUND - MAKE SURE IT IS CLEAN BEFORE USING IT TO FILL YOUR MAGAZINE

EMPTYING MAGAZINES

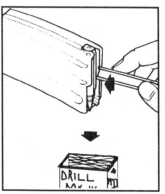

Using an empty CLIP, press down on each SECOND ROUND, to allow the TOP ROUND to drop out. Ensure ROUNDS do not drop into dirt/mud.

A second method is to hold the MAGAZINE in the LEFT HAND, BULLETS pointing away from body, then push the BASE of the ROUND forward so that it disengages from the GUIDE LIPS. Care must be taken as you may have to twist and pull the ROUND clear with your free hand. This is a useful method, especially at night as it makes very little noise.

LOAD, READY and UNLOAD

The weapon is LOADED when it has a MAGAZINE inserted. It is READY to FIRE when the weapon IS COCKED and a LIVE ROUND is in the CHAMBER. It is UNLOADED when the MAGAZINE has been removed and there is no ROUND in the CHAMBER.

On the command "LOAD":

1. You adopt the `LOW PORT' position.
2. Set SAFETY CATCH at `S' (safe). CHANGE LEVER to `R' (repetition).
3. Tilt weapon to RIGHT, take a full MAGAZINE or one with number of ROUNDS ordered, check top ROUNDS are in position correctly, insert it FIRMLY into MAGAZINE HOUSING.
   Ensure the MAGAZINE is clicked fully home and is secure.
4. Fasten your POUCH.

On the command "READY": with the weapon loaded:-

1. Adopt the `ALERT' position - that is :- Advance the LEFT foot, bring the BUTT into the shoulder, point the MUZZLE down.
2. Check CHANGE LEVER is at `R'.
3. Set SIGHTS at 300 or as ordered. Pull the COCKING HANDLE fully to the rear, then release it cleanly to go forward. Do not assist the

SKILL AT ARMS

COCKING HANDLE forward or a stoppage may occur.
4. Set the SAFETY CATCH to `F', place your finger on the TRIGGER and observe.

NOTE: You may be ordered to return the SAFETY CATCH to `S', if so, put your forefinger along outside of TRIGGER GUARD.

On the command "UNLOAD":-
1. Re-position your finger outside the TRIGGER GUARD.
2. Put the SAFETY CATCH to `S'.
3. Check that the CHANGE LEVER is at `R'.
4. Unfasten the POUCH. Adopt the LOW PORT position, tilt the weapon to the RIGHT. Grip the MAGAZINE with the LEFT hand, press the MAGAZINE CATCH with your thumb and remove the MAGAZINE and put it in your POUCH.

NOTE THE MAGAZINE MUST BE REMOVED AT THIS STAGE FOR SAFETY REASONS.
5. Keeping the weapon pointing in a SAFE direction COCK the weapon carefully, to prevent the ROUND ejecting too far, and engage the HOLDING OPEN CATCH. Tilt the weapon to the LEFT and visually check that the BODY and CHAMBER are clear, then operate the BOLT RELEASE to allow the WORKING PARTS to go forward. At night check the BODY and CHAMBER are clear by inserting your finger.

NOTE: Should you have gloves on or have any difficulty in feeling that the CHAMBER is clear, put the weight of your PULLTHROUGH into the CHAMBER, if it drops into the BARREL -the CHAMBER IS CLEAR.
6. Put SAFETY CATCH to `F', operate the TRIGGER, then return the SAFETY CATCH to `S', put SIGHTS down to 300 if necessary.
7. Close DUST COVER, pick up EJECTED ROUND, clean and replace in MAGAZINE, fasten POUCH.

USEFUL TIPS:-To prevent possible injury to the face or eye from EJECTED ROUNDS - DON'T TILT WEAPON TO LEFT WHEN COCKING DURING UNLOAD.

Keep your weapon pointing in SAFE direction, RIGHT HAND should be cupped over EJECTION OPENING to prevent ejected ROUND from being lost especially in the dark.

MAKING SAFE
When ordered to "MAKE SAFE", no matter what `state of readiness' the weapon is in, UNLOAD as you have been taught, then put on a FULL MAGAZINE.

251

SKILL AT ARMS

SAFE HANDLING WITH THE MAGAZINE FITTED.

Once an order has been given to "LOAD", you keep the weapon in that
state until ordered to "UNLOAD".

"SAFETY IS A PERSONAL RESPONSIBILITY"

STRIPPING & ASSEMBLING

The sequence of stripping the weapon is important to prevent damage
to the working parts. It will NOT be stripped further than taught. The
weapon is stripped into the following groups/assemblies:-

**MAGAZINE. SIGHTS. TRIGGER MECHANISM HOUSING (TMH)
BARREL. BREECH ASSEMBLY. GAS SYSTEM. BOLT CARRIER
ASSEMBLY. RECOIL ROD ASSEMBLY.**

THE WEAPON STRIPPED - see illustration on next page.

General Information.

In order to maintain your weapon in a satisfactory working condition,
périodic stripping and cleaning is necessary. In addition to ensuring
that the component parts are clean and lubricated, any undue wear can
be detected and the relevant part replaced as necessary.

The only tools to be used are those provided in the Tool Roll. In your
early stages of training NO time limits are imposed during practicing
Stripping and Assembling.

As the weapon is stripped the parts must be laid out on a clean and dry
surface, it follows that it must be clean when assembled.

Stripping other than that you have been instructed to do will NOT be
carried out.

The regular care and cleaning of will ensure that it is in a serviceable
condition at all times.

Your ability to look after a weapon will be reflected in the high standard
of Weapon Training required to pass your Training Tests.

Regular stripping and assembling does cause "wear and tear" on any
weapon.

This is especially important with the SUSAT, stripping and assembling
should not be carried out without due reason.

Any defects noticed by you must be reported immediately to your unit
Armourer.

THE WEAPON STRIPPED

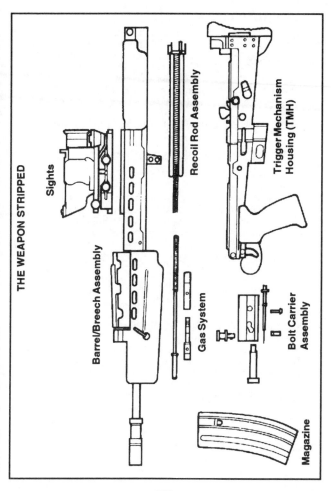

Sights

Recoil Rod Assembly

Trigger Mechanism Housing (TMH)

Barrel/Breech Assembly

Gas System

Bolt Carrier Assembly

Magazine

SKILL AT ARMS

STRIPPING and ASSEMBLING

1. Check SAFETY CATCH is at `S' and the CHANGE LEVER is at `R'.
2. Cock weapon, engage HOLDING OPEN CATCH, inspect BODY and CHAMBER to ensure all clear. Operate BOLT RELEASE to allow WORKING PARTS to go forward. DO NOT operate the TRIGGER. DO NOT close DUST COVER.
3. The SAFETY CATCH must remain on `S' and the HAMMER must remain cocked throughout the time the weapon is in a stripped state.
4. The SUSAT and or the IRON SIGHT should not be removed unless it is impossible to clean the weapon correctly without doing so.

TRIGGER MECHANISM HOUSING (TMH)
See illustration on the next page.
To STRIP:-

1. Ensure the weapon is horizontal and upside down. Fully withdraw the TMH (TRIGGER MECHANISM HOUSING) rear LOCKING PIN, then re-insert the pin approximately 5mm into the BODY, so that the GROOVE nearest the BODY is flush with t he outside of its housing - a distinct click should be heard. This ensures that the end of the PIN retains the RECOIL ROD ASSEMBLY while the TMH is being removed.
2. Finally withdraw the TMH FORWARD LOCKING PIN and separate the TMH from th e BODY by pulling the BUTT upwards and disengaging the TMH from its FRONT CATCH.

To ASSEMBLE:-

1. Check that the TMH FRONT LOCKING PIN is fully withdrawn. Insert front end of TMH into CATCH behind HAND GUARD. Raise back of TMH and press the BODY and TMH together. Fully insert the TMH REAR LOCKING PIN, then the front LOCKING PIN.
2. Test the action by COCKING the weapon and engaging the HOLDING OPEN CATCH, then operate, the BOLT RELEASE, set the SAFETY CATCH at `R' and operate the TRIGGER.
3. Put the SAFETY CATCH to `S' and close the DUST COVER.
NOTE: When/if applicable refit the SUSAT, ensuring that the LOCATING PLUNGER engages the correct recess in the SIGHT BASE to maintain correct EYE RELIEF.

SKILL AT ARMS

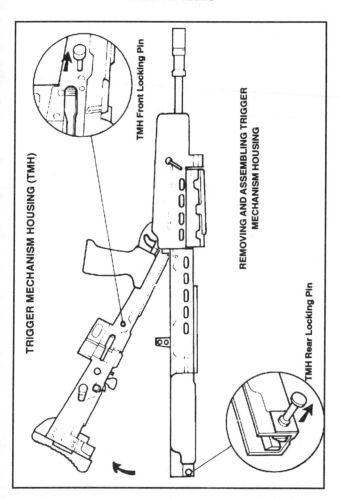

TMH Front Locking Pin

TRIGGER MECHANISM HOUSING (TMH)

REMOVING AND ASSEMBLING TRIGGER MECHANISM HOUSING

TMH Rear Locking Pin

SKILL AT ARMS

RECOIL ROD and BOLT CARRIER ASSEMBLIES - see illustration
below and over page.
To STRIP:-
1. Remove the TMH as detailed, keeping the weapon horizontal and
   upside down
2. Place a hand over the rear of the RECOIL ROD ASSEMBLY.
   Fully withdraw the TMH LOCKING PIN, then under control,
   remove the RECOIL ROD ASSEMBLY. Do NOT separate the
   SPRING from the RECOIL ROD ASSEMBLY.
3. Pull the COCKING HANDLE to the rear to unlock the BOLT, then
   withdraw the HANDLE from the CARRIER.
4. Place hand over the rear of the BODY, raise the MUZZLE and slide
   out the BOLT CARRIER ASSEMBLY.
5. Hold BOLT CARRIER ASSEMBLY in hand, withdraw FIRING PIN
   RETAINING PIN - use COMBINATION TOOL if necessary and
   withdraw the FIRING PIN from the rear of the BOLT.
6. Pull BOLT fully forward in the CARRIER and remove the CAM
   STUD. Separate the BOLT from the CARRIER.

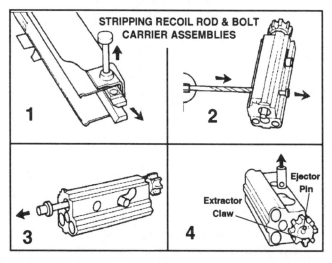

STRIPPING RECOIL ROD & BOLT CARRIER ASSEMBLIES

1

2

3

4

Ejector Pin

Extractor Claw

SKILL AT ARMS

ASSEMBLING RECOIL ROD & BOLT CARRIER ASSEMBLIES.
TO ASSEMBLE

1. Align the EJECTOR on the BOLT with the CAM STUD recess in the CARRIER.

2. Insert the BOLT into CARRIER, align the CAM STUD HOLE in the BOLT with the front of the CAM RECESS in the CARRIER.

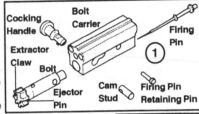

3. Hold the CAM STUD so that the FIRING PIN HOLE in the STUD is aligned to allow the FIRING PIN to pass through it. Push the CAM STUD through the recess in the CARRIER and into position in the BOLT.

4. Insert the FIRING PIN through the back of the CARRIER and ensure that it is fully seated. Replace the FIRING PIN RETAINING PIN from the left side of the BOLT CARRIER. When correctly seated the RETAINING PIN is flush with the sides of the CARRIER.

5. With the weapon horizontal and upside down, first ensure that the BOLT is fully forward in the CARRIER. Then place the CARRIER into the weapon and push far enough forward to align the COCKING HANDLE RECESS adjacent to the COCKING GUIDE in the BODY.

6. Insert the COCKING HANDLE through the side of the BODY and into the RECESS in the CARRIER. Push the CARRIER fully forward until the LOCKING SPINES on the BOLT have entered and locked into the BARREL EXTENSION.

7. Align the RECOIL RODS and SPRING with the holes in the rear of the CARRIER. Push the RECOIL ROD ASSEMBLY into the weapon until the end of the ASSEMBLY is flush to the end of the BODY. Push in the TMH REAR LOCKING PIN to engage the end of the ASSEMBLY, but not sufficient to obstruct the centre area which accommodates the LUG of the TMH.

257

SKILL AT ARMS

STRIPPING AND ASSEMBLING THE GAS SYSTEM

See illustrations on the next page.

TO STRIP:-

1. Ensure that the weapon is horizontal but upright. Open the GAS ASSEMBLY TOP COVER.
2. Grip the GAS CYLINDER with the left hand and with the right hand push the PISTON to the rear against the action of its RETURN SPRING. Move the PISTON out of alignment with the CYLINDER, release the pressure and withdraw the PISTON, complete with SPRING, from the weapon. Do not separate the SPRING from the PISTON.
3. Remove the GAS CYLINDER from the GAS PLUG by pulling it to the rear. Make a note of the GAS SETTINGS positions on the GAS PLUG.
4. Remove the GAS PLUG by pressing the PLUNGER on the front of the PLUG and at the same time withdraw the PLUG from the rear of the GAS BLOCK, removing it from the weapon.

TO ASSEMBLE.

1. Insert the GAS PLUG into the rear of the GAS BLOCK. Depress the PLUNGER and at the same time push the PLUG through the BLOCK. Rotate the PLUG until the PLUNGER is aligned with the recess marked `N' (Normal) on the front of the GAS BLOCK.
2. Fit the CYLINDER onto the rear of the GAS PLUG and hold it in position with the left hand.
3. Turn the weapon on its side and carefully feed the SPRING END of the PISTON back into the CENTRAL HOLE above the BARREL EXTENSION. Push the PISTON to the rear to compress the SPRING, then align and engage the PISTON with the CYLINDER REAR RECESS. Close the TOP COVER.

NOTE: Should you have difficulty in locating the CENTRAL HOLE you can see through the VENTILATION SLITS in the BODY.

STRIPPING & ASSEMBLING MAGAZINE

To STRIP

1. Hold the MAGAZINE in the LEFT hand with the BOTTOM PLATE uppermost.
2. Push in the RETAINING STUD and slide off the BOTTOM PLATE in the direction of the forward edge. Remove the SPRING and PLATFORM from the MAGAZINE.

STRIP & ASSEMBLE THE GAS SYSTEM

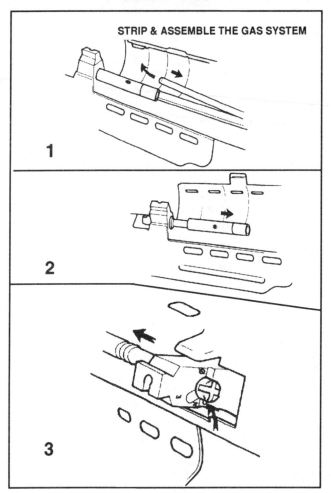

SKILL AT ARMS

To ASSEMBLE
1. Ensure that the PLATFORM is aligned correctly, then insert the
   PLATFORM and SPRING into the MAGAZINE.
2. Push down the RETAINING STUD and slide on the BOTTOM
   PLATE. Ensure that the STUD engages in its recess in the
   BOTTOM PLATE.

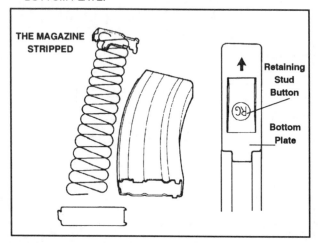

OPERATIONAL STRIPPING.

During tactical training or on operations, it may be undesirable to strip
the complete weapon at any one time, in order to carry out
maintenance. Accordingly, it is possible to strip only one part at a
time, provided that the basic SAFETY PRECAUTIONS are taken. The
GAS ASSEMBLY may be stripped provided the weapon is unloaded
and the BOLT CARRIER ASSEMBLY is held to the rear. The TMH
may be removed without removing any other part. As with normal
stripping all parts should be placed, in the sequence of stripping, on a
clean surface.

Your weapon can be stripped in any sequence providing the
NORMAL SAFETY PRECAUTIONS are first carried out.

SKILL AT ARMS

Stripping is only carried out for a purpose, IE, CLEANING and MAINTENANCE. Never strip your weapon further than you have been taught.

USE OF CLEANING EQUIPMENT
- see illustration over page.

THE TOOL ROLL is provided to carry all the items required for the cleaning of the weapon. The illustration sets out the items to be found in the TOOL ROLL which are described in the following paragraphs.

The **CLEANING ROD** - the 3 section Rod used with either the BORE or CHAMBER BRUSHES. (Two sets of RODS needed to clean a full BARREL length). Do not use if the screwed section joints are not close and smooth. Insert into MUZZLE end of Barrel, twist only clockwise, taking care not to rub it against the side of the bore at the MUZZLE. The **BORE CLEANING BRUSH** is only to be used to clean the BORE of the WEAPON, oil may be applied to assist in removing fouling and stains within the BORE. It can also be used with the PULLTHROUGH, in which case it is only to be drawn from the CHAMBER end of the BARREL.

The **CHAMBER/BARREL EXTENSION BRUSH** is ONLY to be used for cleaning the CHAMBER, the BARREL EXTENSION or the interior of the GAS BLOCK. It is to be used ONLY with the CLEANING ROD.

The **PULLTHROUGH** can be used instead of the ROD to draw a FLANNELETTE PATCH or the BORE BRUSH through the BARREL, it must first be unravelled and stretched to remove any knots or kinks.

A **FLANNELETTE PATCH** can be fitted folding it in half lengthways and putting it into the eyelet with equal parts of the flannelette protruding either side.

FLANNELETTE PATCHES are mainly used to dry clean and lubricate the barrel. They must not be used in a size larger than 50mm x 50mm or they will jam in the barrel.

NYLON PAD (SCOTCHBRIGHT). Used primarily for removing carbon fouling, but can also be used with oil to remove rust. Must not be used on weapon parts coated with a protective finish as the pad will remove the finish.

The **NYLON BRUSH** is used with FLANNELETTE to clean the inside of the BODY. A piece of lightly oiled FLANNELETTE is used to clean the outside of the weapon.

COMBINATION TOOL. A multipurpose tool used when cleaning the weapon, fitting and adjusting SIGHTS, and adjusting GAS SYSTEM.

SKILL AT ARMS

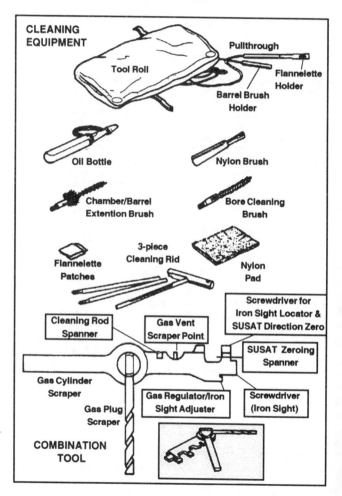

CLEANING EQUIPMENT

Tool Roll

Pullthrough

Flannelette Holder

Barrel Brush Holder

Oil Bottle

Nylon Brush

Chamber/Barrel Extension Brush

Bore Cleaning Brush

Flannelette Patches

3-piece Cleaning Rid

Nylon Pad

Cleaning Rod Spanner

Gas Vent Scraper Point

Screwdriver for Iron Sight Locator & SUSAT Direction Zero

SUSAT Zeroing Spanner

Gas Cylinder Scraper

Gas Plug Scraper

Gas Regulator/Iron Sight Adjuster

Screwdriver (Iron Sight)

COMBINATION TOOL

SKILL AT ARMS

CLEANING THE WEAPON.
FIRST CARRY OUT THE NSP's (Normal Safety Precautions)
1. Using the NYLON BRUSH remove any loose fouling or debris from
   the weapon parts. (Less the SUSAT)
2. Using a piece of lightly oiled FLANNELETTE, clean the outside of
   the weapon.
3. Using the CHAMBER/BARREL EXTENSION BRUSH and
   CLEANING ROD, insert it into the CHAMBER. With a clockwise
   rotating action, withdrawing the BRUSH with the MUZZLE pointing
   up will dislodge fouling or debris which will come out with BRUSH.
4. Using the NYLON BRUSH and FLANNELETTE, clean the inside of
   the body.
5. Clean the BARREL with the BORE BRUSH, then use the
   PULLTHROUGH and dry clean FLANNELETTE.
6. Examine the barrel for cleanliness. Look through the MUZZLE end
   by holding it up to the light about 150mm away from your head,
   keep both eyes open and follow the lands and grooves in the
   barrel throughout their length. If required clean the BARREL again.
7. Carbon fouling is removed with COMBINATION TOOL SCRAPERS
   and the NYLON PAD. Wipe clean the PISTON, GAS CYLINDER
   and GAS PLUG, then lightly oil.
8. Dry clean the whole weapon and examine it for damage etc.
9. Lightly oil the WEAPON and MAGAZINE, but NOT the SUSAT, or if
   fitted the IRON SIGHT APERTURES and POST.
10. Assemble the weapon and test for correct functioning. Put the
    SAFETY CATCH to FIRE (F), operate the trigger, put the
    SAFETY CATCH to SAFE (S) and check that the CHANGE
    LEVER is at 'R'.
11. Using NYLON BRUSH and oily swabs, clean the SUSAT
    BRACKET, ensuring that NO OIL gets on the rubber EYE PIECE
    or LENS. Dry clean the exterior and use LENS CLEANING
    CLOTHS or TISSUES to clean the LENS, lightly oil the SHOE,
    then refit the sight.
NOTE: Should stains or scratches appear on the SUSAT LENS it must
be reported.

CLEANING IN ADVERSE CONDITIONS.

Heavy rain and damp conditions: Keep MUZZLE and SIGHT
COVERS fitted for as long as possible. In an emergency the weapon
can be fired with the MUZZLE COVER fitted. Inspect frequently for
rust and remove it as normal.

Tropical humid conditions:
In these conditions daily care and cleaning is essential to maintain
your weapon cleaning as already described. Special types of oil are
issued to combat the rust that is caused by the damp.

Extreme cold conditions:
Carry out cleaning as normal, use oil sparingly. Special oil will be
issued for working in low temperatures. Your MUZZLE COVER is to be
kept on to prevent snow entering BARREL. A build up of condensation
on the SUSAT will occur if it is covered, therefore do not fit the cover in
these conditions.

Dry, sandy or dusty conditions:
Dry clean your weapon. The heat will make it sweat in the sun, clean
off any oil that appears. Any rust that appears, clean it off leaving no oil
on your weapon. Check your MAGAZINES by emptying them, if
necessary, strip them and clean out any dust or sand. Remove the
TMH and clean out any dust or sand. If practical - keep MUZZLE and
SIGHT COVERS on. Should you get sand or dust on the SUSAT
LENS do not to rub the LENS.

DESCRIPTION OF AMMUNITION

It is obvious that you must be able to immediately recognise different
types of ammunition that you will be using. Especially when you are
filling a MAGAZINE - under pressure - with loose rounds or using a
CHARGER.

The weapons fire rimless 5.56mm ammunition. The manufacturers
information is stamped on the base of each cartridge. Ammunition is
normally supplied in cardboard cartons of 20 rounds or in bandoliers
containing a CHARGER and 150 ROUNDS in clips of 10 ROUNDS.

TYPES OF AMMUNITION.

There are four types of ammunition issued, they are as follows:-
BALL - This has a smooth brass cartridge case, a jacketed bullet
with a GREEN TIP and percussion cap in the base.
TRACER - Similar to BALL rounds with a GREEN & RED painted tip.

SKILL AT ARMS

BLANK - A black plastic cartridge case, with a brass base, or a brass case, both incorporating a percussion cap in the base, there is no bullet.
DRILL - A silver coloured grooved case, a copper jacketed bullet and no percussion cap.

CARE OF AMMUNITION.

Always look after ammunition; keep it clean, dry and free from oil.
Never let it lie in the direct rays of the sun as this can cause inaccuracies when firing.
Do NOT use a round as a tool.
Do NOT apply pressure to the base of a round, either with a clip or another round. There is a possibility of detonating the percussion cap and thereby firing the round.
Tampering with ammunition is dangerous and strictly forbidden.

FUNCTIONAL FAILURES - IMMEDIATE ACTION

If the weapon fails to fire, or stops firing carry out the IMMEDIATE ACTION (IA) drills. It is only with practice that these become second nature to you. The IA drills are described below:- The most important rule is to - ALWAYS LOOK AT THE POSITION OF THE COCKING HANDLE.
1. If the COCKING HANDLE is fully to the REAR, and MAGAZINE is EMPTY - change MAGAZINE - operate BOLT RELEASE - aim - test and adjust - continue firing.
2. If the COCKING HANDLE is NOT fully to the REAR - cock the weapon - engage the HOLDING OPEN CATCH - look into BODY and CHAMBER:-
a. If CHAMBER empty and there are ROUNDS in MAGAZINE - check MAGAZINE fitted correctly - operate BOLT RELEASE - re-aim - test and adjust - continue firing.
b. If LIVE ROUND or EMPTY CASE is in BODY or CHAMBER - remove MAGAZINE - clear obstruction - replace MAGAZINE - operate BOLT RELEASE - re-aim - test and adjust - continue firing.
3. It is important that ANY ROUND which has been involved in a stoppage or used as a tool, whether it appears damaged or not, is **NOT** to be loaded into a MAGAZINE or any attempt made to fire it.

GAS STOPPAGE.

If after carrying out the IA the weapon fires one or two rounds and
then stops again, and after repeating the IA the same condition
arises:-
1. Operate the BOLT RELEASE, put SAFETY CATCH to `S' and using
a ROUND or the COMBINATION TOOL - turn the GAS PLUG so
that the PLUNGER engages the `E' EXCESS GAS SETTING.
2. Put SAFETY CATCH to `F' - aim - test and adjust - continue firing.
3. As soon as is practicable the GAS ASSEMBLY must be cleaned
and reset to the `N' (NORMAL) setting.

FURTHER ACTION

If an obstruction in the CHAMBER cannot be removed during the IA, or
obstructions occur repeatedly, or the weapon will not fire after carrying
out the IA, then:-
1. UNLOAD the weapon - remove TMH - BOLT - BOLT CARRIER .
2. Inspect and check EXTRACTOR - EJECTOR - RETAINING PINS -
FIRING PIN PROTRUSION and the CHAMBER.
3. If BOLT parts are damaged or loose, fit serviceable SPARE BOLT
ASSEMBLY.
4. If the obstructed CHAMBER is due to a broken/damaged
EXTRACTOR:- Replace the BOLT with the spare assembly, cock
the weapon to allow the EXTRACTOR to grip the base of a
ROUND and remove the obstruction, engage the HOLDING
OPEN CATCH and visually inspect the CHAMBER through the
EJECTION OPENING.
If the CHAMBER is clear, reload and operate the BOLT
RELEASE, set the CHANGE LEVER as required, put the
SAFETY CATCH to `F', test and adjust, and continue to fire.
If the CHAMBER does not appear to be obstructed and there are no
damaged parts, examine the CHAMBER and if there is a SEPARATED
CASE - refer your weapon to the armourer.
If continued stoppages occur, the weapon should be thoroughly
cleaned and examined. Particular attention must be paid to the parts of
the GAS SYSTEM.
These should be cleaned and gauged, using the COMBINATION
TOOL SCRAPERS, after every 200 ROUNDS fired, regardless of
satisfactory functioning of the system.

SKILL AT ARMS

THE SMALL ARMS COLLIMATOR (SAC)

The Francis Barker SAC provides a method of boresighting (zeroing) that can be carried out by day or night. There is no need to strip the weapon, saving time, ammunition and valuable range time.

It allows you to record your zero by day or night and regain that zero— that is if you are sufficiently trained and skilled to use it. Having used the SAC, when you fire your PW/LSW with the target correctly sighted YOU WILL get a hit. This will have been achieved without having fired a shot to zero your weapon.

The need for accuracy has become more important by the growing use of optical and night vision sights which are more sensitive to rough handling than iron sights and therefore need more frequent checking and setting.

It goes without saying your weapons need to be zeroed correctly at all times irrespective of the duties or operations you are engaged in. Your ability to use the SAC is without doubt a great advantage for you to be confident that your weapon is correctly zeroed. Any deviation from the average zero position can be recorded to give a personal check zero position for each firer. This approach will improve accuracy over using an average standard reference position.

OTHER BENEFITS

You will be familiar with the sayings such as "it must be cost effective", "it should save time" etc. Any time you are hanging about, waiting - especially on a Range is costly and frustrating to say the least. You must accept that the SAC is a piece of kit that every soldier who fires their PW should use as a matter of course.

It does need treating with respect and using correctly, after which you will soon be aware of its great benefits. The consequences of having more time on the Range will create opportunities to fire other practices such as; firing from other positions; firing at a moving target etc,.

There might even be time to organise a "Pool - Bull" target!.

FITTING A SMALL ARMS COLLIMATOR TO A LSW

CARE & HANDLING

The Collimator, Small Arms, LIA1 is a sealed unit and **no attempt** must be made to adjust or strip any component beyond that as instructed.

The Spigot must not be damaged in any way.

SAFETY and MAINTENANCE

WARNING

THIS EQUIPMENT CONTAINS A GASEOUS TRITIUM LIGHT SOURCE (GTLS), THEREFORE THE INSTRUCTIONS NOT TO ADJUST OR STRIP THE **SAC** WILL BE STRICTLY OBSERVED. IMMEDIATE ACTIONS TO BE TAKEN ON DISCOVERY OF A DAMAGED GTLS ARE AS FOLLOWS:-

1. DO NOT TOUCH THE GTLS.
2. DO NOT INHALE THE ESCAPING GAS.
3. VENTILATE AND EVACUATE THE AREA.
4. INFORM THE APPOINTED RADIATION PROTECTION SUPERVISOR.
5. WASH HANDS THOROUGHLY, DO NOT USE SOAP.

BRIEF DESCRIPTION

The Collimator Small Arms Cased, LIA1, consists of Collimator, Small Arms, LIA1, (SAC) and Confidence Checker housed in a moulded case for transit purposes. Also included in the case are a small pack of lens cleaning tissue.

The SAC is an optical/mechanical instrument that comprises an anodised aluminium alloy casting which houses the optical collimator assembly in which the graticule pattern is contained.

The optical collimator assembly is mounted to the upper body of the device whilst the lower body provides a mounting for the

1. Optical Collimator Assembly
2. Spigot. 3. Betalight Assembly
4. Bumper Rubber

Graticule Pattern

ACEGIKMOQ
ACEGIKMOQ

sprung steel spigot. The spigot is designed to precisely fit the 5.56mm barrel and the forward end of the spigot is equipped with a bumper rubber to ensure correct insertion.

The body of the SAC also provides a housing for the graticule illumination assembly (Betalight Assembly) which is required when using an unfiltered CWS or IWS.

OPERATING INSTRUCTIONS

In order to achieve accurate results the following procedure should be carried out in a prone supported firing position. It is VERY important that the left hand is not used to grip the hand-guard but should simply support the rifle. The help of a 'buddy' is required to enable adjustment of the sight.

To use the SAC proceed as follows:

1. Apply a light coating of oil to the shaft of the spigot.
2. Ensure rifle is unloaded, carry out NSP normal safety precautions
3. Adopt the prone supported firing position.
4. Your 'buddy' should fit the SAC by pushing the spigot into the rifle muzzle until the flash eliminator is in contact with the bumper rubber. You check that the graticule pattern is upright. Your 'buddy' carefully rotates the SAC back and forth and finally to the upright position, this will have the effect of settling the spigot in the bore of the rifle and will result in a more accurate reading.

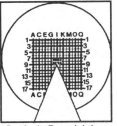

Graticule Boresighting mark using SUSAT

5. If boresighting, you tell your 'buddy' to adjust the sights until the pointer exactly corresponds with the boresighting datum.

The boresighting datum is the point where the horizontal line 9 and the vertical line I intersect as shown in the illustration above.

6. If simply recording a reading after zeroing by live firing you should note as accurately as possible the position of the sight pointer on the graticule pattern

Recording Zero

In the example on the left it shows the correct zero position is F5 (using SUSAT)

7. When checking zero you simply note the position of the pointer and if necessary ask your 'buddy' to adjust the sight until the previously recorded setting is achieved.

8. It is most important that after the sight has been adjusted the SAC is removed and replaced by your 'buddy' so that you may again check that the sight relationship is correct. It is often the case that when the lock nuts on the horizontal adjustment screws of the SUSAT are tightened the sight moves slightly in direction. Careful checking at this stage will ensure an accurate result.

9. Remove the SAC and replace in transit case.

10. Make careful note of the graticule readings.

Night Sights

When using the SAC with CWS the tip of the inverted V on the CWS graticule should be used instead of the pointer and in the case of the IWS the top of the upper vertical bar. When operating CWS or IWS without the daylight filter in place it will be necessary to remove the Betalight assembly from its housing and screw it into the forward end of the optical assembly in order to illuminate the graticule. When carrying out boresighting or checking in dusk or equivalent conditions it will be necessary to shroud the sight and operate with the filter removed in order to discern the graticule. A poncho or shelter sheet draped over you and your 'buddy' will protect the sight from the otherwise high light level.

Checking Alignment

Each SAC is equipped with a confidence checker which is carried in the transit case. This device enables you to carry out a simple check to ensure that the spigot is still correctly aligned to the graticule. The confidence checker consists of a shaped device through which two holes are drilled. The larger hole at the bottom of the checker will accept the SAC spigot and the smaller hole at the top of the checker is designed as a viewing hole. In order to check the alignment push the spigot into the larger hole of the checker until the device butts against the optical assembly of the SAC. Ensure the confidence checker is upright and look through the viewing hole. If the complete circle encompassing the graticule

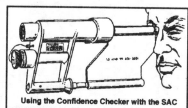

Using the Confidence Checker with the SAC

270

pattern can be discerned the SAC alignment is correct. If it is not possible to discern the circle around the graticule pattern the complete equipment is to be handed to the unit armourer for checking.

The only maintenance you are permitted to carry out on the SAC is limited to cleaning.

CLEANING

There are no special tools required. Standard lens cleaning tissue, contained in the case, should be used to clean the objective lens.

If there is mud or grit on the objective lens, it should be removed with clean water. Soap or weak detergent may be used to remove grease stains or smears.

The body of the SAC is similarly cleaned. Entrapped debris may be removed by loosening the dirt with a soft bristled brush.

Total submersion of the SAC is to be avoided.

Replacement of parts, to be carried out by Unit Armourers, is limited to:-

Replacement of the Betalight Assembly.

Replacement of the Bumper Rubber.

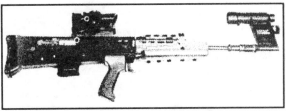

SA 80 WITH SUSAT SIGHT AND FITTED WITH SMALL ARMS COLLIMATOR

"If I pull the trigger will the target in my sights be hit" ?
"No, unless your sights have been properly zeroed "
"What chance of going on a zeroing range today"
"Very little chance - it's no problem - use an SAC"

271

THE DAYS OF THE ZEROING TARGET ARE NUMBERED ... NOW THAT THE **SMALL ARMS COLLIMATOR** IS IN USE

"don't waste your time, ammo and targets - use your SAC"

THE SA80 WITH SUSAT SIGHT - FITTED WITH THE SMALL ARMS COLLIMATOR

AIMING WITH THE IRON SIGHT

1. With both your eyes open identify the target and roughly align the weapon adjusting the body position so that the weapon points naturally at the target without effort.
2. Position your cheek on the CHEEK PIECE so that the eye is approximately 25mm from the APERTURE.
3. Look through the centre of the APERTURE and centralise the TIP of the FORESIGHT. The BACKSIGHT will be too close to the eye for the edges of the aperture to be clearly seen; however a clear area in the centre of the aperture will be apparent.
Ensure that the FORESIGHT is upright and clearly in focus. Keep the left eye open.
4. It may be necessary to move your head slightly in order to achieve SIGHT ALIGNMENT; it is essential, however, once it has been achieved, that the position of your head remains unchanged.
5. Maintaining this alignment, focus on the tip of the foresight lining it up with the target or more correctly called the POINT of AIM (POA), this completes the 'AIM PICTURE'. You will find that when doing this the target will become blurred for a few moments.
6. Check that the tip of the FORESIGHT is still in the centre of the aperture
7. The adjustment of your sights can give you a more 'COMFORTABLE AIM PICTURE' or eye relief, you must test and if necessary adjust your sights with the aid of your instructor. This will help you to be consistent with your aim and improve your results.

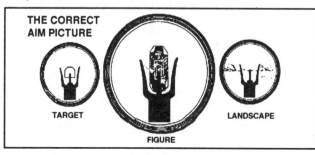

THE CORRECT AIM PICTURE

TARGET

FIGURE

LANDSCAPE

SKILL AT ARMS

IF after GENUINE attempts you are unable to aim keeping BOTH
    EYES OPEN, you should close the left eye. The 'BOTH EYES
    OPEN' technique is generally recommended as better with the
    IRON SIGHT.

AIMING WITH THE SUSAT

Look along the barrel with both eyes open, select the target and
roughly align the weapon on the target. Look through the EYEPIECE
with your disengaged eye, resting your eyebrow against the rubber
EYEPIECE.
Focus the POINTER of your sight until it is clear in your vision. Keep
the POINTER upright, align the TIP of the POINTER with your POA -
Point Of AIM, ensure that you have a CLEAR - CIRCULAR view
through the SIGHT LENS.

AIMING WITH THE EBS - EMERGENCY BATTLE SIGHT.

As already mentioned the EBS is an integral part of the SUSAT,
mounted on the top of the OPTICAL BODY, and that it is matched to
the OPTICAL CENTRE during manufacture.

Sighting View

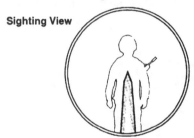

It is not easy to use this sight and a great deal of practice is required
to become skilled at getting the CORRECT ALIGNMENT with the
weapon and at the same time finding the CORRECT AIM PICTURE.
The position of the EBS means that you have to adopt a different
position with your CHEEK or the EYEPIECE of the SUSAT will
interfere with your eye when aiming.
The 'Rules for Aiming' with the EBS are very simple and are as
follows:-

SKILL AT ARMS

1. Look over the top of the SUSAT and roughly align the MUZZLE of
   the weapon with the target.
2. Close your disengaged eye and look through the APERTURE
   BACKSIGHT of the EBS.

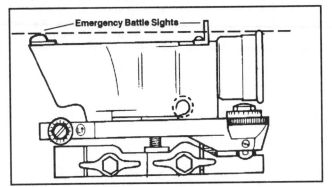

3. Align the tip of the EBS FORESIGHT BLADE in the centre of the
   APERTURE, keeping the SIGHTS UPRIGHT.
4. Focus on the TIP of the FORESIGHT, Align it on your POINT OF
   AIM on the target at the same time maintaining the TIP of the
   FORESIGHT in the CENTRE of the APERTURE.

NOTE: You may have difficulty in 'focusing' and the Target may
appear blurred and if you have your eye too far away from the
APERTURE it will appear too small to see through.
As already pointed out it is only with practice that you will become
accustomed to your EBS . If it is any consolation to you, this was the
type of sight used with great effect by your predecessors.

USE OF COVER - MUZZLE CLEARANCE.

The diagram on the following page is produced to make you aware of
the fact that your LINE of SIGHT - the dotted line - on the weapon is
high in relation to the AXIS of the BORE of the BARREL or the
FLIGHT PATH of the BULLET when fired.

SKILL AT ARMS

Firing from behind low cover it may well be possible/essential to have a clear LINE of SIGHT to the target, but, at the same time have the FLIGHT PATH of the BULLET obstructed by the cover. Obstruction may be less noticeable a few metres in front of the position than directly in front of the MUZZLE.

It is therefore important to always be mindful of the MUZZLE CLEARANCE and make allowances for it when selecting a FIRE POSITION, at the same time consider the possible increased exposure to view.

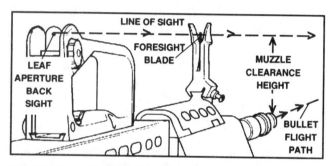

SETTINGS & ADJUSTMENTS.

Zeroing the Weapon The purpose of zeroing is to superimpose the true position of the MEAN POINT of IMPACT (MPI) on the CORRECT ZERO POSITION so that with the appropriate setting and use of wind allowance, a group of shots fired will form centrally at all of the ranges selected.

To determine the true position of the MPI, you should fire a number of shots, not less than 20, at the same AIMING MARK and under the same conditions.

You must be capable of consistently firing five rounds at 100 metres and achieving an average of 150mm group using the SUSAT sight or a 200mm group using an IRON SIGHT. It is essential for you to zero your own weapon for the following reasons:-

1. Variations in your aiming.
2. The effect of 'weapon jump', influenced by your physical build .
3. The firing position you adopt for your own comfort.

SKILL AT ARMS

4. The control you have, dictated by the way you hold the weapon.

Zeroing should be carried out:-

1. When you are initially issued with the weapon.
2. Before and, whenever possible, during active service.
3. If the sights are changed.
4. When there is any doubt of the weapons accuracy.

ZEROING RANGE.

The ideal range for zeroing is 100 metres, which combines clarity of aim with lack of wind effect. A range of 25 metres may be used if a 100 metre range is not available.

CORRECT ZERO POSITION (CZP)

The correct positions of the MPI in relation to the POINT of AIM (POA) at 100 metres and at 25 metres, with sight settings shown are as below:-

Type of Sight	Sight Setting	CZP - SA80 & LSW	
		100 metres	25 metres
SUSAT	300 metres	100mm above	25mm below POA
IRON SIGHT	200 metres	100mm above	25mm below POA

If the MPI obtained does not coincide with the CZP given above, then the sights of the weapon require adjustment.

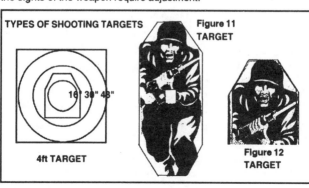

TYPES OF SHOOTING TARGETS

16" 30" 48"

4ft TARGET

Figure 11
TARGET

Figure 12
TARGET

SIGHT ADJUSTMENT

The sights of the weapon are adjustable for elevation and for direction. The Combination Tool should be used to make these adjustments.

ELEVATION - see diagram below

To move the MPI up, turn the VERTICAL ADJUSTMENT NUT in the direction indicated by the arrow marked 'U'. To move the MPI down turn the ADJUSTER in the direction indicated by arrow 'D'.

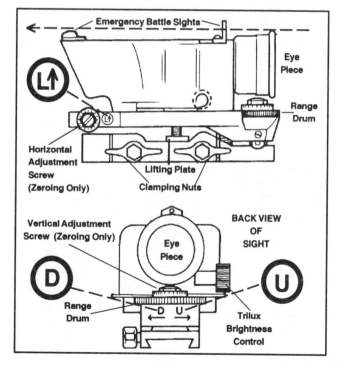

SKILL AT ARMS

One graduation moves the MPI approximately 13mm vertically at 25 metres or 50mm at 100 metres.

DIRECTION.

To move the MPI to the left, loosen the LOCK-NUT and turn the HORIZONTAL ADJUSTER SCREW in the direction as shown by the arrow 'L' as illustrated in the diagram on the previous page.
To move the MPI to the right turn the ADJUSTER as shown by the arrow 'R' - **on the opposite side of the SIGHT BASE.**
When the required adjustment has been made, turn the opposite ADJUSTMENT SCREW against the direction of its arrow, then tighten the LOCK-NUTS.
One graduation moves the MPI approximately 13mm horizontally at 25 metres or 50mm at 100 metres.

IRON SIGHT

ELEVATION. To move the MPI up, depress the LOCKING PLUNGER on the FORESIGHT, using the COMBINATION TOOL, then rotate the VERTICAL ADJUSTMENT SCREW in the direction as indicated by the arrow 'U. To move the MPI down, turn the SCREW in the direction of arrow 'D'. One graduation will raise or lower the MPI approximately 13mm at 25 metres or 50mm at 100 metres.

DIRECTION. To move the MPI to the left, depress the LOCKING PLUNGER on the HORIZONTAL ADJUSTMENT SCREW, using the COMBINATION TOOL, turn the screw in the direction as indicated by the arrow 'L'.
To move the MPI to the right turn the screw in the opposite direction.
One graduation moves the MPI horizontally approximately 13mm at 25 metres or 50mm at 100 metres.

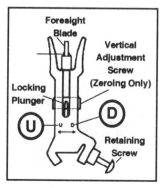

SKILL AT ARMS

EYE RELIEF ADJUST-MENT.

To adjust either the SUSAT or the IRON SIGHT to obtain the CORRECT EYE RELIEF carry out the following:-

1. Loosen the CLAMPING NUTS/SCREWS.
2. Operate the LIFTING PLATE (SUSAT), or unscrew the RETENTION STUD (IRON SIGHT), and slide the SIGHT forward or backward as required.
3. Adjust the SIGHT so that the RETENTION STUD is located in the hole in the SIGHT RAIL that gives you the best possible EYE RELIEF.
4. Tighten the CLAMPING NUTS/SCREWS.
5. Optimum EYE RELIEF is achieved by moving the position of your head.

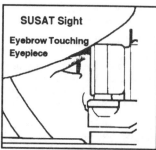

SUSAT Sight

Eyebrow Touching Eyepiece

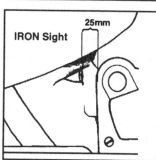

IRON Sight

25mm

SAC Inserted in a Rifle with an Optical Sight

SKILL AT ARMS

FIRE CONTROL

As a Rifleman in action you would normally carry six full magazines, one on your weapon and five in pouches. You would also be carrying a bandolier containing 150 rounds which is worn slung over your equipment. It is used to re-supply the LSW or to refill your own magazines during a lull in operations.

You may also be issued with TRACER ROUNDS for use with the LSW or used for target indication. It is important to always keep in mind the conservation of all supplies, especially ammunition. The high rates of fire that are possible must be strictly controlled at all times.

This can be achieved by good Fire Discipline and Fire Control Orders indicating the "types of fire" to be used in battle.

DESCRIPTION OF TYPES OF FIRE.

DELIBERATE.

A slow rate of fire not more than 10 rounds per minute. The order usually given after the FIRE FIGHT is won to prevent the enemy returning accurate fire, or from observing your dispositions or moving from their own positions. Always count the rounds you fire to know how many you have left in your magazine.

The FIRE ORDER will be on the assumption you're "READY", been given the RANGE, and TARGET INDICATED; is - "FIRE".

When ordered to "STOP", SAFETY CATCH to 'S', change MAGAZINE if necessary, adopt ALERT position, observe, await further orders. If ordered - "GO ON", put your SAFETY CATCH to 'F' and carry on firing.

SNAP SHOOTING.

This is shooting when a target appears for just a short time. If you are a skilled shot you should get off two accurate shots at the target.

The FIRE ORDER - as you are awaiting the appearance of the target - will be - "WATCH and SHOOT".

When given the command "STOP" and "GO ON" your actions are as for DELIBERATE SHOOTING

RAPID FIRE.

Principally used in order to WIN the 'FIRE FIGHT' or when any number of the enemy are attacking your position. It is not wildly firing at random, but carefully aimed shots to makes every one count. Firing must be strictly controlled to ensure that no more ammunition is used than necessary to achieve the desired result.

SKILL AT ARMS

You should, provided you are a skilled soldier, be able to get off 20 well aimed shots in a minute at several targets.

With RAPID FIRE practice you should develop a rhythm of operation with your weapon, this in turn will help with your breathing control, correct aim, holding and trigger operation. Your "follow through" will be carried out as a natural and correct sequence.

With practice, shallow breaths between shots during RAPID FIRE and breath restraint can result in being able to 'get off' two or three shots. Care should be exercised not to cause undue strain.

The FIRE ORDER after, the RANGE and TARGET has been indicated, is in two parts:- "RAPID" - "FIRE" - one after the other. On the command "RAPID" check CHANGE LEVER is at `R' and aim at target.

On the command "FIRE", you fire as fast as possible with well aimed accurate shots, moving from one target to another as each one falls. Continue to fire until there are no targets to fire at or you given the order to "STOP".

Counting the rounds and changing MAGAZINES must be carried out as for DELIBERATE FIRE.

After continuous fire, allow the weapon to cool at any a lull in the firing by COCKING it, and engaging the HOLDING OPEN CATCH, thus clearing the breech, allowing air to circulate. If you didn't catch the ejected ROUND - clean it - and put it in your pouch or a magazine. If ordered to "GO ON", operate the BOLT RELEASE and continue to fire.

AUTOMATIC FIRE.

Used mostly in close quarters battle, especially during the final stages of an assault, or springing an ambush, or when faced by a mass attack. Used to great effect in house clearing, clearing trenches bunkers and woodlands. It is the responsibility of your Section Commander to decide on the rate/volume of fire - dependent upon the ammunition available. You are also to use your initiative in the effective use and conservation of ammunition.

The FIRE ORDER given will be "BURSTS" - "RAPID" - "FIRE". On the command "BURSTS" the CHANGE LEVER is set to `A' and on "FIRE", fire in short burst of two to three rounds.

The actions you carry out on the order: "STOP" and "GO ON" are the same as for RAPID firing.

FIGHTING at CLOSE QUARTERS.

Firing at Targets Crossing your front. Under operational conditions the majority of shots fired will be against moving targets at short ranges, a proportion of them will be crossing your front. The target they present will move quickly from cover to cover, with the least amount of exposure for the shortest possible time. You must develop quick reactions and anticipate the moves that the enemy will make.

This coupled with the ability to develop techniques to "out wit" and engage the enemy, making every round count.

While moving across close country or through an urban area you will often be adopting different positions to fire from, standing, kneeling, sitting or lying.

This will test your ability to react quickly and fire accurately under such conditions when engaging a moving target. Again, it will only be with constant practice that you will develop the skills required and to maintain a high state of readiness.

Making allowances for a Crossing Target.

When you fire at a moving target its movement continues across your front during the time it takes the bullet to reach it. An allowance for this must be made by you "aiming off" in front of the target. If you don't the shots will miss by passing behind it.

Aiming in front so as to make allowances for the movement of the target is known as the "LEAD".

Depending upon the speed at which the target is moving, will be the amount of "LEAD" that you will have to allow to make a hit. To make it more difficult - the target may be moving obliquely - at a angle across your front.

All that can be offered to you in this case is - only with practice at such a target will you be able to develop the right 'touch' or 'technique' when firing at moving targets.

Obviously targets at longer ranges are much more difficult to hit. Should you be using an IRON SIGHT with the a target beyond 300 metres you will need to aim higher than normal. If you are using a SUSAT sight you will need to increase the range setting, while maintaining the normal elevation.

METHODS OF ENGAGING DIRECT & OBLIQUE CROSSING TARGETS.

As previously explained, crossing targets are successfully hit when the correct amount of LEAD has been taken into consideration and your POINT of AIM has been adjusted and applied to the target.
There are several methods used for engaging moving targets they are explained below:-

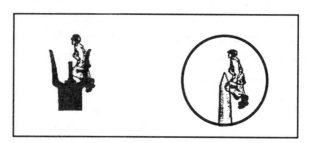

The BASIC Method

Aim behind the target, swing through the target to the leading edge as in the illustration above. Do not check the swing, open fire and if required increase or decrease the 'LEAD' while firing several shots, continue to fire until the target is hit or disappears.

The AMBUSH Method

Used when it is difficult to follow or swing with the target, especially when you are in the prone or sitting position with perhaps both elbows rested. You select a POINT OF AIM on its anticipated route, ahead of the target, come into the aim, wait for the target to appear, start firing just before the target reaches your selected POA. Continue until it is hit, or disappears or if you know that you have missed it - in which case the target has moved ahead of your POA, in other words you need more practice!!

SKILL AT ARMS

The SHOT GUN Method

Favoured by those who are experienced and successful 'poachers'. Under operational conditions very often there is not time nor space to use your sights, therefore with BOTH EYES open, look only at the TARGET, keep your head up, left hand gripping firmly and well forward, weapon pointing naturally at the target - 'FIRE' - all in one action. Speed and accuracy are the basis of this technique, which can be very effective up to 150 metres.

FIRING BURSTS.

In certain situations automatic fire can be very effective. In situations such as ambushes, house clearing and night fighting, When operating in these conditions and in anticipation of action your CHANGE LEVER would be set at **'A'**.

Normally and in fact the most accurate position is to fire from the shoulder.

You can obviously fire your weapon in any position provided it is held correctly, you are comfortable with it and you get the right results. Remember:-

1. With the Rifle it has a tendency to 'climb' as you fire a burst, therefore - AIM LOWER, it might be better to get off several well aimed shots.
2. If firing BURSTS , remember, SHORT BURSTS - of TWO or THREE rounds.
3. Don't get caught out with an empty MAGAZINE - change it.
4. DON'T attempt to fire from the HIP - you will become a casualty through the COCKING HANDLE hitting your RIGHT ARM.

"DON'T WASTE AMMUNITION - SOMEONE HAS TO CARRY IT"

SKILL AT ARMS

SA 80 & LSW TRAINING TESTS

PURPOSE OF TRAINING TESTS

You have to be fully trained and highly skilled with your personal
weapons at all times. It is only with practice that you will attain a high
standard and only with regular practice that you will maintain those high
standards and pass your Annual Personal Weapons Test first time.
Don't miss any opportunity to take part in firing practices it will help you
to achieve this aim.

These tests will enable your instructors to assess your safety
standards, handling and application of fire with both weapons. You
are required to be regularly tested under a variety of conditions. This
will give your examiners a good measure of how well you have been
trained.

The tests are used to assess your standards with either the Rifle or
the LSW, it is not necessary for you to be tested on both weapons.

TEST No 1 SAFETY

Conditions. The weapon will be laid on the ground, with a
MAGAZINE fitted, LOADED, SAFETY CATCH NOT APPLIED the
CHANGE LEVER at '**R**' will be told to PICK UP the rifle, you should:
pick up the weapon, put the SAFETY CATCH to '**S**',
take off the MAGAZINE and check that there is no ROUND in the
CHAMBER. You will then be told to hand it to the examiner. When
doing so you must carry out the following:-

1. Pick it up with the MUZZLE POINTING in a SAFE direction.

2. Check that the
SAFETY CATCH to '**S**'.

3. Cock weapon, operate the HOLDING OPEN CATCH, check it
   yourself, then show - "prove it" to the examiner, that the BODY,
   CHAMBER and BOLT FACE are clear. EASE SPRINGS, and
   hand over the weapon to the examiner.

ASSESSMENT.

You will ONLY Pass this test if you carry out ALL the safety
precautions and actions correctly.

SKILL AT ARMS

TEST No 2 PREPARATION FOR FIRING - CLEANING
Conditions: Weapon with MAGAZINE. Cleaning Tool Roll, Flannelette and Oil.
1. Strip the weapon - including the SLING - as you have been taught for daily cleaning.
2. Dry clean the whole of the weapon, looking out for any damage.
3. Lightly oil the WORKING SURFACES of the BOLT, GUIDE RODS and CAM STUD.
4. Put the weapons together and test that it functions correctly.
5. Re - fit the sling.
ASSESSMENT
Standards: The main purpose is to test your ability to strip and assemble the weapon correctly. No time limit is set for this test. Skilled - up to two mistakes made. Average - three or four mistakes made. Fail - over four mistakes. You will only pass this test if **NO** mistakes are made that affect SAFETY PRECAUTIONS or ACTIONS.

TEST No 3 MAGAZINE FILLING - this is a timed test.
Conditions: MAGAZINE CHARGER , MAGAZINE. and 30 ROUNDS in clips On the order "GO", using an EMPTY MAGAZINE, you will fill it with 30 ROUNDS.
a. Filling by using the CHARGER.
b. Filling by HAND.
Leave the MAGAZINE filled ready for the next test.
ASSESSMENT.
a. Standards: With the CHARGER. Skilled - 20 sec. Average - 21 to 30 sec. Fail - over 30 sec. b. By HAND. Skilled - 60 seconds or less. Average - 61 to 75 sec. Fail - over 75 sec.

TEST No 4 LOADING - STANDING POSITION - a timed test
Conditions. Put ONE FULL MAGAZINE in a fastened POUCH. On the order "LOAD", timing will commence until you have completed the LOAD. Your POUCH must be FASTENED - the time taken to do this is NOT included in the time limit.
ASSESSMENT.
Standards 1. SKILLED - 10 seconds or less. AVERAGE - 11 to 15 seconds. FAIL - over 15 seconds. 2. TWO SECONDS will be added to

your total time for each mistake. You will only pass this test if **NO** mistakes are made that affect SAFETY PRECAUTIONS or ACTIONS. NOTE: The weapon is left LOADED ready for the next test.

TEST No 5 GAS STOPPAGE & IMMEDIATE ACTIONS (IA's)
Conditions: This test is only concerned with IA's and GAS STOPPAGES. NO time limit, but all actions must be carried out correctly and efficiently.
1. Using the LOADED weapon from the previous test, the order given will be :- "Down - Ready - Test and Adjust - Rapid Fire".
2. Order "weapon firing alright - weapon stops", you examine position of the COCKING HANDLE. Order given "Not fully to the rear", on examination of the BODY and CHAMBER, Order "ROUNDS in MAGAZINE, CHAMBER clear. You will be allowed to complete the drill and fire. Then given the order "weapon fires one or two ROUNDS and stops again" - "NOT fully to the rear" - "ROUNDS in the MAGAZINE, CHAMBER clear".
3. You should operate the BOLT RELEASE, apply the SAFETY CATCH and using the COMBINATION TOOL, adjust the GAS REGULATOR.
4. The test is not complete until the SAFETY CATCH is set at 'F', the weapon re-aimed and the TRIGGER operated.
5. You will then be given the order "STOP".
ASSESSMENT
1. Standards: Skilled - All actions correct. Average - One or two mistakes. Fail more than two mistakes.
2. You will only pass this test if NO mistakes are made that affect SAFETY PRECAUTIONS or ACTIONS.

TEST No 6 UNLOADING - LYING POSITION - a timed test.
Conditions: Following the previous test you will still be in the LYING POSITION, LOADED and READY. The test will start when you are ordered to "UNLOAD". Timing will be from the order "UNLOAD" until you have finished the UNLOAD. When finished, stand up, collect the ejected ROUND, inspect it and put it back in the MAGAZINE. Fasten your POUCH - time taken to fasten your pouch is not included in the time limit.

SKILL AT ARMS

ASSESSMENT.
1. Standards: Skilled 12 seconds or less. Average - 13 to 18 seconds.
   Fail - over 18 seconds.
2. TWO seconds will be added to your time for each mistake made.
3. You will only pass this test if NO mistakes are made that affect
   SAFETY PRECAUTIONS or ACTIONS.

TEST No 7 APPLICATION OF FIRE
Conditions: Using a figure target, your examiner will ask you to
indicate on the target where your POI (POINT OF AIM) would be, as a
result of two different questions he asks you relating to AIMING OFF
FOR WIND at different strengths and ranges, and a third question on
firing at a target crossing your front.
Examples of the questions are set out below:-
Question 1.
a. A fresh wind is blowing from Right to Left, the distance to the target
   is - 200 m, indicate your POA.
b. A strong wind is blowing from Left to Right. The distance to the
   target is - 200 m, indicate your POA.
Question 2.
a. A strong wind is blowing from Right to Left. The distance to the
   Target is - 300 m, indicate your POA
b. A fresh wind is blowing from Right to Left, the distance to the Target
   is - 300 m, indicate your POA.
Question 3.
As these tests can involve 'aiming off' the target area, you MAY have a
second target to use for your POA indication.
a. Aiming at a Crossing Target, using the BASIC method, the distance
   to the target - 250 m, target walking.
b. Aiming at a Crossing Target, using the AMBUSH method, the
   distance to the target is - 80 m, target - running slowly.
ASSESSMENT.
Standards: Skilled - All correct. Average - two correct answers. Fail -
Less than two correct answers.

REMEMBER - *PRACTICE MAKES PERFECT.*
Study these TRAINING TESTS, get them off 'word perfect', and then
pitch your training to meet the needs of the tests.

COMPETITION/SPORT SHOOTING

Target Shooting is one of the very few sports that you are able to keep up throughout your life. After your time in the Army, Territorial Army or in fact any of the Services there are many Rifle Clubs throughout the country which you could join.

If you have been a good shot don't discard the skill, there are plenty of clubs and other organisations, especially the uniformed Youth organisations who would be glad to have your help, there is always something to look forward to with shooting.

It must be remembered that the success of most things we do, be it our job of work, a chore, a sport or a hobby, invariably goes to those who are both keen and determined to do what ever it is to the best of their ability.

This especially applies to shooting, where the amount of care and practice you have is directly related to the results you achieve. No special skills are required, just keenness, practice and perseverance will bring you the rewards.

Competitions have always been used by the Army as a means of improving the standard of Marksmanship. The Boer War taught us a lesson in the need to have accurate riflemen in the face of overwhelming odds, as a consequence a period of feverish activity took place when Competition Shooting was the 'order of the day'.

The reputation the British soldiers had for their high standard of marksmanship during the initial fighting of the 1914-18 war, due to the continuous programme of Shooting Competitions that our regular and volunteer troops had taken part in prior to the war.

This standard of training was not maintained, as the newly arrived troops did not have time to be fully trained before being committed to battle. When they came 'out of the line' for R&R, those that were able, took part in shooting competitions to improve their skills.

Competitive shooting makes a valuable contribution as an integral part of your marksmanship training. If you are to keep up your standards in order to pass your Annual Personal Weapons Test (APWT), it makes good sense to get all the practice you can, what better way is there than holding down a place in your unit shooting team.

Army/TA shooting is split into two distinct activities; Shooting as a Sport or Competition Shooting and Qualification/Operational Firing. We must say at the outset that it is very difficult to try and treat them separately when you get down to the serious business of the skills required for shooting.

SKILL AT ARMS

The reason being that many of the shooting principles generally apply equally to both Shooting as a Sport and Qualification / Operational Firing, because of this you may feel that they are both mixed up together.

The basic skills required are very much the same, but applied for a different purpose, we make no apologies about this, just ask you to bear it in mind throughout this Shooting Section.

We need to say at this juncture that no units have an unrestricted supply of ammunition, and point out that it is just as much credit for you to be a Marksman with a .22 weapon as it is with the GPMG or the SA80, in the context of maintaining your skill as a marksman. What is important is for everyone to make good use of what range allocations and ammunition you do have available, for as many as possible to have the chance to take part in shooting on a regular basis. It follows that if an opportunity presents itself to do some firing take every advantage of it to maintain and improve your own standards.

Perhaps the greatest difference between 'Shooting as a Sport' and 'Qualifying/Operational Firing' is that you have to be physically fit to carry out 'Qualifying/Operational firing' practices, as they involve practices running down the range or tactical firing on ETR ranges or Close Quarters Battle Ranges (CQBR).

Under the stress of firing in battle conditions, it is recognised that your shooting becomes erratic and below normal standards, not very good at a time when it needs to be well 'on target'. This form of stress can not be reproduced in normal training, but if you are a member of a team who get into a top competition , then the 'pressure will be on'. This provides a similar reaction to that of stress, and when you get down to fire 'shoulder to shoulder', you will quickly learn what 'competition stress' is all about.

The training you have to combat the stress factor should be to develop your personal skills in the determination to win as a member of the team. To build your self discipline giving you confidence in your own and the weapons ability and the concentration to bring it all together at the right time.

If you are a Recruit - a word of warning - don't be 'put-off' if at first you don't get a reasonable result. You must stick at it, as it is more than ever necessary in shooting. The reason being that your score suffers directly by the errors you make, there is no second chance, the mistake you make you pay for right away.

If you make less mistakes than the others - you will win.

SKILL AT ARMS

Hopefully, this Skill at Arms section dealing with shooting will help you to:-

1. Think positively about your training and what you could do to improve it.
2. Give you information and ideas for you to apply in your own training.
3. Improve your results, giving you more confidence in your ability.
4. Arouse your interest in pursuit of better results.
5. To pass on your skills to others who may be just starting to shoot.
6. Respect the patience and interest others have given to train you, and meet their expectations of you in return.

Once you start to improve - nothing will hold you back - only you can make the choice.

Don't miss a chance to have a practice shoot, no matter what type of weapon or range - PRACTICE MAKES PERFECT.

PERSONAL QUALITIES.

It is within the ability of almost anyone to become a good shot, provided they are 'mentally' and 'physically' fit. Mental Fitness -because it is to a great extent the 'mental control' that is required once you have learned the skills needed. The determination and keenness to succeed relies on Mental Fitness.

Physical Fitness in this context, is the need to have those parts of the body working sufficiently well to hold, sight and fire the weapon accurately.

Many firers find out - for the first time - that their eyesight is not as good as they imagined, have yours checked at regular intervals.

You will be constantly told that "your ability to shoot well depends entirely upon being able to GROUP TIGHTLY" or " you must have a good GROUPING capacity".

To explain this, imagine that perhaps the ideal method of holding and firing a weapon might be to have it clamped firmly in some device on the firing point - so as it cannot move, load and fire it at a target 100 metres away.

You may not believe it, but a weapon fired under these 'ideal' conditions would not put all the shots through the same hole in the target, it would produce shots spread out in a "GROUP".

It is not suggested that you can hold your weapon as firmly as some device, but firstly it is essential to learn to shoot when in the prone or lying position. The techniques and skills are dealt with later.

SKILL AT ARMS

DIAGRAM OF A 4ft TARGET ILLUSTRATING A "GROUP"

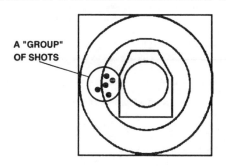

A "GROUP"
OF SHOTS

You will have been taught by your instructors how to handle the weapons SAFELY and to master the basic skills. Once you are qualified in these skills, then you will start to be given the training in some depth by coaching you for marksmanship during live firing practices. Your 'coach' will modify the techniques to suit your individual needs.

You will find that until you are able to achieve a satisfactory 'GROUPING CAPACITY', you will not be allowed to progress on to other practices.

During your service the same will apply when taking your Annual Personal Weapon Test, if you are unable to group correctly, you will have to undergo remedial shooting training.

Your first objective must be to attempt to fire a group of five shots; having done this the second must be to concentrate on reducing the size (spread) of the shots in your first group, no matter how good it was, to an even smaller size.

On a .22 range of 25 metres should be firing a 1" group, once you have mastered this by getting it central on the target, then you are on your way.

GROUPING IS THE FOUNDATION OF ALL GOOD SHOOTING - UNLESS OR UNTIL YOU ARE ABLE TO ACHIEVE THE REQUIRED STANDARDS, IT IS DOUBTFUL WHETHER OR NOT YOU WILL EVER BECOME A MARKSMAN.

SKILL AT ARMS

GOING ON THE RANGE.

Every Range has their own set of Range Standing Orders, controlling all aspects of safety for those using the Range and the public at large. It is the responsibility of all units and personnel using the range to familiarise themselves with the range Orders.

Ignorance of Standing Orders is no defence. The most important action when first arriving in the vicinity of the Firing Point is that Safety Drills are carried out.

You will be inspected - your pockets and all personal equipment, webbing etc., will be checked to make sure that no DRILL ROUNDS are brought onto the Range.

Likewise, when finishing on the range for the day and just before you leave, you will be inspected again for any live ammunition or empty cases -even if you have been on the range in support of those firing as a working party.

At the actual time of your inspection by the Range Officer or Instructor you will make the following declaration to them, saying:- "NO LIVE ROUNDS OR EMPTY CASES IN MY POSSESSION, - SIR" (that is assuming you DO NOT have any live rounds or empty cases lurking in your pouches - if you do - NOW is the time to produce them).

These and other Range Rules apply equally to all personnel on the Range, you will see your instructors and officers inspect each other in your presence.

MARKSMANSHIP PRINCIPLES.

The Definition of a Good Shot - What is Essential?

"To fire a shot without it disturbing your aim". To achieve this:-

1. Your FIRING POSITION and the HOLD you have must be FIRM ENOUGH to SUPPORT the weapon.
2. The weapon must point naturally in the direction of the target, without any undue physical effort.
3. The alignment of your sights and aiming must be correct.
4. You control the rhythm of your breathing and operate the trigger correctly.
5. The shot will be fired and 'followed through' without undue movement disturbing your aim.

You must learn these Marksmanship Principles, until they become firmly established in your mind. The application of them demands great concentration on your part, this combined with the determination to be a Marksman will ensure success.

SKILL AT ARMS

LYING POSITION and HOLDING.

You must develop the control you have over HOLDING the weapon, to keep it steady. This is the foundation upon which to carry out the other activities, Viz BREATHING, AIMING, TRIGGER OPERATION, FOLLOW THROUGH.
Only when you have mastered the correct HOLDING will you start to improve upon your results. GET THE BASIC'S RIGHT - FIRST.

THE LYING POSITION.

The lying position is the basic shooting position as it gives the firer the best support for the weapon, it is least tiring and presents the smallest image as a target to the enemy.
To maintain steadiness and be able to achieve a perfect hold, the first essential is that you are comfortable and feel that your weapon is a part of you. The importance of this cannot be over emphasised.
The position to be adopted on the ground, is with your body slightly oblique to the line of fire from which you are able to achieve the CORRECT AIM in the shortest time.
When getting on the ground hold the PISTOL GRIP with the Right hand, lie down, breaking your fall with the LEFT hand, keep the weapon parallel to the ground, make sure that no dirt get into the MUZZLE.
When you are down on the ground, tilt the weapon to the right, and support it by placing your LEFT hand under the HAND GUARD across the palm of your hand and hold with your fingers together. The grip should be no more than a stable platform for the weapon. NO attempt should be made to grip the HAND GUARD tightly or pull it backwards with the left hand. The position should be one of support.
The LEFT elbow is positioned as close as possible - in a comfortable position - to a point as near as possible, directly below the weapon. This position is intended to support the weight of the weapon on the bone of the arm, rather than using your muscular effort to support and hold it - which can't be sustained for very long.
You must be aware that this may produce a 'strained' position which is not comfortable for you, if so, you will not produce your best results, therefore adopt a comfortable position within the constraints of the correct hold.

SKILL AT ARMS

GET AND STAY COMFORTABLE.

The BUTT should be in a position against the muscle between the shoulder joint and the lower edge of your collar bone - it should not come into contact with the bone itself.

Your RIGHT hand is the controlling hand and is the most important factor in good shooting. It should be high up on the PISTOL GRIP, with the web of the skin between thumb and forefinger positioned at the back of the PISTOL GRIP.

The grip must be firm, pulling back into the shoulder, but take care NOT to twist the weapon causing the SIGHTS not to be upright.

The first joint of your forefinger should be naturally on the TRIGGER. The position of the RIGHT ELBOW is determined after taking the correct grip with your hand on the PISTOL GRIP. Your elbow also helps to keep your right shoulder in the correct position all the time. Your body should be slightly at a angle to the 'line of fire', and your muscles in a relaxed state.

As you may not be accustomed to regular visits to the range, you may find it difficult to relax as there is always a certain amount of excitement in shooting. However in spite of this it is a part of the Self Discipline that you will need to master every time you get down to fire, BE - COOL - CALM, and COLLECT your THOUGHTS.

Your LEFT leg should be in line with your body, your RIGHT leg is positioned to form a continuation of the line of fire. Relax your leg muscles and turn your toes outwards with your heels on the ground. This position gives you the maximum amount of contact between your body and the ground, affording the most comfortable position. This often puts extra pressure on your chest in contact with the ground.

It can affect your breathing rhythm and you may feel that it restricts your breathing. If this is so, bend your right knee and bring your leg up slightly. This will raise the right side of your body just enough to make your breathing easier.

Keep your head in an upright position, this is it's natural position used instinctively to maintain your sense of balance, and to correctly position your eyes immediately behind the sights.

Don't press your cheek hard against the CHEEK PIECE of the BUTT. Rest it lightly in a position that is comfortable and that you can keep for the time you are firing a practice. Don't get your eye too near to the BACK SIGHT. The distance should never be LESS than 25mm away.

SKILL AT ARMS

AUTOMATIC ALIGNMENT WITH THE TARGET.

The Marksmanship Principle - "that requires the rifle to point naturally at the target" needs little explanation as you will know how to adopt the correct firing position, but, if you are in a position that you have to strain even the smallest muscle to achieve the CORRECT AIM PICTURE it can affect your results.

At the moment you fire your weapon it will move against or be affected by that 'small muscle strain'. This strain is in force at the very moment you fire, in fact before the round leaves the MUZZLE of the weapon, the weapon will move against this strain and as a result your correct aim will be "off" and your results affected.

On firing it cannot be helped that your weapon will move, but natural alignment will go a long way to ensure that the movement is kept to a minimum.

Once you have had some experience of firing it will become easier for you to get into a correctly aligned position each time you fire. Until that time arrives you will have to practice 'testing and adjusting' until you find the most 'comfortable position'.

A useful tip to help find a 'comfortable position' is to shut your eyes and come up into the aim. As your eyes are shut you will instinctively adopt the most comfortable stance.

On opening your eyes, the AIM PICTURE should be on or very near the POINT OF AIM (POA) you had. If not your position should be altered.

Other ways to adjust your position are as follows:-

Aim at the target and then relax your hold. You should not notice any great change in your aim.

If there is, then it is an indication that you need to adjust your position. If you need to correct lateral - LEFT to RIGHT errors. Keep your left elbow still, move your body slightly to the LEFT or RIGHT into the error as required.

To correct VERTICAL errors, keep BOTH your elbows still, and lift your body slightly forward or backwards - into the error - as required. Keep your BUTT in the same position in your shoulder.

The more you practice, it will become second nature to automatically adopt the correct position without a great deal of adjustment, but you should still go through this procedure every time you get down to fire.

SKILL AT ARMS

SIGHT ALIGNMENT - AIMING

The CORRECT AIM PICTURE requires several different actions to be carefully coordinated at the same time, not just once, but time after time using exactly the same formula on each occasion. It is a lot to ask of our human make up to perform this, that is why you have to practice and have the patience to develop the skill.

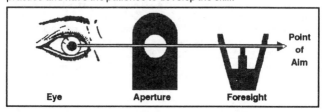

| Eye | Aperture | Foresight |

To achieve this CORRECT AIM PICTURE you have to align:-
1. Your EYE.
2. The CENTRE of the APERTURE BACKSIGHT.
3. The CENTRAL POINT of the TIP of the FORESIGHT.
4. Place the sights - so aligned on the POINT of aim on the target. See diagram above.

The correct focusing of your eyesight is essential to carry out the aiming. It is important to understand that you are asking your eyes to focus on two objects at different distances both at the same time. The objects are the TARGET, or the TIP of the FORESIGHT.

FORESIGHT.

The critical part of SIGHT ALIGNMENT is the connection between the BACK SIGHT APERTURE and the FORESIGHT. Any errors you make are multiplied in proportion to the range of the target, so it is most important to make sure that the FORESIGHT is in clear focus at the moment of 'SHOT RELEASE'.

The tendency is to focus on the target and in so doing draw your attention away from the connection there should be between the FORESIGHT and the APERTURE BACKSIGHT. With sufficient practice and experience your eye will automatically line up the centre of the APERTURE in the BACKSIGHT, BUT, don't get carried away by thinking this does not need regular practice and concentration - it does!.

SKILL AT ARMS

CHARACTERISTICS OF THE WEAPON.

Particularly in Competitive shooting, the ability to fire your weapon and for it to produce a 'GROUP' of shots within a certain specified maximum area, is the essential requirement for you and your weapon to achieve .

You have to have complete confidence, not only in your own capability, but also your weapons ability to achieve this goal. Once this confidence is achieved the weapon becomes an extension of your body.

TESTING YOUR INDIVIDUAL WEAPON.

A short range is better to test weapons, 30 or 100 metres - they are not affected by errors due to the wind. Check that the weapon you are about to use is in fact *'your weapon'*.

Ensure that the Barrel and CHAMBER are dry cleaned for firing. Check that the weapon is functioning correctly, and if appropriate, that the magazine is correctly filled.

A Grouping Practice of five or more rounds should then be fired at any type of target having an easily defined Aiming Mark.

Should you make a faulty shot, this should be declared to your coach. Weapons of the same type often have slight variations when fired, also the weather conditions, wind etc, may have to be taken into consideration as it can effect how your weapon fires. With practice under a variety of conditions, you will get to know how your weapon performs and become accustomed to its own characteristics.

Having spent considerable time with your weapon and come to terms with it and the results you are able to 'jointly' produce, what now can be done to improve your results?.

You must develop the control you have over HOLDING the weapon, to keep it steady.

This is the foundation upon which to carry out the other activities, Viz: *BREATHING, AIMING, TRIGGER OPERATION, and FOLLOW THROUGH.*

Only when you have mastered the correct HOLDING will you start to improve upon your results.

GET THE BASICS RIGHT - FIRST.

You will also find out that the benefits of good holding will become more apparent when you are firing Rapid and Snap shooting practices.

299

CONTROL OF BREATHING.

We all breathe naturally at a steady rate with very little change in the rate of the number of breaths we take per minute, it has a natural rhythm - that is UNLESS we do something to upset it and it takes very little to do just that.

Operational Shooting Practices invariably involve running down the range. You will experience that when you are out of breath - no matter how fit you are -that it is more difficult to concentrate on what you are doing.

When you come up into the aim, your sights are not in focus, in fact may be blurred. You are far from being steady - never mind getting the right AIM PICTURE.

The reason for this is a lack of oxygen in the blood stream. It must be rapidly replaced by CORRECT BREATHING, which in turn reduces the tension and strain, allowing you to get back to the normal rhythm of breathing in the shortest possible time.

You will now appreciate that it is very important to keep your breathing under control when you are shooting. The need to be 'cool - calm - and collected' especially when leading up to the point at which you actually make the decision to fire the shot.

To assist you in this refer to the diagram below and the notes. Practice the timing for 'Breathing for Firing' as shown in the diagram until it becomes second nature, then apply it when you are shooting.

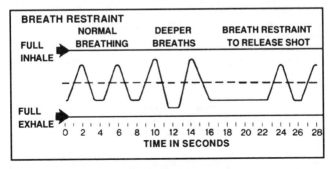

SKILL AT ARMS

THE BREATHING CYCLE

There are three stages in the normal breathing cycle that are important to consider when shooting.

1. During normal breathing your lungs are neither completely filled nor emptied.
2. When breathing out there is a natural pause.
3. The time for the whole 'cycle' takes about five seconds. It is plain to see that the ideal time to fire a shot will be when your body is having a natural pause in the breathing cycle. The idea is to slightly extend that pause by a second, to six seconds.

TRIGGER OPERATION.

During the six seconds of BREATH RESTRAINT you have to perfect the CORRECT AIM and correctly operate the trigger so as to release the shot without any alteration to your aim or the grip with your Right hand.

To achieve the CORRECT SHOT RELEASE :-

1. Put your SAFETY CATCH to **'F'**.
2. Place your finger naturally on the TRIGGER.
3. Take a few slow deep breaths, at the same time take up the TRIGGER SLACK.
4. Hold your breath, PERFECT THE AIM, at the same time steadily apply increasing pressure to the TRIGGER until the weapon fires.
5. Maintain the pressure on the TRIGGER after the shot is released and concentrate on the AIM PICTURE until the weapon has settled; this is known as the 'FOLLOW THROUGH'.
6. Release the TRIGGER and continue to breathe normally. If for some reason you decide not to fire, relax and start again.

REMEMBER: This can only be achieved by the independent movement of the TRIGGER FINGER whilst the remainder of your body is perfectly still.

There are several different name given to the control of the trigger, Viz; 'let-off', 'final-pressure', 'trigger-pressing', 'trigger-squeezing'. You may call it what you will, the fact is that - all trigger control is dependent for its efficiency on GOOD HOLDING.

No amount of super efficient 'trigger squeezing' etc., will make up for bad holding - REMEMBER - HOLDING is the FOUNDATION of good shooting.

SKILL AT ARMS

Should you be involved in a long period of firing there is no doubt that some form of fatigue will become apparent. Usually you will notice that your eyes become tired, especially if you are inclined to remain in the aim too long.

As your eye gets tired its power of clear vision rapidly reduces. It can become upsetting if your results become erratic.

This is when it is important for you to strictly control the amount of time that you allow yourself for firing the number of rounds in each practice. Once you are in the aim - discipline yourself to get off your shots in say, the space of ten seconds - dependent upon your individual skills, preference and the conditions of the practice.

This approach will have its rewards when you fire Rapid or Snap Shooting practices. It is better to take a more leisurely approach, come down off the aim and start again. While out of the aim, relax and give your eyes a rest. It is always said that to look at the grass near to you on the range is good for the eyes, green being a restful colour.

Don't look down the range or at distant objects as your eyes have been accustomed to being focused on near objects such as your sights, therefore look at objects close by.

THE FOLLOW THROUGH

It is possible that you may respond to TRIGGER action or other influences at the very moment the weapon is fired and the BULLET is still in the BARREL. This can cause a shot to be misplaced, even so, it is essential that the shot is 'followed through' to the target. It requires you to concentrate during the period of TRIGGER operation and SHOT RELEASE.

As the shot is fired, the TRIGGER must be held to the REAR, keep your eyes open and look out for any movement of the FORESIGHT. This movement is usually in an upwards direction.

Remain still until the weapon has settled down. If your HOLD and POSITION are correct your SIGHT will normally settle on to the POA (Point Of Aim). Afterwards, continue to breath normally. If for some reason you decide not to fire, come off the aim, relax and start again.

ERROR RECOGNITION.

This aspect of shooting is especially important when taking part in your early training, but just as important in competitive shooting. When firing your practices on the range you should have an experienced shot with you as a 'Coach', who will be down by your side on the firing point.

SKILL AT ARMS

The 'role' of the coach is essentially to watch over you and what you are doing, to help and encourage you to carry out the actions and drills, safely and correctly as you have been taught, and to watch for faults in your technique and record your shots.

In advanced competition shooting you will come to rely on your coach for advice on matters such as changes in the wind and sight corrections.

When firing a shot there is some RECOIL ACTION produced by the explosion of the round in the breech and the BULLET leaving the MUZZLE, plus the reaction of the weapons mechanism.

Assuming you are HOLDING the weapon correctly, the direction and amount of the weapons movement should be limited, then the position of your shots in the GROUP should be within your normal GROUPING CAPACITY.

If you concentrate on your AIM PICTURE each time you press the TRIGGER you will be able to see which way the weapon moves. As a result of this IF you do NOT HAVE a correct AIM PICTURE at the time of firing, you will immediately be aware that the shot will be outside your normal GROUP.

During practices on the range this has special significance as, when you realise that you have made an error you 'declare' it to your Coach by telling him that the shot has gone "low right" etc. If it was a genuine mistake - then it should not happen again - should it !

THE SLING - AN AID TO GOOD SHOOTING.

Many of the 'Top Shots' in the world who shoot at Bisley use a sling. Its purpose is in support of the weapon.

Current thinking favours the use of a SINGLE POINT SLING, where it is attached to the weapon at the fore end, leading over the wrist to a point high on the left arm well above the elbow.

This helps to keep the LEFT arm vertical under the weapon and does not exert any sideways pressure.

Some firers may prefer the TWO POINT SLING, where it is secured at the fore end and on the butt, they make the point that it gives more stability -especially in the wind. In the end it is a matter of choice which one you prefer, the important point to remember is that no matter which you use, it must be kept well up on your left arm or it will become uncomfortable and cause havoc with your shooting.

Having accepted that you are happy with a sling as an aid to your shooting, you will have to check it each time you use it, to ensure that

303

SKILL AT ARMS

it has been adjusted correctly, giving you the support that is comfortable to shoot with. If you share the sling with other firers, mark the settings for your own use to make sure it fits you next time.

CARE and CLEANING.

This subject has already been dealt with is some detail, but it must be emphasised that your CARE and CLEANING when you are involved in competitive shooting must be meticulous.
This extra care of your weapon may reveal something that could put you out of the competition - if you had not found it. It will pay dividends to be extra careful with all aspects of Care and Cleaning.

SHOOTING RECORDS

It is important to maintain your own Shooting Records in order that you see the progress you are making and to highlight those areas or practices that you need extra training or shooting practice.
If you do not keep a record it will be an indication of your lack of interest in keeping up your standards, which in the long run will make it more difficult for you to pass you APWT.

ABOVE ALL - CARRY OUT YOUR SKILL AT ARMS AND SHOOTING - SAFELY.

The Army Rifle Association is the official body based at the School of Infantry, who are responsible for organising the Service Weapon Competitions and Target Shooting Competitions. Central shooting matches are organised for units, Corps and District at Skill at Arms Meetings (SAM's). Teams who pass muster then go on to the Regular Army Skill at Arms Meeting (RASAM), similarly, the Junior Soldier units have their Junior Soldier Skill at Arms Meeting (JSSAM) all of whom meet annually, usually at Bisley.
The Territorial Army follow the same pattern as the Regular Army. Each district hold their Skill at Arms Meetings viz North East District (NEDSAM). The winning teams going on to the Territorial Army Skill at Arms Meeting (TASAM) normally held annually at Bisley.
NOTE: In view of current changes taking place in the Services this information on Shooting Competitions may not be correct. Please check with your unit Skill at Arms Instructors.

SKILL AT ARMS

ANNUAL PERSONAL WEAPON TEST (APWT)

As a guide only, we set out in the following pages information and conditions of the Stage 2 Rifle APWT. Please check this information with your instructors as it may be subject to changes or variations.

It is compulsory that all ranks below that of Lt Colonel successfully complete their APWT firing their personal weapon to the standards as set out in the respective Skill at Arms manuals.

The term 'Personal Weapon' is in fact the weapon you are issued with for operational purposes. You will also be expected to train on an 'Alternative Weapon' which is applicable to your particular Arm of Service, thus ensuring that in an emergency you have a 'second string to your bow'.

If you have an above average score in your APWT you could go on to qualify as a MARKSMAN. This will entitle you to wear the Marksman Badge - assuming it is authorised for your particular Arm of Service to wear them. Don't forget you will have to achieve the same good results the following year to keep your badge!

Your weapon training instructors will explain in detail the Practices, Ranges, Rules, Dress etc., that you will be required to comply with as a part of your APWT.

Essentially there are two 'Stages' or 'Phases' carried out by you in your shooting programme, as explained below:-

1. The first stage is the standard set for everyone to achieve as a recruit in their initial training.

2. The second stage is compulsory for the infantry and will be completed at the end of your special to arm training.

 You will subsequently have to take the test every year. Members of other Arms and Service may complete their APWT as directed by higher authority.

Your 'Alternative' weapon already mentioned, requires that you are able to "handle and fire" the weapon safely, this is referred to as your Alternative Personal Weapon Assessment (APWA).

You will be tested on any of the practices from your previous tests - as applicable - and dependent upon the facilities and ammunition available at the discretion of your commanding officer.

SKILL AT ARMS

FIRING REQUIREMENTS

1. *APWT*. Combat Infantry(CI). Rifle APWT (CI) is to be fired by all Infantry soldiers during their Infantry Phase 2 Training. It is to be fired annually by all combat infantry and RLC Soldier Pioneer Support personnel where their personal weapon is the Rifle.

2. *APWA* Combat Infantry(CI) Practices number 1, 4, 7, 9 and 10 of the Rifle APWA (CI) are to be fired annually by all combat infantry whose personal weapon is the LSW or the Pistol.

Combat infantry whose personal weapon is the LSW are to fire the test using their personal weapon LSW, but the bipod is NOT to be lowered during the firing of any of the practices.

RANGES

Both the above tests can be fired on the ETR (Electronic Target Range), Gallery Range or CGR. If the test is fired on a range converted to AMS the firing point monitors are NOT switched on.

RULES

1. Dress and equipment is Combat Dress, belt order webbing (CEFO), combat helmet, combat body armour (where issued) and ear muffs.
2. No extra time given for stoppages.
3. Coaching and signalling are not allowed.
4. SUSAT only is to be used.
5. If fire trenches are not available, prone position is to be used.
6. Practices 11 and 12 (Night Deliberate and Snap) may also be fired on the same occasion, and in addition to Rifle LF 14 (Firing at the Limit of Night Visibility (LNV).
7. Allocation of amunition for the APWA includes 20 rounds for registration, from which 5 rounds are to be fired at each range prior to the test shoot.

AMMUNITION

APWT(CI) 90 rounds.   APWA(CI) 70 rounds.

SCORING

One point per hit, except in Practice 10 where the scoring is one point per successful engagement of each exposure.

Standards: APWT(CI) HPS = 80. Pass = 56. Marksman = 68.

APWA(CI) HPS = 40. Pass = 20.

ANNUAL PERSONAL WEAPON TEST (APWT) - RIFLE

PRACTICE 1: SNAP
Range and Position adopted: 100m Standing and Kneeling. Unsupported/Squatting.
Ammo: 10 rounds.
Target and Exposure: a. Figure 12. b. 5 x double exposures of target. c. In each double exposure the targets are up for 4 seconds down for 4 seconds and up for 4 seconds. d. Irregular intervals between double exposures.
Instructions: a. Firer in the standing alert position. b. Order *"Watch and Shoot"*. c. On the appearance of the target, the firer is to fire one round standing at the first exposure then adopt the kneeling unsupported position and fire one round at the second exposure. d. Firers must adopt the standing alert position between double exposures. e. Targets fall when hit.

PRACTICE 2: RAPID
Range and Position adopted: 100m Sitting Unsupported.
Ammo: 5 rounds.
Target and Exposure: a. Figure 12. b. 1 x 10 second exposure.
Instructions: a. Firer in the nominated position. b. Order *"Five rounds rapid, Watch and Shoot"*. c. Fire 5 rounds at the exposure. d. Target up and hold.

PRACTICE 3: SNAP / RAPID
Range and Position adopted: 200m Prone.
Ammo: 10 rounds.
Target and Exposure: a. Figure 11. b. 5 x 4 second exposures with irregular intervals, followed 15 seconds later by 1 x 10 second exposure.
Instructions: a. Firer in the nominated position. b. Order *"Watch and Shoot"*. c. Fire one round at each exposure. d. Targets fall when hit. e. After fifth exposure order *"Stop, 5 rounds rapid, Watch and Shoot"*. f. Fire 5 rounds at the exposure. g. Targets up and hold.

SKILL AT ARMS

PRACTICE 4: SNAP
Range and Position adopted: 200m. Kneeling Unsupported.
Ammo: 10 rounds.
Target and Exposure: a. Figure 11. b. 5 x double exposures.
c In each double exposure the targets are up for 8 seconds, down for
4 seconds, up for 4 seconds. d. Irregular intervals between double
exposures.
Instructions: a. Firer in the standing alert position, 5m to the rear of
the firing point, loaded, ready. b. Order *"Watch out"*.
c. The appearance of the target is the signal to run onto the firing
point, adopt the kneeling supported position and fire one round at
each exposure. d. Between double exposures, order *"Apply safety
catches, stand up, dress back 5m, adopt the standing alert position"*.
e. Targets fall when hit.

PRACTICE 5: SNAP (NBC)
Range and Position adopted: 200m. Fire Trench.
Ammo: 5 rounds.
Target and Exposure: a. Figure 11. b. 5 x 4 second exposures with
irregular intervals.
Instructions: a. Firer in the nominated position, wearing respirator
and gloves. b. Order *"Watch and Shoot"*. c. Fire one round at each
exposure. d. Targets fall when hit.

PRACTICE 6: RAPID (NBC)
Range and Position adopted: 300m. Fire Trench.
Ammo: 5 rounds.
Target and Exposure: a. Figure 11. b. 1 x 10 second exposure.
Instructions: a. Firer in the nominated position, wearing respirator
and gloves. b. Order *"Five rounds rapid, Watch and Shoot"*.
c. Fire 5 rounds at the exposure. d. Target up and hold.

PRACTICE 7: SNAP
Range and Position adopted: 300m. Fire Trench.
Ammo: 5 rounds.
Target and Exposure: a. Figure 11. b. 5 x 4 second exposures with
irregular intervals.

Practice 7 continued)
Instructions: a. Firer in the nominated position. b. Order *"Watch and Shoot"*. c. Fire one round at each exposure. d. Targets fall when hit.

PRACTICE 8: SNAP
Range and Position adopted: 300m. Prone.
Ammo: 5 rounds.
Target and Exposure: a. Figure 11. b. 1 x 8 second exposure followed 5 seconds later by 4 x 4 second exposures with intervals of 5 to 10 seconds between exposurers.
Instructions: a. Firer in the standing alert position, 5m to the rear of the firing point, loaded, ready. b. Order *"Watch out"*. c. The appearance of the target is the signal to run onto the firing point, adopt the nominated position and fire one round at each exposure. d. Targets fall when hit.

PRACTICE 9: RAPID/SNAP
Range and Position adopted: 300m. Prone
Ammo: 10 rounds.
Target and Exposure: a. Figure 11. b. 1 x 15 seconds exposure followed 10 seconds later by 5 x 4 seconds exposures with intervals of 5 to 10 seconds between exposures.
Instructions: a. Firer in the standing alert position, 5m to the rear of the firing point, loaded, ready. b. Order *"Five rounds rapid, Watch out"*. c. The appearance of the target is the signal to run onto the firing point, adopt the nominated position and fire 5 rounds at the exposure. d. Target up and hold. e. After the first exposure order *"Stop. Watch and Shoot"*. f. Fire one round at each of the remaining exposures. g. Targets fall when hit.

PRACTICE 10: SUPPRESSION
Range and Position adopted: 400m. Prone.
Ammo: 15 rounds.
Target and Exposure: a. Figure 11. b. 5 x 15 seconds exposure with irregular intervals.
Instructions: a. Firer in the nominated position. b. Order *"Watch and Shoot"*.

PRACTICE 10 SUPPRESSION Instructions (continued)
c. Fire up to 3 rounds at each exposure. d. Targets fall when hit.
e. HPS FOR THIS PRACTICE IS 5 - ONE POINT PER EXPOSURE.

PRACTICE 11: NIGHT DELIBERATE
Range and Position adopted: LNV (Limit of Night Visibility).
Kneeling Unsupported.
Ammo: 15 rounds.
Target and Exposure: a. Figure 11 stick-in (draped).
b. 5 x 6 second exposurers with irregular intervals.
Instructions: a. Firer in the nominated position. b. Order *"Watch and Shoot"*. c. Fire one round at each exposure. d. Targets do not fall when hit. e. Record the scores.

PRACTICE 12: NIGHT SNAP
Range and Position adopted: LNV (Limited Night Vision).
Kneeling Unsupported.
Ammo: 5 rounds.
Target and Exposure: a. Figure 11 stick-in (draped). b. 5 x 10 second exposures with irregular intervals.
Instructions: a. Firer in the standing alert position. b. Order *"Watch out"*. c. The appearance of the target is the signal for the firer to adopt the nominated position and fire one round at each exposure. d. Between exposures, order *"Stand up, adopt the standing alert position"*. e. Targets do not fall when hit. f. Record the scores.

A MOVING TARGET - Fig 20

A = Height 1365mm (approx 4ft 6ins)
B = 610mm (approx 2ft)
C = 260mm (approx 11ins)
D = 560mm (approx 22ins)
E = 280mm (approx 12ins)

SKILL AT ARMS

THE 5.56mm SA 80 WEAPON SYSTEM COMPARED WITH THE 7.62mm EQUIVALENTS

	RIFLE		MACHINE GUN	
	5.56mm SA80	7.62mm S.L.R.	5.56mm L.S.W.	7.62mm G.P.M.G.
Weight (kg)				
Weapon (less Mag & Optical Sight)	3.8	4.3	5.4	10.9
Sight Optical	0.7	-	0.7	-
Sight Iron	0.3	Integral	0.3	Integral
Empty Magazine	0.12	0.26	0.3	-
Loaded Magazine	0.48	0.76	0.48	0.87
(filled with)	(30 rds)	(20 rds)	(30 rds)	(30 rd belt)
Weapon (complete with sight and loaded magazine)				
	4.98	5.06	6.58	11.77
Length (mm) Weapon	785	1140	898	1230
Mechanical Features				
Firing Modes	S.S/Auto	S.S	S.S/Auto	Auto
Method of Operation	Gas	Gas	Gas	Gas
Type of Locking	Rotary Bolt Forward Locking	Falling Breech Blk Rear Lock'g	Rotary Bolt Forward Lock'g	Dropping Link Rear Lock'g
Method of Feed	Magazine	Magazine	Magazine	Belt
AMMUNITION				
Calibre (mm)	5.56	7.62	5.56	7.62
Types:	Ball	Ball	Ball	Ball
	Tracer	Tracer	Tracer	Tracer
	Blank	Blank	Blank	Blank
	Training		Training	
Round Weight (g)	12	25	12	25
Firing Characteristics (approx) Muzzle Velocity (m/sec)				
	940	835	970	845
Recoil Energy (joules)	4	17	4	9

THE GENERAL PURPOSE MACHINE GUN
(GPMG) (Light Role).

The GPMG provides the main fire support for the Infantry section and is used throughout the British Armed Forces in many and various roles which include an anti-aircraft role demonstrated during the Falklands conflict where it increased the protection given to the ships of the task force.

The GPMG is a 7.62 mm calibre, belt fed, bipod mounted, fully automatic, gas operated, machine gun which is capable of fast accurate fire to ranges up to 800m in the light role and up to 1800m in the Sustained Fire (SF) role.

Note, however that the SF role requires the addition of a tripod, different butt and a dial sight for recording targets. These notes deal only with the light role.

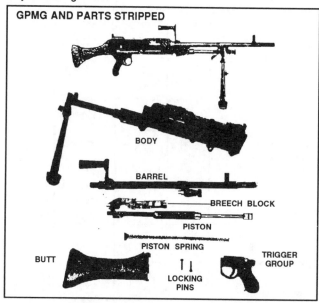

GPMG AND PARTS STRIPPED

BODY

BARREL

BREECH BLOCK

PISTON

PISTON SPRING

BUTT

LOCKING PINS

TRIGGER GROUP

SAA GPMG

NOTE - Carry out NSP's (NORMAL SAFETY PRECAUTIONS) before starting any lessons with a weapon.

NORMAL SAFETY PRECAUTIONS

Kneel behind the gun, grasp the pistol grip with the left hand, open the top cover by pushing in the cover catches with the right hand, cock the gun by pulling the cocking handle fully to the rear, lift the feed tray.

Look inside and inspect the chamber and body to ensure they are clear, lower the feed tray and close the top cover. Hold the cocking handle with the right hand, press the trigger and allow the working parts to go forward under control.

Close the ejection opening cover unless stripping is to follow at once.

STRIPPING, ASSEMBLING AND CLEANING THE GPMG.

Stripping Sequence

1 Check the weapon as above to make sure it is safe.
2 Make sure the working parts are forward.
3 Remove the sling.
4 Remove the butt.
5 Remove the return spring, piston and breech block. It is usual to clean these parts and reassemble before going on to the barrel group.
6 Cock the gun.
7 Remove the barrel.
8 Unscrew the gas regulator and remove the collars, plug and regulator. These would now be cleaned and then reassembled. The trigger group can also be stripped and cleaned after firing.
9 With the working parts forward remove the retaining pin.
10 Remove the trigger group by pivoting the group slightly downward.

CLEANING

The GPMG is equipped with a Spare Parts Wallet (SPW) which contains cleaning materials and spare parts. The contents of the SPW are :-

Oil can. Cleaning rod in two parts. Bore cleaning brush.
Chamber cleaning brush. Cylinder cleaning brush.
Gas port cleaner. Clearing plug. Spare firing pin.
Combination tool. Spare extractor, stay and spring.
Spare link pin Piston and cylinder cleaning tool.

SAA GPMG

Two spare collars. Gas regulator cleaning tool.
The GPMG is prone to becoming clogged up with carbon due to the large number of rounds it fires. The gas parts are particularly bad with the carbon becoming very hard and very difficult to remove however it must be removed so persevere and get several of the other members of your section or group to help you.

1   Assemble the chamber cleaning brush to the rod and clean out the chamber.
2   Clean the barrel with 100mm by 50mm (4 x 2 inches) flannelette inserting the pullthrough at the chamber end only and pulling in one motion.
3   When clean, oil the barrel using 100mm x 38mm (4 x 1$\frac{1}{2}$ inches) flannelette.
4   Clean and oil the flash hider.
5   Put flannelette round the cylinder brush and using the rod clean out the cylinder from the front. Oil the cylinder.
6   Clean the rest of the gun with an oily rag.
7   Reassemble the gun setting the gas to 6 if the normal setting is not known.
8   Clean, check and re-pack the SPW.

ASSEMBLY SEQUENCE

1   Check the numbers on the breech block and the body.
2   Replace the piston and breech block into the body.
3   Insert and secure the return spring.
4   Replace the butt.
5   Insert the plug into the seating on the barrel.
6   Replace the collars and screw the regulator fully home, then unscrew to No 6.
7   Check the numbers on the barrel and the body and that there is no obstruction in the barrel.
8   Replace the barrel (weapon should be cocked).
9   Ease springs.
10 To replace the trigger group check that the safety catch is at "F", insert the pistol grip and replace the retaining pin.
11 When fully assembled test the gun by cocking it and pressing the trigger with the recoil mechanism under control.
12 Lastly close the ejection opening cover.

SAA GPMG

GPMG AMMUNITION BELT

Ammunition for the GPMG is issued already belted in 200 round liners. These belts are broken down into the required lengths by holding the rounds either side of the point of separation and twisting them in opposite directions.

Belts are usually broken down into 50's and distributed throughout a section for use when moving or can be left in 200's in their tins when used in defence. Belts can be rejoined, but should not be made up from used links except in battle situation.

THE GPMG SIGHT PICTURE

SIGHT SETTING

The back sight is used in the lowered position for ranges 200 to 800m in the light role and is raised for use at greater ranges in the SF role.

LOADING AND UNLOADING

The prone position is adopted for loading, straight behind the gun with the legs together and heels uppermost. Hold the pistol grip with the right hand with the forefinger lying outside the trigger guard, put the butt in the shoulder with your cheek on the butt, place the left hand - palm down - on the butt with thumb underneath. Get comfortable with both elbows on the ground, with the forearms forming an "A" shape.

SAA GPMG

On the command "LOAD":-
1   Tilt it to the right
2.   Open the top cover (right hand)
3.   Pick up the ammunition belt and check that it is not loose or damaged with your (left hand)
4.   Place the belt in the feed tray (left hand) with the first round against the cartridge stop and close the top cover (right hand).
5.   Replace the hands in their correct positions
6.   Hold the gun upright

On the command UNLOAD:-
1.   Open the top cover by pushing in the cover catches but do not lift it.
2.   Raise the butt into the shoulder and cock the gun
3.   Lower the butt
4.   Raise the top cover and remove the belt
5.   Clear the feed tray of empty links
6.   Close the top cover
7.   Raise the butt into the shoulder align the sights and squeeze the trigger.
8.   Lower the butt
9.   Close the ejection opening cover
10. Lower the sights and stand up.

Sometimes on the range you will be required to Clear the gun. To do this you should unload the gun then raise the top cover to its upright position, stand up and report "Gun Clear".

On the command "MAKE SAFE": unload, then reload but **DO NOT** cock the weapon.

Loading and Unloading with a two man team.

When a Number 2 is provided for the gunner he should lie on the left of the gunner and assist with loading and unloading.

To load, the gunner raises the top cover, the No 2 places the belt in the feed tray keeping his fingers clear of the top cover as the gunner closes it. During the unload the No2 removes the belt from the feed tray.

HOLDING AIMING AND FIRING

Although the GPMG rests on a bipod you must be able to hold the weapon, aim and fire in bursts against both stationary and moving targets.

SAA GPMG

Holding and Aiming

1   You will be given a range or the order to load.
2   Aiming is as for the rifle since the sights are of the same type.
3   To begin roughly adjust the weapon on to the target by placing the left hand under the weapon, lifting and moving the gun in line with the target.
4   Adjust for height by moving the elbows apart or together or for large adjustments alter the nut between the bipod legs.
5   Move your shoulder firmly up to the butt of the gun.
6   Pull the butt into the shoulder, backwards and downwards with the left hand on the butt and the left elbow as far forward as possible.
7   Hold the pistol grip firmly with the right hand, forefinger over the trigger, and pull the gun backwards and upwards.
8   Lock the position by twisting the wrists against each other and rest the cheek on the butt/left hand.
9   To test your position rock backwards and forwards slightly; the foresight should move up and down on the point of aim.

FIRING

1. On the command fire and when you have finished adjusting, squeeze the trigger, holding it long enough to fire a burst of two or three rounds, then release the trigger without disturbing the position.
2. As soon as you have fired, open both eyes and look for the fall of shot.
3. Make any necessary adjustments and then continue firing at a rate of 25 rounds per min or 100 per min if Rapid fire is ordered.
4. **When ordered to "STOP"**, cock the gun, put the safety catch to safe and rest the butt.
5. **When ordered to "GO-ON"**, aim and continue firing.
6. If a No2 is available he should keep the gun fed with ammunition by clipping on more belts and ensure that they feed into the gun correctly.

IMMEDIATE ACTION AND GAS STOPPAGES

The **IA** drills for the GPMG are as follows.
If the gun stops or fails to fire:-
1.   Cock the gun.
2.   Lower the butt.
3.   Open the top cover, clear the feed tray and close the top cover again as quickly as possible.

4. Raise butt into the shoulder and align the sights then press the trigger.
5. Lower the butt, reload and carry on firing.

The following stoppages will be remedied by using the "IA":-

1. Expended belt.
2. Damaged rounds.
3. Poor feed.
4. Misfired round.
5. Hard extraction.
6. Damaged link.

If the gun cannot be cocked open the top cover, clear the feed tray, close the top cover and complete the IA.

GAS STOPPAGE DRILL

If after completing the **IA** the gun fires a few rounds and stops again do the following:

1. Cock the gun.
2. Put the safety catch to **"SAFE"**.
3. Lower the butt.
4. Adjust the regulator 3 clicks. If hot use the nose of a round in the holes in the regulator.
5. Put the safety catch to **"FIRE"** and carry on.

Do not try to reuse damaged rounds, put them to on side and hand them in after firing. If after carrying out the stoppage drill it recurs you should look closely at the rate of fire and cleanliness of the gun and either adjust or clean the gun.

OTHER STOPPAGES

Stoppages caused by broken parts are rare, however, they do sometimes occur and are usually due to the following.

1. An obstruction in the body, empty case in the chamber. Cleared by unloading, inspecting and removing the obstruction.
2. Broken parts, obstruction in the barrel, separated case. Cleared by unloading, inspecting, removing the obstruction and replacing any broken parts.

A separated case will require the use of the clearing plug.

3. Feed pawl and springs. If after carrying out the IA the gun will not fire and you cannot fully cock the gun, inspect the feed pawls and springs to see that they are working correctly. You may have to clean and oil them before reloading.

SAA GPMG

4. Runaway gun. A mechanical fault may cause the gun to continue firing after the trigger has been released, if this happens hold the gun firmly into the shoulder and twist the belt at its point of entry to the feed mechanism to cause the gun to stop.

When the gun has stopped, reload, adjust for more gas, cock the gun and carry on firing.

GPMG TRAINING TESTS

The purpose of these training tests are to measure the standards that you have attained in safety and handling of the GPMG. You will be tested during your Recruit training and thereafter annually.

TEST No 1. SAFETY

Stores: Gun loaded, cocked and safety catch at SAFE. Gun either in the corner of a room or on the firing point.
Conditions: You will be ordered to bring the gun to the centre of the room, or to another position on the firing point. You should - without further directive - carry out the normal safety precautions on the gun.
ASSESSMENT: You will **FAIL** if the safety actions are not carried out correctly.

TEST No 2. STRIPPING, CLEANING & ASSEMBLING.

Stores: GPMG Weapon. Spare parts wallet complete. One 7.62mm Drill Round.
Conditions: You will be ordered to strip the gun as for daily cleaning. The following questions will be asked:-
1. What size of flannelette is used to clean the bore.
2. What size of flannelette is used to oil the cylinder.
3. What spare parts for the gun are contained in the section wallet.
You will them be ordered to assemble the gun.
ASSESSMENT: Main purpose to assess your ability to strip and assemble the gun. You are assessed follows:- SKILLED made no mistakes. AVERAGE made 1 to 3 mistakes. FAIL made more than 3 mistakes.
NOTE. No qualification is awarded if any mistakes affect safety.

TEST No 3. LOADING.

Stores: GPMG Weapon. Belt of 15 DRILL rounds. Stop Watch.
Conditions: This is a TIMED TEST. You are tested lying behind the gun. Safety catch at FIRE. Belt on the ground on the left of gun. Ordered to LOAD. Time is taken from the time of the order LOAD, until you have both hands in their proper position on the gun and the gun is upright.
ASSESSMENT: SKILLED - 8 seconds or less. AVERAGE - 9 to 12 seconds. FAIL over 12 seconds.
NOTE. Two seconds are added to the overall time for each mistake. No qualification is awarded if any mistakes affect safety.

TEST NO 4. IMMEDIATE ACTION & GAS STOPPAGES.

Stores: As for TEST No 3.
Conditions: This is a TIMED test. You are tested lying behind gun, gun loaded and firing. Order GUN STOPS. When the IA has been done, order GUN FIRES A FEW MORE ROUNDS AND STOPS AGAIN. Time taken from AGAIN until you have aimed and fired the gun. Mistakes made in the IA count for the test.
ASSESSMENT: SKILLED -8 seconds or less. AVERAGE - 9 to 10 seconds. FAIL - over 10 seconds.
NOTE: Two seconds are added to the overall time for each mistake. No qualification is awarded if any mistakes affect safety.

TEST No 5. UNLOADING.

Stores: As for TEST No 3.
Conditions: This is a TIMED test. You are tested lying behind gun, gun loaded and firing. Ordered to STOP and when actions have been carried out correctly, given the command UNLOAD. Time taken from the UNLOAD until you are standing up behind gun.
ASSESSMENT: SKILLED - 8 seconds or less. AVERAGE - 9 to 12 seconds. FAIL - over 12 seconds.
NOTE: Two seconds are added to the overall time for each mistake. No qualification is awarded if any mistakes affect safety.

TEST No 6. PREPARATION FOR FIRING.

Stores: GPMG Weapon. Spare Parts Wallet complete. One 7.62 DRILL round. Flannelette. Oil.
Conditions: You will be ordered to prepare gun for firing.

SAA GPMG

Without further direction you should:-

a. Strip the gun as for daily cleaning, clean and leave dry.
b. Open the dust cover, clean and oil the guide ribs then close the dust cover.
c. Oil the bearing surfaces of the breech block and piston extension, locking lever and locking shoulder, feed arm and feed channel, the return spring and the trigger mechanism.
d. Set the gas regulator at its correct setting, check there is no obstruction in the barrel and that it locks firmly into position.
e. Check sights for tightness.
f. Ensure ball of the firing pin is seated correctly in its recess.
g. When the gun is assembled, press the trigger and move the working parts backwards and forwards a few times

ASSESSMENT: The sequence used need not be the same as laid down in the conditions above, but all aspects are to be correctly completed. SKILLED - Up to 2 mistakes. AVERAGE - 3 to 5 mistakes. FAIL - Over 5 mistakes.

NOTE: No qualification is awarded if any mistakes affect safety.

"ere corp - ave' we got one of them SAC's"

SKILL AT ARMS

CHARACTERISTICS OF THE 81 mm MORTAR

Fire-power Characteristics

Accuracy. The 81 mm mortar is a very accurate weapon. The sight system includes the Mortar Fire Data Computer (MFDC).

Consistency. Because of the very fine machining of rounds and the barrel, produces accurate fire comparable with a field gun.

Beaten Zone. The effective beaten zone of one section of mortars at maximum range is approximately 200 metres square. At shorter ranges and with lower charges the beaten zone is smaller.

Flexibility. The range varies from 180-5660 metres for HE and WP ammunition. The mortar can engage targets over a 6400 mils arc.

Ammunition. The mortar fires three main types of amrnunition - High Explosive, White Phosphorus Smoke and Illuminating. The HE and WP matched charges. The illuminating ammunition has a range of 4050 metres, a burning time of 43 seconds, will illuminate area of 400 metres radius. The brightness is 400,000 candle power.

High Rate of Fire. The mortar can fire more than 20 rounds a minute; Under normal circumstances Rate 12 should be used; this will give from one to 12 rounds of fire in a minute.

Danger Area. The HE round has a high lethal capability up to a radius of 40 metres from the point of burst and it can be expected to cause casualties up to 190 metres from the point of burst.

Ability to Fire at Obscured Targets. The mortar has the capability of firing on previously adjusted targets when they are obscured by darkness, fog or battlefield smoke. Targets not previously adjusted can be engaged, but the fire will be less accurate.

Response Times.

Being a battalion asset fire is guaranteed to the battalion. This often is not the case with artillery fire. Response times compare well with artillery. Their role in general is to give:

Final Protective Fire (FPF). If the mortars are laid on a target the time to have effective fire will be from 20-60 seconds.

Defensive Fire (DF). Approximately three minutes, and individual skills and the time of flight.

Time of Flight. This varies between 12 and 51 seconds.

SKILL AT ARMS

Deployment Characteristics

High Trajectory. The high trajectory enables it to fire from behind high cover. Engage targets in dead ground or defiladed from other weapons.

Ground. When firing the ground must be firm and stable. Very rocky ground and marshes must be avoided.

Mobility. Mortar detachment are self-contained, in a 1 tonne Landrover and trailer or FV 432.

Weight of Stores. The main parts of the mortar are light weight compared to the ammunition which is both bulky and heavy. Help is necessary for carrying ammunition.

Vulnerability. The mortar needs carefully located, preferably in dead ground. High trajectory, long flight time, easily recognised sound and muzzle flash make the mortar vulnerable to sound ranging, mortar-locating radar and visual detection.

Organization. At company level mortar fire is controlled by the MFCs. An MFC party consists of two MFCs and a driver. They are equipped with radios and optical devices, including SPYGLASS.

Allocation. Mortar sections are allocated at priority call to companies by the mortar platoon commander.

CHARACTERISTICS OF MILAN

General Introduction.

MILAN is a second generation, semiautomatic wire guided missile system. This means that after launch, the operator only has to track the target by keeping the cross hairs on it. He does not have to fly the missile as in older systems.

There are three main component parts:

   a. The Firing Post - which contains the launch, tracking and guidance system.

   b. The Missile - in its separate tube.

   c. MILAN Infra-Red Adapter (MIRA) - a thermal imaging sight which forms an integral part of the system.

Range. When fired the missile is armed at 20 metres it can only be used in an emergency at less than 400 metres, because it is not until this range that the missile has settled onto its correct flight path. The maximum range is 1950 metres.

SKILL AT ARMS

Accuracy. The system has a high degree of accuracy against all targets due to its semiautomatic nature and to the operator's x7 magnification in the sight.

Effect on Armour The missile has a 115 mm HEAT warhead which will penetrate 352mm armour. It will penetrate the side armour of most known AFVs. It should be sited in defilade,

Concealment. MILAN's small size and low silhouette make it easy to conceal.

Handling. The firing post weighs 18 kilograms and the MIRA sight 7 kilograms. Both are carried by the MILAN operator. Each missile weighs approximately 12 kilograms and two missiles are carried by his No 2. Since MILAN is a relatively light, compact and robust system, ideal for airmobile and airborne operations.

Flexibility. MILAN can be used in the open or fired from a trench. It can be mounted on various vehicles such as the FV 432 , or in the MILAN Compact Turret mounted on SPARTAN (MCT(S)). The post has an all round traverse of 6400 mils.

Pre-Firing Checks. A simple visual pre-firing inspection is required on the MILAN ammunition tube. The firing post can be tested by the MILAN operator by using a simple 'GO/NO GO' Unit Test Equipment

Limitations

Time of Flight. The time of flight to maximum range is approx 12 seconds. This precludes the engagement of fleeting targets and it results in a slower rate of fire. It also requires the firer to be protected during the missile's flight.

Rear Blast Area. On launch the missile tube is ejected to the rear and there is a small back blast. A zone 5.5 metres behind, 533 mils either side of the axis and 0.5 metres above the level of the ammunition tube must be clear of men, equipment and obstacles.

Decoy. The Heat from a burning tank or building may decoy the missile if close to the flight path. The MILAN tracker confuses the battlefield IR source for the IR tracking flare on the missile. This can be partially overcome by experienced and well trained operators.

METHOD OF INSTRUCTION

INTRODUCTION

This section on Methods of Instruction (MOI) is as used by the Army, it is easy to understand and use, provided you apply the well tried and practised framework called a **Lesson Plan**.

Instructing becomes interesting and very much simplified, but if you fail to use a Lesson Plan and ignore taking sufficient time for preparation, neither you nor those you are instructing will gain anything.

As an NCO, it will add to your skills and improve your confidence and performance.

Provided you learn how to apply this system of MOI, it will remain as a skill for you to call on in a variety of situations throughout your service.

You may have the use of an Overhead Projector or even a Video Camera and Computer, but even so you will still have to plan and prepare your presentation in a logical and professional manner, don't get side tracked by the technology!

QUALITIES REQUIRED

The main qualities you need as an instructor are enthusiasm, self confidence and to know your subject. Good Planning and Preparation breed self-confidence and makes those under instruction feel confident in your ability.

Your enthusiasm will stimulate interest for the class to listen and learn.

Your Manner and Bearing is important.

Look up when you speak, your voice will travel further. Vary the pitch of your voice to stress a particular point.

Avoid distracting mannerisms, such as saying "OK or RIGHT" after each statement or tapping with a pen on the table, scratching your ear or nose!!

Watch and listen to other instructors for any of their mannerisms or bad habits. Make sure you don't fall into any yourself. Ask any of your other instructors to *sit in* on one of your lessons now and again to give you a critique. This will stop any bad habits developing.

Your appearance/turnout is very important, if you are well turned out and "look the part" you will command respect and attention.

METHOD OF INSTRUCTION

YOUR ATTITUDE

Your attitude must be right to command attention and make the class want to listen.

Avoid sarcasm and favouritism, getting a cheap laugh by making a fool of someone is not good, have a joke by all means and try to win over the confidence of the class. Avoid passing remarks that can offend or have a double meaning at someone else's expense.

Encourage them to join in by being friendly and fair, but firmness at all times is always advisable.

Instruct : **clearly, completely, patiently, giving information at a suitable pace, one *stage* at a time.**

YOUR SQUAD MUST ENJOY BEING INSTRUCTED.

CHECK YOUR OWN PERFORMANCE

Be observant - apply yourself to the task, pay attention to detail - don't cut corners, never be satisfied with standards, always look for ways and means of improving your own performance, the training aids you use, and the questions you ask.

Carry out a rehearsal, especially of any difficult parts.

BASIC POINTS ON SUCCESSFUL INSTRUCTION

REMEMBER THE SIX "P"s:-

PRIOR PREPARATION & PRACTICE PREVENTS POOR PERFORMANCE

PREPARE and PLAN

1. What is the objective to be achieved?
2. Which is the best method ? (lecture, lesson, discussion, exercise, demonstration)
3. Where is the instruction to take place ?
4. What is the size of the class?
5. What time is available.
6. What equipment or aids are available?
7. Are the aids suitable, simple, large enough or even necessary ?
8. What handout notes do I need to produce.
9. What is the present standard of the classes knowledge.
10. Prepare your list of questions and answers for **this lesson** and have your questions and answers ready from **the previous lesson.**

METHOD OF INSTRUCTION

QUESTIONING TECHNIQUE

When instructing a squad you will at times need to ask questions.
There is a simple technique to adopt. It is important that all members
of the squad are '*kept on their toes*', you must therefore **first ask the
question to the whole squad,** wait or pause for a few moments for
them **ALL** to think of the answer, then **select or nominate one of
them** to give it.

REMEMBER: ASK - PAUSE - NOMINATE.

LESSON PLAN

1. Prepare a Lesson Plan.
2. Use logical stages.
3. Use correct question techniques ASK - PAUSE - NOMINATE who
is to answer.

METHOD OF INSTRUCTION

Skills Lessons - for example - Drill, Skill at Arms, remember and use
the sequence:

EXPLANATION — DEMONSTRATION — IMITATION — PRACTICE

A SIMPLE LESSON PLAN

The framework of a lesson plan is set out over page with headings
and information for you to follow.
Set it out on a large sheet of paper adding the lesson details to the
'skeleton' for the lesson you are taking.
The plan is divided into three stages:-

STAGE 1 - BEGINNING

Subject ...... Class/Squad ...... Time ..... Location ..... Dress ....
Stores required and Training Aids .... Time allowed ....
Prelims: Safety Precautions: Roll Call: Class formation: Seating
plan: Comfort of the class: Lighting levels: Standard of Visual Aids.
Revision: Check their knowledge/skills in the subject previously
taught — they soon forget.
Introduction: Make sure class know your name.
Objective: It must be clearly stated and understood, definite, limited
and attainable in the time allowed and capability of the squad.
The reason why: A realistic reason: Incentive to achieve results:
Benefits to be gained from the lesson.

METHOD OF INSTRUCTION

STAGE 2 - THE MIDDLE

The main instruction to be taught. Time allowed ..... Divide the subject
into several **"STAGES"**, select from each stage the **"KEY POINTS"**
that you must bring out in your instruction - such as SAFETY, to
ensure a complete understanding of the lesson.

Rule up sheets of paper as the example below setting out the
STAGES or BLOCKS of information as headings on the subject, and
the KEY POINTS; number them in descending order of importance to
stress the important points to be made, such as safety, particular
information like figures, codes, references. Note the correct training
aid to use at this particular point, use it as a prompt, drawing as
many lines spacing them out as you require.

Don't forget to write large enough and clearly, as you may be using
this when standing up — *not held in your hand reading from it!.*

LAYOUT OF A LESSON AIDE MEMOIRE or PROMPT SHEET

SUBJECT or TOPIC to INSTRUCT/TALK ABOUT	
STAGES	**KEY POINTS**
BREAK DOWN THE 1 LESSON TO AS	IMPORTANT POINTS NOT TO BE MISSED NUMBER THEM IN DESCENDING ORDER OF IMPORTANCE
MANY 2 STAGES AS YOU	STRESS SAFETY, ANYTHING THAT CAN CAUSE DAMAGE
LIKE 3	"MEMORY TICKLER" FOR SIZES, MEASUREMENTS. TRAINING AIDS. REFERENCES, COLOURS ETC.
4	

METHOD OF INSTRUCTION

CHECK YOUR TRAINING AIDS

Make sure you have all your training aids, maps, compasses, spare bulb if using an OHP, etc.

At the end of each STAGE of instruction, confirm that the key points have been understood, by using good Question Technique.

Correct any errors as they occur ASK THE QUESTION - PAUSE - NOMINATE who is to answer.

Ask sufficient questions to the squad. If you don't it reduces the odds of those individuals who are likely to be asked, as a result they are not *"kept on their toes"*.

STAGE 3 - THE END

Invite questions from the class - if you are asked a question and do not know the answer, do not try to 'bluff' your way out of it. Admit you do not know, but find out and let them know - ***AND MAKE SURE YOU DO***.

Ask your PREPARED questions to the class - using the right technique - confirm that they have learned by your instruction, by oral tests, written tests or by practical performance tests.

NOTE: PREPARED questions means preparing them in advance **WITH THE ANSWERS**.

YOU DON'T HAVE TIME TO THINK *CORRECTLY* ON YOUR FEET

Summary - bring out and stress the achievement of the objective.

Look forward - state when and what is the next lesson/subject.

ONCE YOU HAVE SPENT TIME ON WRITING
A LESSON PLAN AND REHEARSED IT
— STICK TO IT - YOU WON'T MAKE MISTAKES
AND IT'S SO MUCH EASIER

KEEP ALL YOUR LESSON PLANS AND CAREFULLY
FILE THEM FOR EASY REFERENCE.
THE NEXT TIME YOU TAKE THAT LESSON —
HALF YOUR WORK IS ALREADY PREPARED

AFV and AIRCRAFT RECOGNITION

TECHNICAL INFORMATION

The silhouette illustrations on the following pages should be familiar to you, to such an extent that you are able to recognise each one individually by their particular characteristics. We did say "should be". It is your responsibility to know how to recognise 'friend' or 'foe' in the very short space of time that you would actually have available to identify them.

Some of the information will not tell you how to recognise vehicles or aircraft, but through persistent practice at every available opportunity your skills will improve - TO KNOW, - IS TO SURVIVE.

Arms sales throughout the world by those nations who have them to sell, means that the equipment may have been supplied by different manufacturers from a variety of countries. You can imagine the logistic problems their Q.M will have, but if you are ever in an 'operational theatre' you will most certainly have the additional problem of trying to identify a 'wolf in sheep's clothing'.

NATO

BATTLE TANKS

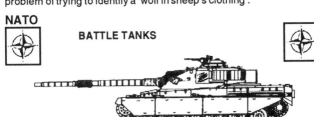

CHIEFTAIN

Manufactured by: UK. Crew of 4, Commander, Gunner, Loader/Operator. Weapons: 1x120mm rifled gun. (APDSFS, APDS, HESH/HE, Smoke, Canister with separated ammo. 1x12.7mm rmg. 1x7.62 coaxial mg. 1x7.62 AA mg. Weight 55.8 tonnes. NBC protection system. IFCS firing system laser range finder and ballistics computer, day and night sights. Dual purpose searchlight. Stabilised Gun, laser Range Finder

AFV and AIRCRAFT RECOGNITION

CHALLENGER.

Manufactured by: UK. Crew of 4, Commander, gunner, loader, driver. Weapons: 1x120 rifled gun. (APDS, APDSFS, HESH, Smoke, Canister) 2 x .762mm (coaxial and AA). Weight 62,000kg. NBC protection system. IFCS integrated firing system, with laser range finder.

LEOPARD 1A4

Manufactured by: Germany. Crew of 4, Commander, Gunner, Loader/ Operator, Driver. Weapons: 1x105mm rifled gun (APDS, APDSFS, HEAT, HESH), 1 x 7.62mm coaxial mg, 1 x 7.62mm AA. Weight 40,000kg. NBC protection system. IFCS firing system. Wades to 2.25m without preparation. Variants are the ARV, AEV with dozer blade and auger; bridge layer. The same chassis is used for the Gepard AA system.

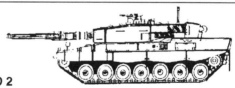

LEOPARD 2

Manufactured by: Germany. Crew of 4, Commander, Gunner, Loader/ Operator, Driver. Weapons: 1 x 120mm smooth bore (APDSFS, HEAT) 1 x 7.62 coaxial Reheinmetall MG3 Machine Gun. 1 x 7.62 AA mg, Grenade Launcher. Combat Weight 55,000kg. IFCS firing system with laser range finder. NBC protection system.

AFV and AIRCRAFT RECOGNITION

Comparison views of the Main Battle Tanks

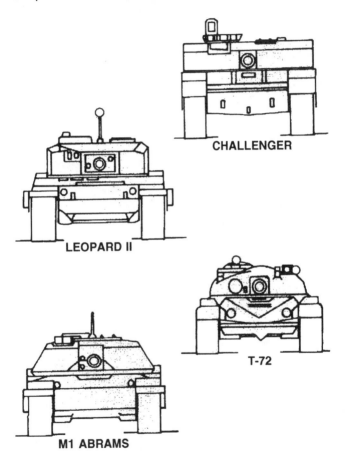

CHALLENGER

LEOPARD II

T-72

M1 ABRAMS

332

AFV and AIRCRAFT RECOGNITION

M1 ABRAMS

Manufactured by: USA. Crew of 4, Commander, Gunner, Loader, Driver. Weapons: 1 x 105mm rifled gun (improved APDSFS, HEAT, HESH, Smoke, Canister), 1 x 12.7mm AA and 2 x 7.62mm mgs (coaxial and AA). Weight 54,430kg. IFCS firing system with laser range finder, night viewing and fighting aids.

M 60 A3

Manufactured by: USA. Crew of 4 Commander, Gunner, Loader, Driver. Weapons: 1 x 105 rifled gun (APDS, HESH, HEAT, Smoke, Canister), 1 x 7.62mm coaxial mg, 1 x 12.7mm Commander's mg. Weight 49,000kg. NBC protection system.
This tank is being replaced in the American Army by the M1 Abrams.

ARMOURED PERSONNEL CARRIERS

SPARTAN

Manufactured by: UK. Crew of 3, Commander, Driver, Gunner, plus 4 Infantrymen. Speed 87 kph. Weight 8170kg. Weapons: 1 x 7.62 mg. NBC protection system. Can be fitted with surveillance radar; night driving aids.

AFV and AIRCRAFT RECOGNITION

SAXON

Manufactured by: UK. Crew of 2 Commander and Driver, plus 8 Infantrymen. Speed 96 kph. Weight 10,670kg. Weapons: 1 x 7.62mm mg in fixed cupola. Firing ports in sides and rear. Air conditioning system.

M 113

Manufactured by: USA. Crew of 2 Commander and Driver, plus 11 Infantrymen. Speed 68 kph. Weight 11,160kg. Armament 1 x 12.7mm mg. Amphibious; night driving aids. This vehicle has many variants, as a light recce vehicle with a Scorpion turret fitted. Fitters vehicle with a crane. Mortars carrier. AA system vehicle. Flamethrower vehicle. Command vehicle with raised roof. Tracked Rapier and many other adoptions.

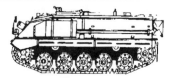

10. F 432.

Manufactured by: UK. Crew of 2, Commander and Driver, plus 10 Infantrymen. Speed 52 kph. Weight 15,280kg loaded. Weapons: 1 x 7.62 mg (some have turret-mounted 7.62). Amphibious - using track propulsion and floatation screen with max speed of 6.6kph. NBC protection system. Night driving aids. Many variants of this vehicle, Repair vehicle. Ambulance. Command Vehicle.
Surveillance with radar. Ptarmigan Communications System. Recovery. Swingfire, and many others roles using the F432 as the base chassis.

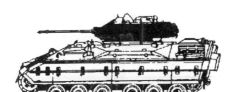

M2 BRADLEY

Manufactured by: USA. Crew of 3, Commander, Gunner, Driver, plus 7 Infantrymen. Speed 66 kph. Weight 22.680kg. Armament 1 x 25mm cannon, twin TOW ATGW missile launcher, 1 x 7.62 mm. coaxial mg. Fully amphibious, propelled by its tracks, max speed 6.3 kph. Night viewing and fighting aids. 6 weapon ports in hull sides and rear using specially adapted 5.56mm M16A1 rifle. Variants as a Multiple Launch Rocket System platform and as a vehicle to fire TOW 2 having NBC protection.

MARDER

Manufactured by: Germany. Crew of 4, Commander, Driver, 2 Gunners and 6 Infantrymen. Speed of 75 kph. Weight 28,200kg. Weapons: 1 x 20mm cannon, 2 x 7.62mm mg (coaxial and rear mounted). Night driving and fighting aids. NBC protection system; can ford to depth of 2.5metres using snorkel. Variants have a Milan ATGW launcher mounted on side of turret. Vehicle fitted with 25mm cannon. Early warning with Siemens radar mounted on hydraulic arm.

AFV and AIRCRAFT RECOGNITION

WARRIOR MCV-80

Manufactured by: UK. Crew of 2, Commander and Driver. plus 8 Infantrymen. Speed of 75 kph. Weight 20,000kg. Weapons: 1 x 30mm Rarden gun, 1 x 7.62 mm coaxial mg. Has NBC protection system and night driving aids.

RECONNAISSANCE VEHICLES

SCORPION

Manufactured by: UK. Crew of 3, Commander, Gunner, Driver. Speed 87 kph. Weight 7960 kg. Speed 87 kph. Weapons: 1 x 76mm rifled gun (HESH, HE, Smoke), 1 x 7.62mm coaxial mg. Night fighting and driving aids. Amphibious using floatation screen with max speed of 6.44 kph. NBC protection system.

SCIMITAR

Manufactured by: UK. Variant of the SCORPION, same detail except armament; mounting a 30mm Rarden Gun.

336

AFV and AIRCRAFT RECOGNITION

M 109 A2.

Manufactured by: USA. The M 109 **Self Propelled Gun** has a crew of 6, Commander, Driver, 4 Gun Crew. Weight 23,800 kg. Speed of 56 kph. Weapons: 1 x 155mm howitzer, 1 x 12.7mm or 7.62mm AA mg.

AS 90

Manufactured in UK.. The AS90 **Self Propelled Gun** has a crew of 5. A maximum road speed of 53kph; road range of 420km. Calibre of gun 155mm. Fires unassisted projectile out to a range of 24kms. Fitted with navigation and gun laying electronics.

SURFACE TO AIR MISSILES

PATRIOT

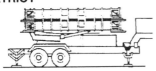 

Manufactured in the USA The Patriot Missile system. 2-4 missiles per launcher. Missile length 5.18 m, each carries over 90KG of HE The system proved itself against Skud Missiles in the Gulf War.

AFV and AIRCRAFT RECOGNITION

ROLAND

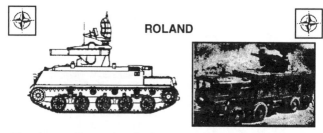

Manufactured internationally. Can be mounted on several base units: AMX-30. Marder.MAN (8x8) 10 ton truck. Missile length 2.4m. Warhead 3.3KG. Missiles per launcher 2. Max range 6300 metres.

RAPIER

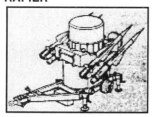 

The Rapier missile system provides low level air defence over the battlefield. It can be towed as illustrated above or mounted on a tracked vehicle which of course is a better option. (see illustrations below) The system comprises of an Optical Tracker, a Fire Unit, Radar and a Generator.

Rapier is operated by the Royal Artillery.

RAPIER TRACKED VEHICLE

AFV and AIRCRAFT RECOGNITION

MLRS (Multi Launch Rocket System

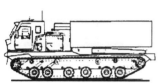 

The MLSR is built on a American Tank chassis the M2 Bradley. It is loaded with six 227mm rockets at a time and can fire a volley of 12 Rockets. Reloading is carried out with a mechanical loading system. In due course this may replace some guns currently in service with the Royal Artillery. The Rockets are transported in a special vehicle; Heavy Expanded Mobility Tactical Truck (MEMTT) which also pulls a Trailer loaded with Rockets.

ANTI - TANK WEAPONS

MILAN

The Milan Anti-Tank system was a joint project by France, Germany and Britain. It has a semiautomatic guidance system by means of wires connected to the missile. The operator keeps his aiming mark on target and the weapon guidance system does the rest. This has proved to be a very effective weapon against all known battle tanks. No doubt the future developments of this system will have a marked effect on armoured warfare.

AFV and AIRCRAFT RECOGNITION

SWINGFIRE

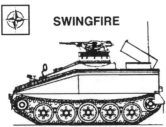

Swingfire designed and developed in the UK. This is another weapon using a wire guidance system controlled by the operator. It can be mounted like the Milan on a variety of chassis. The maximum effective range is 4000m.

COMMAND VEHICLE

SULTAN

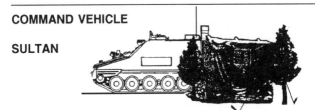

The Sultan is the Command Vehicle version of the Combat Vehicle Recce Tracked series. It is a comparatively small vehicle, the APC version — the Spartan carries a crew of 3 plus 4 soldiers. Recognition features: 5 road wheels. High slab sided, sloping front. canvas extension fitted at rear.

RECCE VEHICLE

LUCHS

Country of origin, Germany. Has a crew of 4. Powered by Diesel/Petrol. The main armament is 1 x 20mm cannon. Secondary armament 1 x 7.62mm mg (coaxal). In service with the German army.

AFV and AIRCRAFT RECOGNITION

AIRCRAFT

TORNADO ADV

Manufactured by: UK.
Similar in appearance to T-2/F-1 Phantom Identification
Features:- Two high
mounted square air-intakes.
Twin exhausts - end short
of tail. Whole tail area
overhangs twin exhausts.
Tail plane is down swept.
Flat bottomed fuselage.
Chisel-type nose.

HARRIER.

Manufactured by: UK.
Similar in appearance to the
Hunter, Forger and
Etendard. Identification
features: Downswept
sloping wings and tailplane.
Huge half-circular air
intakes. Small Dolphin
shaped nose. Small
fuselage projection behind
tail. Wing tip folded wheels.
(Sea Harrier has
conventional pointed nose)

A-10 THUNDERBOLT II

Manufactured by: USA.
Identification Features: Two
large rear-mounted 'dumpy'
turbo fan engines. Twin
vertical tail fins - well
spaced. Straight wings and
tail fins, tail plane - at
bottom of fuselage. Cock pit
mounted well forward.

AFV and AIRCRAFT RECOGNITION

JAGUAR.

Manufactured by: UK. Similar to the Tornado IDS, Flogger, F-111, Fencer. Identification Features:- Short dumpy body. Swing wing. Twin exhaust. Taked-back rectangular air intakes. Huge sloping tail fin. Fat pointed nose. Flat bottomed fuselage.

AEW DEFENDER

Manufactured in the UK a development of the Defender Mk1 used for a variety of training and observational roles as well as general utility purposes. The recognition features are a Twin Turboprop Engines. Large Nose Radome. High Wing. Fixed Tricycle Undercarriage.

KEEP UP TO DATE WITH YOUR RECOGNITION SKILLS

· · · ·

MISTAKEN IDENTITY COSTS LIVES

HELICOPTERS

LYNX

Manufactured by: UK.
Identification Features: Long slim 'chin' type nose. Long drawn out cabin. High mounted tail boom - slopes downwards. Half stabiliser. Skids (Army) Wheels (Navy).

PUMA.

Manufactured by: France. Similar to Wessex, Super Frelon. Identification Features: Retractable undercarriage. Protruding wheel sponsons. Air intakes - similar to HIP. Square stocky appearance. Half stabiliser - can be left or right.

CHINOOK CH-47

Manufactured by: USA. Similar to SEA KNIGHT. Identification Features: Twin Tandem rotors. Large rear - conning tower. Flat bottomed fuselage. Fixed wheels front and rear. Twin outboard engines, mounted at bottom of rear conning tower.

AFV and AIRCRAFT RECOGNITION

GAZELLE.

Manufactured by: French.
Similar to: Alouette 111,
Dauphin.
Identification Features:
Enclosed tail rotor - (polo mint
type). Long drawn out cab -
75% glass. Body like a
'chicken drum stick'. Open
engine. 'H' shaped full
stabilisers. Bow shaped
skids.

BLACKHAWK UH-60A

Manufactured by: USA. There
are no helicopters of similar
shape in the Western
Powers. Identification
Features: Long humped-
backed appearance. Canted
tail rotor. Large slab low set
tailplane Engines mounted on
side of rotor housing.

IROQUOIS UH-1D

Manufactured by: USA.
Similar to Scout/Wasp, Bell
205, Bell 212.
Identification Features: Very
high mounted rotor. Long
stretched cabin. Tail boom
comes from the bottom of the
fuselage - sloping upwards.
Full rectangular stabilisers.
Skids pass under the bottom
of the cabin.

344

AFV and AIRCRAFT RECOGNITION

APACHE AH-64

Manufactured by: USA. Similar
to: AH-1 COBRA, HAVOC
M1-28.
Identification Features: Long,
angled cockpit canopy. Trailing
main wheels under forward
fuselage. Low-set tailplane
under tall fin.

HUEY COBRA AH-1

Manufactured by: USA. Similar
to HIND. Identification Features:
Pointed small nose. Long
tandem cockpit. Conning tower
top. Tail boom runs from the
bottom of the fuselage. Two
mid-mounted stub wings. Very
thin and long fuselage. Fitted
with Skids. Used as an assault
helicopter, carries eight troops.
Has rocket and antitank
capability.

F 16 FIGHTING FALCON.

Manufactured by: USA. Similar
to the SKYHAWK. Identification
features: Long pointed nose.
Large blister cockpit. 'Mouth'
type air intake under cockpit.
Small delta-type wings and
tailplane. Tailplane is down
swept Single round exhaust

AFV and AIRCRAFT RECOGNITION

COMMONWEALTH OF INDEPENDENT STATES (CIS) BATTLE TANKS

T 72.

Origin CIS. Crew of 3, Commander, Driver, Gunner. Weapons: 1 x 125mm smooth bore gun (APDSFS, HEAT), 1 x 7.62mm coaxial mg, 1 x 12.7mm AA mg. Weight 40.000 kg. Speed 70 kph. Night fighting and driving aids. NBC protection system. Has ability to snorkel. Auto loader and optical range finder.

T-64A

Origin CIS. Crew of 3, Commander, Driver, Gunner. Weapons: 1 x 125mm smooth bore gun, (FSAPDSF, HEAT & HE), 1 x 7.62mm coaxial mg, 1 x 12.7 AA mg. Weight 38,000kg. Cross Country Speed 45 kph. Night fighting and driving aids. NBC protection system. Has ability to snorkel. Auto loader and optical range finder. A bulldozer blade can be fitted, gives added protection and useful to dig itself in. Low silhouette, rounded turret set midway on body.

T-80.

Origin CIS. Crew of 3, Commander, Driver, Gunner. Weapons: 1 x 125mm smooth bore gun (APDSFS, HEAT),
1 x 7.62mm coaxial mg, 1 x 12.7mm AA mg. Weight 40.000 kg. Speed 70 kph. Night fighting and driving aids. Possibly fitted with Laser range finder. NBC protection system. Has ability to snorkel. Reactive armour and Kobra ATGW system.

AFV and AIRCRAFT RECOGNITION

SELF PROPELLED GUNS

2S-1 SELF PROPELLED HOWITZER

Origin CIS. SELF PROPELLED GUN. Crew of 3, Commander, Driver, Gunner, plus additional crew members carried in separate vehicle. Weight 20,000kg. Speed 70kph. Weapons: 1 x 122mm gun, range 16732 yds. Gun barrel does not extend forward of chassis. Night driving aids. NBC protection system. Amphibious capability, max water speed 5 to 10 kph. Can fire HEATFS and rocket assisted projectiles. Variants are; ACRV-2 command and recce; mine clearing with rocket-propelled mine clearing system; chemical recce vehicle.

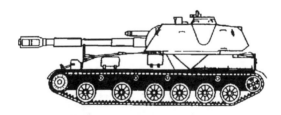

2S3 SP HOWITZER

Origin CIS. SELF PROPELLED GUN. Crew of 3, Commander, Driver, Gunner, plus additional crew carried in a separate vehicle. Weight 27,000kg. Speed 70 kph. Weapons: 1 x 152mm gun. Night driving aids and NBC protection system. Variants on the same chassis are other SP guns, heavy mortars and rocket launchers.

AFV and AIRCRAFT RECOGNITION

ZSU-23-4.

Origin CIS. SELF PROPELLED AA GUN. Crew of 4, Commander, Driver, Gunner, Radar Operator. Weight 14.000kg. Speed 44 kph. Weapons: 4 x 23mm cannon. Night driving aids; NBC protection system. The guns are radar controlled and have an effective range of 3000m. Optical sights are also fitted.

ARMOURED PERSONNEL CARRIERS (APC)

BMP 1

Origin CIS. Mechanised Infantry Combat Vehicle. Crew of 3, Commander, Gunner, Driver, plus 8 Infantrymen. Weight 12,500kg. Speed 55 kph.
Weapons: 1 x 73mm smoothbore gun with launching rail for, Sagger ATGW missile. 1 x 7.62mm coaxial mg. Amphibious, propelled by its tracks, max speed of 8 kph. NBC protection system. Night fighting and driving aids. Low silhouette with pointed nose.

BMP 2.

Origin CIS. Mechanised Infantry Combat Vehicle. Crew of 3, Commander, Gunner, Driver, plus 6 Infantrymen. Weight 12,500kg. Speed 55 kph. Weapons: It has a two man turret armed with a 30mm cannon and a Spandrel ATGW launcher. Amphibious, propelled by its tracks, max speed of 8 kph. NBC protection system. Night fighting and driving aids.

AFV and AIRCRAFT RECOGNITION

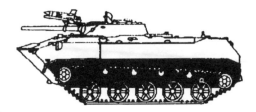

BMD

Origin CIS. Airborne Infantry Combat Vehicle. Crew of 3, Commander, Gunner, Driver, plus 6 Infantrymen. Weight 9000kg. Speed 80 kph. Weapons: 1 x 73mm smooth bore gun, 1 x Sagger ATGW launcher, 3 x 7.62 mm mgs - 1 coaxial, 2 hull-mounted. Amphibious capability, propelled by water jets at rear of hull, max speed 6 kph. Night fighting and driving aids. NBC protection system. Adjustable ground clearance suspension system.

BRDM 2

Origin CIS. Recce vehicle. Crew of 4, Commander, Gunner and two drivers. Weight 7,000kg. Max speed 100 kph. Armaments; 1 x 14.5mm, 1 x 7.63mm coaxial mounted mg. Amphibious capability, propelled by a single water jet from rear of hull, max speed of 10 kph. Night fighting and driving aids.
NBC protection system. 2 x 2 retractable cross country wheels. There are many variants of the BRDM; BRDM-1 with an open turret used as a NBC recce vehicle, an Armoured Command Vehicle, as a base vehicle for missile launching.

AFV and AIRCRAFT RECOGNITION

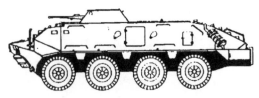

BTR 60

Origin CIS. Armoured Personnel Carrier. Crew of 2 Commander and Driver, plus 14 Infantrymen. Weight 10,300kg. Max speed 80 kph. Weapons: 1 x 14.5 mm mg, 1 x 7.62mm coaxial mg. Amphibious capability, propelled by single water jet at max speed of 10 kph. NBC protection system. Night fighting and driving aids.

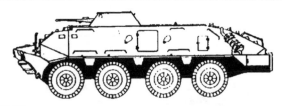

BTR 70

Origin CIS. Armoured Personnel Carrier. This vehicle is a development of the BTR 60. It has a longer hull and a larger engine compartment. Variants are as an Armoured Command Vehicle, a radio vehicle with telescopic antennae and as a base vehicle for mortars.

"TO KNOW IS TO SURVIVE"

FOR ABBREVIATIONS - SEE END OF POCKET BOOK

AFV and AIRCRAFT RECOGNITION

AIRCRAFT

FISHBED MiG-21

Origin CIS.
Similar to FISHPOT and
FLAGON. Identification
Features: Delta wing with
swept back tail plane. Air
intake in the nose with
protruding nose cone.
Single exhaust. Tail swept
back tail fin.

FLOGGER D MiG-27

Origin : CIS.
Similar to the FLOGGER-B.
TORNADO, F111, and
FENCER. Identification
Features: Long pointed or
chisel type nose. Large
rectangular air intakes
forward of wings. Swing
wings with cutout in leading
edge when swept. Tail fin
fillet and ventral fin
underneath.

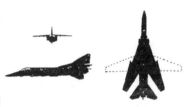

FENCER Su-24

Origin CIS.
Similar to F111, Tornado,
Flogger. Identification
Features: Swing wing.
Long pointed nose. Large
rectangular full depth air
intakes. Twin - side by side
- exhausts, 'boxed in'. Twin
ventral fins.

AFV and AIRCRAFT RECOGNITION

FROGFOOT Su-25

Origin CIS.
Similar to: JAGUAR,
AERMACCHI. Identification
Features: Chisel-type nose
with a slight uptilt. Two
underslung engines close to
fuselage. Oval appearance
to air intakes. Tapered
shoulder wing with tip pods.
Cropped triangular tail fin.

CUB AN-12

Origin CIS.
Similar to: HERCULES,
BELFAST. Identification
Features: Four turbo prop
engines. High mounted wing
with a straight trailing edge.
Wing tips droop. Tail fin fillet.
Rear gun turret.

CANDID Il-76

Origin CIS.
Similar to STARLIFTER,
GALAXY, 747, BAe 146.
Identification Features: Very
large. Four underslung turbo
fans. Tail plane on top of the
tail fin. Glass nose with
radome chin. Fat bodied
fuselage. Hump back, high
mounted wings. Cargo
capacity 44 tons.

AFV and AIRCRAFT RECOGNITION

HIND Mi-24   HELICOPTERS

Origin CIS.
Similar to: HUEY, COBRA.
Identification
Features:- Square
greenhouse type nose
(HIND A). Two cockpits on
HIND D. Stub mid mounted
wings (Downswept) with
weapon pylons. Western
type thick tail boom.
Retractable undercarriage.
HIND D has a chin turret.

HIP Mi-8

Origin CIS. Similar to S-61
L/N, S-61R, HAZE.
Identification Features:-
Long coach type body.
Two large round air intakes
- above cabin. Skinny high
mounted tail boom. Fixed
tricycle undercarriage.
MAY have external
weapon pylons.

HOOK Mi-6

Origin CIS.
Similar to: HARKE.
Identification Features:-
Very large. Airliner type
nose. Large spaced
intakes. Stub high mounted
wings. Fixed tricycle
undercarriage.

AFV and AIRCRAFT RECOGNITION

HOKUM

The Ka-50 HOKUM is the latest built CIS helicopter. It has been compared with the AH-64 APACHE.

The notable feature in its design is the stacked contra-rotating main rotor.

Weapons carried include 80 mm air-to-ground rockets, antitank laser guided missiles and air-to-air missiles.

A 30mm cannon is sited in the starboard fuselage.

LOCAL SILHOUETTES TO MEMORIZE

THE ADJUTANT   THE CO & DOG   THE RSM

THE TERRITORIAL ARMY

INTRODUCTION

This section of the Pocket Book is devoted to matters connected
specifically to the **Territorial Army**. You will notice there are only a
few pages, which indicates that the greater part of the content of
this Pocket Book applies to both Regular and TA soldiers.

There is a great difference in the backgrounds of many TA soldier to
that of the Regular Soldier. A member of the TA who has done a
normal day's work, goes home to for a meal and then to a Drill Night
at their local TAC (Territorial Army Centre), the following weekend
may be away on an exercise. Regretfully, some of them do not have
the luxury of that routine and are without regular employment.

It is against this background that the TA soldier is expected to play
their part in the '*one Army*' concept.

The enthusiasm and interest shown by the soldiers of the TA in
attaining a professional level of efficiency and high standards of
training in the time they have available is a great credit to them.

The 'media' seldom comment or recognise the contribution made by
the TA, and therefore those of you who do understand and know of
the effort made by their members, should use every opportunity to
publicise the good job they do.

We cannot speculate on the future, but would not be surprised, if
the 'lot' of the TA soldier were to be enhanced. To put it in context,
we are all conscious of costs, the TA soldier is cost effective and
therefore they present a valuable '*string to the bow*' of the MOD
(Army).

TERRITORIAL ARMY

TERRITORIAL ARMY OATH OF ALLEGIANCE

In many countries the armed forces are seen as, and often used for political ends. In this country however, a soldier makes his Oath of Allegiance, not to the nations political leaders, but to the Monarch, Her Majesty Queen Elizabeth II.

OATH OF ALLEGIANCE

"I swear by Almighty God, that I will be faithful and bear true allegiance to Her Majesty Queen Elizabeth the Second, her heirs and successors, and that I will, as in duty bound, honestly and faithfully defend Her Majesty, her heirs and successors, in person, crown and dignity against all enemies, and will observe and obey all orders of Her Majesty, her heirs and successors, and of the generals and officers set over me."

In the world we live in today, there are many ways of considering the Oath of Allegiance. Irrespective of your reasons for becoming a member of the Armed Forces, it is occasionally worthwhile reflecting on the meaning of the Oath.

It puts things in perspective and gives us a common reason for being what we are all *Volunteer Soldiers*, whose task it is to retain our freedom and defend our country and the society we live in from aggression either within or without the UK.

Serving here in Britain or as part of NATO or indeed anywhere else in the world, makes no difference. Many of our predecessors measured up to this serious commitment, it is now your responsibility to do the same.

Your commitment is to meet the needs of your personal development in terms of the knowledge and skills required to become a proficient soldier, at the same time to back up those who instruct you in your unit. The experience is entirely in your hands as a full member of the Volunteer Forces, supporting your unit, through the time you have available.

If you have that sense of purpose to become properly trained, and then to maintain that state, you will match up to the TA motto of "Ready and Waiting".

TERRITORIAL ARMY

PAY and ALLOWANCES.

INTRODUCTION

Many people are surprised to find that they will be paid for their voluntary service, particularly after being told that they should treat it as a hobby. In fact many would still serve for no pay because they enjoy it and see it as a useful and rewarding pastime.

You will need a Bank Account if you do not already have one, as your pay is paid directly to your account. You will be paid for the training you do each month, usually it is credited to your account by the middle of the following month.

TYPES OF PAY & ALLOWANCES

Your pay will fall into three main categories:
1. Pay for half, quarter and a full days training.
2. Allowances for expenses.
3. Bounty.
The first is taxable, the second and third are not.

PAY

You will be paid a quarter day for each drill night that you do attend. You may be paid a half day if you attend on a Friday night as part of a weekends training.

You will be paid a full day for completing eight hours in each 24 hour period. Your rate of pay will depend on your rank, grade and class, which in turn depend on your period of service and experience.

RATES OF PAY

Below is shown the three elements that affect your rate of pay, your RANK, CLASS and BAND I.E. period of service.

RANK	CLASS	BAND
Private Soldier	4 Recruit	6 months Pte. - L/Cpl.
	3 Trained Soldier	1 Year Pte. L/Cpl, Cpl.
	2 Trained Soldier	3 Years Pte to WOII.
	1 Trained Soldier	6 Years Pte to WOII.

If you have any queries about your pay see your pay NCO or PSAO. Do not delay, if you want them to check anything for you.

It is very important to keep careful records of the training you do, the claims you make, and the pay and allowances credited to your account.

TERRITORIAL ARMY

This is for two particular reasons. The first, to check that the correct amounts are in fact being credited to your account each month, and secondly for your own personal records you will often require information for a variety of reasons.

CHECK THAT YOUR TRAINING HAS BEEN LOGGED ON

Invariably the Inland Revenue will at some time assess you or ask for some information regarding the past years, it saves you a lot of 'hassle' if you can find it without any problems. Always make sure your name is down on your units nominal role, if it is not - you will not get paid - don't leave it to others to do.

REMEMBER

1. Make sure **you are on** the Nominal Roll.
2. Keep a personal record of your attendance.
3. Notify your PSAO of any changes - especially Bank details.

It is the Volunteers responsibility to ensure that their attendances are properly recorded. Failure to do so may result in loss of pay.

TYPES OF ALLOWANCES

There are several types of allowances, these are:-

1. Residence to place of duty . This will be paid to you for every trip that you make into your drill hall and will be equivalent to bus fare. How you travel is up to you.
2. Training Expense Allowance (TEA) is a small nontaxable allowance paid to all who attend drill nights.
3. Travel allowance. Sometimes you will be asked to travel to training using your own transport away from your TAC. If so you will be give a Form 1771 to fill in. Ask for help in filling it in. Like most forms of this type it is not too difficult, but if it is not correct you may not receive payment.
4. Other Allowances. Subsistence Allowance is paid to those who are travelling, perhaps to a course, and no provision has been made for food etc. This is also claimed on the Form 1771.

BOUNTY

This is a tax free once per year payment which is roughly equivalent to a bonus in civilian life. There are three levels of payment depending on the amount of service you have; one, two, three or more years. Bounty is paid to members of the TA who have been available for training for the whole year, having completed a specified amount of training, and

TERRITORIAL ARMY

who in the opinion of their Commanding Officer is an effective soldier.
The Training Commitment to qualify for Bounty is:-

1. A trained soldier has to in camp training or in exceptional circumstances a short camp of not less than 8 days may be authorised, plus 12 days (out of camp) training. e.g. designated Bounty weekends.
2. Twelve days out of camp training for the trained soldier. Sixteen days for the recruit.
3. A Recruit to qualify for bounty must first have successfully completed a Recruit Cadre, plus 16 days out of camp training.
    These days will usually be at weekends and are often called bounty days as you MUST attend to receive your bounty. They will usually be indicated on your unit's Forecast of Events for you to ensure that you attend.
3. The Battle Fitness Test (BFT).
4. The Personal Weapon Test (PWT).
5. The NBC Defence Test.
6. The First Aid Test.
7. AFV Recognition Test.

When you pass *ALL* your BFT's you will be awarded your Commanding Officers Certificate of Competence which will then be published on Part 2 orders.

PAY AND THE UNEMPLOYED

There is no doubt that those who have jobs benefit the most from the TA, the pay you earn has tax deducted and you keep the rest. If you are unemployed and receiving
The Dole or Social Security, then your training is seen as pay which will affect payments and can in some cases reduce the amount to almost nothing. However, the first £15 per week or £60 per month is disregarded by the DHSS when assessing your benefit.
If in receipt of benefit it is your duty to inform the relevant benefit office of your TA earnings - **it is the law.**
Travel and TEA is regarded as pay.
You are reminded that failing to declare your 'pay' is seen as fraud and in some cases can result in criminal charges being brought against you. A number of unemployed soldiers fall prey to social security inspectors every year, so be warned, make sure you talk to the local social security people about your pay and sign off before going to Annual Training.

TERRITORIAL ARMY

You should take advice before seeing the social services by talking to your pay NCO or PSAO who will be able to advise you on all pay related matters.

Despite all this, many unemployed soldiers continue to serve and fill a very important role as part of the defence of this country. The difficulties for the unemployed volunteer soldier are recognised and some small concessions have been made to try and enhance their conditions in recognition of their voluntary spirit, and to meet their individual needs, discussions are continuing for further concessions to be made.

Remember that if you start off on the right foot in these matters you will no doubt be happier with the rewards.

PAY AND THE STUDENT

If you are a student then you will be financially better off even than your employed friends, the reason for this is that you can apply to the Inland Revenue on a form **P38 Income Tax, PAYE, Students in the Reserve Forces**, to claim back the tax you have paid and to stop paying tax on future earnings while a student.

REMEMBER FOR FUTURE REFERENCE, KEEP DUPLICATE COPIES OF ALL YOUR PAY AND ALLOWANCE RECORDS, CORRESPONDENCE AND TAX RETURNS

WHAT IS EXPECTED OF YOU?

The following notes are produced to give you some guide lines as to what will be expected of you by the Officers of most units in the TA. You must remember that in most cases the Officers and NCOs that command you are, like you, volunteers, and that the TA is their hobby, again, like it is for you.

You should also remember that they will have other interests and commitments, to work and family.

The unit you belong to is like any army unit, it depends on the teamwork of ALL its members to be able to do its job. The organising of training takes a great deal of time and effort which is wasted if you do not turn up.

Try to remember to :-

Attend your Drill Night each week - for training, but perhaps more importantly to find out and make preparations for what is going on at the weekend.

Read your orders as soon as they are sent to you - carry out the

TERRITORIAL ARMY

instructions in them. Always communicate - let your unit know if you are unable to attend a duty or if you are available to go on that exercise.

Let your unit know of any changes in your circumstances - particularly change of address or telephone number, but also marriages, changes in employment, etc.

Look after your uniform - keep it clean and in good condition, do not be afraid of using a needle and an iron. Look smart at all times and be proud of the uniform you wear. Don't wear your uniform except for Drill Nights and Weekend Training, and that means any of it.

Be on time - in the army that means be at least 5 minutes early for any parade, being late is almost considered to be a crime in some units and rightly so.

Obey orders - even if they seem to be unfair, obey them and complain afterwards, you will then be in the right. Ask for an interview with an officer to do this.

Have good manners and behave as you would expect a soldier in the finest army in the world to behave.

To - "hitchhike" - in uniform is not considered as portraying the right image of the soldier, it also makes you easy prey for a terrorist at worst, or hooligans at best, so don't do it.

Develop your own self discipline - if the NCOs are always on your back, ask yourself why and do something about it. Help other members of your unit - the Army believes in the buddy - buddy system, that of helping your mate and him helping you, it makes life a great deal easier.

Be a Full Member of your unit - remember things are organised for you. Whether it is training or a social event get involved and get your family involved whenever you can.

Do your job as well as you can and try to learn the job of the person in charge of you, this is how you will progress and gain promotion. Someone once said that there are shirkers, 'jerkers' and workers. This is just as true in the TA as anywhere else. Shirkers can never be found when there is work to do. Jerkers are full of promises and even start off with good intentions, but always fall short and usually fail. The only people really worth the time of day are the workers, you will notice them, they are the soldiers who stay on for a while after a tough exercise to help with the "post exercise admin" checking the kit, hanging it up to dry, etc., when everyone else has disappeared, be a full member of your unit, be a worker.

TERRITORIAL ARMY

EQUIPMENT and CLOTHING - RESPONSIBILITY

Your uniform is issued to you and other items of equipment like
webbing, sleeping bags, compasses and the like can be drawn from
the stores when required, and will be signed out to you personally
and will be your total responsibility until you return them in good
condition and working order and have your signature struck off.
However, there are a number of items which you will find can make
your job as a soldier more enjoyable and will make you more
effective.

The items vary in price from a few pence to many pounds and can
be obtained from many different sources, it's a good idea to shop
around.

By using your first few months pay you can equip yourself very well
and when others shiver you will be warm, when waiting for a hot
meal you will have a brew on.

Pen Knife - Sharp, light and not too bulky; **Knife/Fork/Spoon set
or Spork** -this combines all three in one; **Note Book** - keep this in
a plastic bag, it should be just smaller than your top combat jacket
pocket: **Half a pencil, a ball pen and a piece of chalk; Pen Light
or torch** - with a red filter if possible and don't keep the batteries in it:
Black Plastic Bin Bags - to wrap your kit in, inside of your large
pack, to keep it dry, they also have other uses, have a few spare.
Foot powder - to keep your feet in good condition. **Extra woollen
socks. Insect repellent** - useful in summer - who said "What
summer"? **Bungees 6** - essential for basha kit. Strong dark cord -
several metres.
Waxed matches - Useful when everybody else has got soggy
matches, make them, don't buy them, you only need a candle and a
box of matches, wax each one individually.
A Candle. Sleeping Mat - often called carrymats, these insulate
you from the cold floor and provide a certain degree of comfort,
make sure it is olive green and not shiny.
Silva or Suunto - mils compass and a Pathfinder Protractor/Romer.
Small gas stove - with screw thread gas cylinder for ease of
dismantling.
Thermal underwear. Thermal Jacket - required for wear under the
new issue combat jacket. **Set of Water/Windproofs** - Jacket and
trousers, not too thin and camouflaged
Steel Thermos flask - these must be good all the Sergeant Majors
have them.

TERRITORIAL ARMY

Canvas walkers gaiters - these give added protection to boot uppers and the bottom part of the leg, green colour again.
A Rucksack or Bergen - these can be very useful, though when you have one the tendency is to take more kit than you need;
A Bivi Bag - made of Gortex the height of luxury, so they tell us, very expensive, but if you have the money, why not. There are many outlets for this type of equipment.

PROTECTIVE CLOTHING

The wet and cold weather clothing now being issued to the Army has already gained the respect of the soldier. Some members of the TA may have these items issued to them, or due to the very high cost the many units have a 'pool' of clothing to be issued on an as/when needed basis. You will find that your normal combat jacket is made of thinner material than previously, consequently you would be well advised to invest in a thermal jacket of some type to wear under your combat jacket for winter training.

The cover design of this Pocket Book was specially commissioned, from a water colour by Carl Marshall Esq, Illustrator of Arnold, Nottingham.

The 'ghost' figures on the back cover represent:

A Pte Light Company, Bethnal Green Vols 1798.

A Rifle Volunteer 1860.

A member of the Imperial Yeomanry 1900.

An Infantry Pte of 'Kitcheners' Army 1916.

A member of the Parachute Regiment circa 1944.

TERRITORIAL ARMY

EMPLOYERS SUPPORT

Today more and more employers are supportive towards the role of the reservist and many employees find they are given either extra paid leave to cover their annual training or perhaps unpaid leave towards their annual training commitment

In many instances you will have to forego part of your annual holiday allocation at your place of work; this being the case if you are married will not find favour with the family, on the other hand some employers are totally hostile at the idea of giving you special leave for your commitment to your unit.

What can you do about it? Perhaps it would be as well when seeking employment to make sure that your employer is sympathetic to the TA soldier and the time they have to put into being efficient in their role.

In a 'climate' where jobs are difficult to find and hold, TA soldiers are occasionally faced with a choice, leave the TA or loose their job. This is understandable, employers have to make the most effective use of their resources. If some of their work force are TA members and changes in working practice, promotion prospects, overtime or weekend working are called for, obviously it requires difficult decisions to be made.

It could be the situation where the majority of employers who are difficult regarding time-off do not have sufficient knowledge of the skills required by the Volunteer Soldier and what part he plays in the defence of the country.

The Ministry of Defence were instrumental in setting up a special body called the National Employer Liaison Committee for the Volunteer and Reserve Forces. Every Territorial Army Volunteer Reserve Association (TAVRA) has an Employer Support Committee to help as a back up in dealing with difficult employers.

As you are at the sharp end it is important to have all the available information and the right answers to ensure that if at any time you are engaged in a discussion with some unenlightened individual, you are capable of putting across the need for the Volunteer Soldier and the role you play requiring time to fulfil your training commitment.

The NELC (National Employer Liaison Committee) published guidelines for the Volunteer Soldier on HOW TO GET YOUR EMPLOYERS SUPPORT and we recommend that you take careful note of this valuable advice which we reproduce on the next page.

TERRITORIAL ARMY

"BRITISH BUSINESS GAINS MUCH FROM ITS
PARTNERSHIP WITH THE RESERVE FORCES"

HOW TO GET YOUR EMPLOYERS SUPPORT

DO

Remind your employer
that the Reserve Forces are
vital for National Defence;

Demonstrate your pride
in your unit; by your bearing,
turn out and sense of
responsibility

Thank your employer for the
support given to you. For
example, an invitation to
social and open days.

Sort out problems between
your Reserve (Forces) and
Civilian obligations.

DON'T

Leave it to the last
minute to tell your
employer about annual
training camp or courses:

mention your dates before
the holiday programme is
planned.

Let your service in the
Reserves, be seen to
interfere adversely with your
civilian occupation.

"A PROFITABLE PARTNERSHIP -
WHY YOUR EMPLOYER SHOULD GIVE SUPPORT".

EVERY EMPLOYER IN THE COUNTRY HAS A STAKE IN NATIONAL DEFENCE.

Companies pay taxes that go to finance the armed services
including the Reserve Forces. Members of the Reserve Forces
cannot serve effectively unless they receive support and
encouragement from their employers which is sought as a
contribution to the defence of the nation.

Active employer support means more enthusiastic, better trained
employees, who take to their civilian jobs the virtues they have
acquired in the Reserves.

TERRITORIAL ARMY

WHAT YOU HAVE TO OFFER

You develop qualities as a result of service in the Reserves that are of direct value to the employer such as:-

- a sense of personal pride and discipline.
- the development of leadership potential and man-management capabilities.
- training in extra skills and trades.
- encouragement of responsibility and decision making.
- improved physical fitness.
- training in verbal and written communications.
- proficiency in the maintenance and use of valuable technical equipment.
- it gives you a worthwhile weekend and evening interest which is also a refreshing change from routine.

These virtues give a measurable commercial benefit to an employer.

WHAT TO DO TO GAIN YOUR EMPLOYERS SUPPORT

It is important that you gain the support of **ALL LEVELS** of management.
The approach to employers will vary with the size of the company or authority concerned.

- **MAKE SURE YOUR EMPLOYER KNOWS THE VALUE OF YOUR INVOLVEMENT WITH THE RESERVE FORCES, AND YOUR ROLE.**
- **DISCUSS WITH YOUR EMPLOYER IN GOOD TIME YOUR RESERVE FORCES CAMP OR COURSE COMMITMENTS.**
- **THANK YOUR EMPLOYER.**
- **IRON OUT PROBLEMS PERSONALLY.**

Be courteous to your employer by giving advanced notice - never less than six months notice of your Reserve Forces commitments that will affect your work, such as annual training camp or courses. Make sure that your employer is thanked, at least annually, perhaps by an invitation to an Employers Open Evening. This should not only be a social event, but also an opportunity to display your unit's skills and equipment.
Any problems that occur with your employer should be ironed out face to face if possible, or with the help of your officer and your TAVRA Employer Support Committee.

ANNUAL TRAINING RECORDS

	YEAR					YEAR					YEAR			
	1	2	D	Spec	Totals	1	2	D	Spec	Totals	1	2	D	Spec	Totals
APR															
MAY															
JUNE															
JULY															
AUG															
SEPT															
OCT															
NOV															
DEC															
JAN															
FEB															
MAR															
Totals															

Annual Camp or Course in Lieu

Qualification		NBC	FIRST AID	CO TEST
APWT	BFT			

ANNUAL TRAINING RECORDS

	YEAR 1	YEAR 2	D	Spec	Totals
APR					
MAY					
JUNE					
JULY					
AUG					
SEPT					
OCT					
NOV					
DEC					
JAN					
FEB					
MAR					
Totals					
Annual Camp or Course in Lieu					

Qualification	APWT	BFT	NBC	FIRST AID	CO TEST

	YEAR 1	YEAR 2	D	Spec	Totals
APR					
MAY					
JUNE					
JULY					
AUG					
SEPT					
OCT					
NOV					
DEC					
JAN					
FEB					
MAR					
Totals					
Annual Camp or Course in Lieu					

Qualification	APWT	BFT	NBC	FIRST AID	CO TEST

	YEAR 1	YEAR 2	D	Spec	Totals
APR					
MAY					
JUNE					
JULY					
AUG					
SEPT					
OCT					
NOV					
DEC					
JAN					
FEB					
MAR					
Totals					
Annual Camp or Course in Lieu					

Qualification	APWT	BFT	NBC	FIRST AID	CO TEST

ABBREVIATIONS

AA	Anti Aircraft
AAD	All Arms Air Defence
accn	accommodation
ACE	Allied Command Europe
ACO	Air Contact Officer
ACP	Ammunition Control Point
ACRV	Armoured Command Recce Vehicle.
AD	Air Defence
Adj	Adjutant
admin	administration.
ADS	Advanced Dressing Station
adv	advance
AEV	Armoured Engineering Vehicle
AFV	Armoured Fighting Vehicle
AGAI	Army General & Administrative Instructions
AKA	Armoured Killing Area
AMF(L)	ACE Allied Mobile Force (Land)
ammo	ammunition
amph	amphibious
am	ante meridian
APC	Armoured Personnel Carrier
APDS	Armour Piercing Discarding Sabot
APDSFS	Armour Piercing Discarding Sabot Fin Stabilized

Apers	Anti personnel
ARV	Armoured Recovery Vehicle
ATD	Army Training Directives
ATGW	Anti-Tank Guided Weapon
Atk	Anti tank
ATN	Army Training News
ATO	Ammunition Technical Officer
armd	armoured
asslt	assault
assy	assembly
att	attachments
AVLB	Armoured Vehicle Launched Bridge
AVRE	Assault Vehicle Royal Engineers
AWOL	Absent without leave
BAA	Brigade Administrative Area
BASO	Brigade Air Support Officer
BC	Battery Commander
BCR	Battle Casualty Replacement
Bdr	Bombardier
bde	brigade
BFPO	British Forces Post Office
BG	Battle Group
BHE	Battle Handling Exercise
bn	battalion
BOLP	Boat Off-Loading Point

ABBREVIATIONS

BQMS	Battery Quartermaster Sergeant
Brig	Brigadier
BSM	Battery Sergeant Major
bty	battery
cam	camouflage
CAM	Chemical Agent Monitor
CAP	Company Aid Post
Capt	Captain
cas	casualty
CASEVAC	Casualty Evacuation
CB	Counter Battery
CDE	Combat Digging Equipment
CEFO	Complete Equipment Fighting Order
CofE	Church of England
CES	Complete Equipment Schedule
CGI	Corrugated Iron
CIS	Commonwealth of Independent States
Col	Colonel
CP	Command Post
CO	Commanding Officer
C/Sgt	Colour Sergeant
COMMCEN	Communications Centre
Conc	Concentration
Coy	Company
Cpl	Corporal
CPX	Command Post Exercise
CQB	Close Quarter Battle
CQMS	Company Quartermaster Sergeant
CRP	Chemical Reconnaissance Party
CSM	Company Sergeant Major
CRW	Counter Revolutionary Warfare
CS gas	Chemical Smoke Gas
CSA	Corps Supply Area
Csups	Combat Supplies
CSWS	Crew Served Weapon Sight
CTAD	Commander Training & Arms Directors
CV	Command Vehicle
CVR(T)	Combat Vehicle Reconnaissance (Tracked)
CVR(W)	Combat Vehicle Reconnaissance (Wheeled)
CW	Chemical Warfare
CWS	Common Weapon Sight
DAA	Divisional Administrative Area
DAER	Daily Ammunition Expenditure Rate
DAT	Director of Army Training
DCI	Defence Council Instruction
DCSR	Daily Combat Supply Rate
def	defence
dets	detachments

DF	Defensive Fire
DFK	Decontamination Kit Personal
Div	Division
DS	Dressing Station/Directing Staff/Direct Support
dvr	driver
DOP	Drop Off Point
DSA	Divisional Supply Area
DTG	Date Time Group
DZ	Dropping Zone
EMP	Electromagnetic Pulse
en	enemy
engr	engineer
EOD	Explosive Ordnance Disposal
eqpt	equipment
ERA	Explosive Reactive Armour
ERV	Emergency Rendezvous
ETA	Estimated Time of Arrival
ETD	Estimated Time of Departure
ETH	Entrenching Tool Hand
FAC	Forward Air Controller
FAP	Final Assault Position
FEBA	Forward Edge of the Battle Area
FFE	Fire For Effect
FofF	Field of Fire
FFI	Free From Infection
FFR	Fitted for Radio
FGA	Fighter Ground Attack
FIBUA	Fighting in Built-Up Areas
FLOT	Forward Line of Own Troops
F&M	Fire and Movement
Fmn	Formation
FOO	Forward Observation Officer
FOT	Forward Ordnance Team
FPF	Final Protective Fire
freq	frequency
FRV	Final Rendezvous
FSCC	Fire Support Co-ordination Centre
FSCL	Fire Support Co-ordination Line
FSG	Fire Support Group
FUP	Forming Up Place
FV	Fighting Vehicle
fwd	forward
GD	General Duties
gd	guard
Gen	General
GMT	Greenwich Mean Time
GPMG	General Purpose Machine Gun
GPMG(SF)	Sustained Fire role GPMG

ABBREVIATIONS

GRID	Grid Reference
HASE	Head Angulation Siting Equipment
HD	Home Defence
hel	helicopter
HE	High Explosive
HEAT	High Explosive Anti-Tank
HESH	High Explosive Squash Head
HF	Harassing Fire
HHLRF	Hand Held Laser Range Finder
HLS	Helicopter Landing Site
HQ	Head Quarters
HMLC	High Mobility Load Carrier
hr	hour
IA	Immediate Action
IC	In Charge
IED	Improvised Explosive Device
IFCS	Integrated Fire Control System
II	Image Intensification
illum	illuminate/illuminating
Instr	Instructor
IO	Intelligence Officer
IPE	Individual Protection Equipment
IPK	Individual Protection Kit
IR	Infra-Red
IRG	Immediate Replenishment Group
IRIS	Infra-Red Intrusion System
IT	Infantry Training
ITO	Individual Training Organisation
IW	Individual Weapon
IWS	Individual Weapon Sight
JSP	Joint Services Publication
junc	junction
LAD	Light Aid Detachment
LAW	Light Anti-Armour Weapon
LO	Liaison Officer
LOE	Limit Of Exploitation
LP	Landing Point
LRATGW	Long Range Anti-Tank Guided Weapon
LRV	Light Reconnaissance Vehicle
LS	Landing Site
LSW	Light Support Weapon
Lt	Lieutenant
Lt Col	Lieutenant Colonel
lt	light
LZ	Landing Zone
Maj	Major
MAOT	Mobile Air Operations Team
MAPCO	Map Code
MAW	Medium Anti-Tank Weapon

ABBREVIATIONS

MBSD	Multi-barrelled Smoke Discharger		NBC	Nuclear, Biological and Chemical
MBT	Main Battle Tank		NOD	Night Observation Device
MCT(S)	Milan Compact Turret on Spartan		N of K	Next of Kin
MDS	Main Dressing Station		NSP	Normal Safety Precautions
MEXE	Military Engineering Experimental		NVP	Night Vision Plan
	Establishment		obj	objective
MFC	Mortar Fire Controller		OMB	Outboard Motor
MFDC	Mortar Fire Data Controller		OC	Officer Commanding
MG	Machine Gun		offr	Officer
MMG	Medium Machine Gun		O Gp	Orders Group
mg	Ranging Machine Gun		OHC	Over Head Cover
MIRA	Milan Infra-Red Adapter		OHP	Over Head Protection
ML	Mortar Line		OIC	Officer In Charge (pl,tps,patrol etc).
MO	Medical Officer		OOM	Order Of March
MOD	Ministry of Defence		OP	Observation Post
MPI	Mean Point of Impact		Ops	Operations
MRATGW	Medium Range Anti-Tank		PADS	Position & Azimuth Determining
	Guided Weapon			System
MRG	Main Repair Group		pl	platoon
MSR	Main Supply Route		PLCE	Personal Load Carrying Equipment
MTO	Mechanical Transport Officer		POL	Petrol Oil and Lubricants
NAIAD	Nerve Agent Immobilized Enzyme		POA	Point of Aim
	Alarm Detector		pte	private
NAPS	Nerve Agent Pre-treatment Set		PUP	Pick Up Point
NCO	Non Commissioned Officer		PW	Prisoner of War

ABBREVIATIONS

QM	Quartermaster		Sgt	Sergeant
QRs	Queens Regulations		SHS	Split Hairpin Shelter
RAP	Regimental Aid Post		SITREP	Situation Report
RC	Roman Catholic		sig	signaller
recce	reconnaissance		SLR	Self Loading Rifle
RES	Radiation Exposure State		SL	Start Line
regt	regiment(al)		sldr	soldier
replen	replenishment		SMG	Sub-Machine Gun
Rfn	Rifleman		smk	smoke
RGS	Remote Ground Sensors		SNEB	Squash Nosed Explosive Ballistic
RMA	Regimental Medical Assistant		SOCs	Secure Orders Cards
RMO	Regimental Medical Officer		SOP	Standing Operating Procedure
RP	Regimental Police		SQMS	Squadron Quartermaster Sergeant
RSM	Regimental Sergeant Major		SQMS	Staff Quartermaster Sergeant
The rat rations			SSM	Squadron Sergeant Major
RUMA	Reinforcing Units Marshalling Area		STAP	Surveillance & Target Acquisition Plan
RV	Rendezvous		str	strength
RVD	Residual Vapour Detector		SUSAT	Sight Unit Small Arms Trilux
SA	Small Arms		Surv	Surveillance
SAA	Small Arms Ammunition		TA	Territorial Army
SAC	Small Arms Collimator		TACP	Tactical Air Control Party
SAM	Surface to Air Missile		TAOR	Tactical Area of Responsibility
SAWES	Small Arms Weapons Effects Simulator		TCV	Troop Carring Vehicle
sect	section		Tech	Technical
SF	Sustained Fire		TEWT	Tactical Exercise Without Troops

374

ABBREVIATIONS

TI	Thermal Imaging
tlr	Trailer
tk	tank
TOW	Tube Launched Optically Tracked Wire Guided
TOBIAS	Territorial Observation By Intrusion Alarm System
tp	troop
tpt	transport
trg	training
UKLF	United Kingdom Land Forces
U/S	Unserviceable
USOP	Unit Standing Operating Procedure
UTE	Unit Testing Equipment
VCP	Vehicle Check Point
veh	vehicle
VOR	Vehicle Off Road
VT Fuze	Variable Time Fuze
Wng O	Warning Order
wpn	weapon
WP	White Phosphorous/ Water Point
wdr	withdraw

ADDITIONAL ABBREVIATIONS

SHOOTING RECORD

SAC Personal Zero Reference

Date	Weapon Fired	SUSAT No	Type of Practice Fired	Type of Range	HPS	Score or Group Size	Remarks

SHOOTING RECORD

SAC Personal Zero Reference

Date	Weapon Fired	SUSAT No	Type of Practice Fired	Type of Range	HPS	Score or Group Size	Remarks

Names Addresses & Telephone Numbers

Name ....

Address ....

....

Tel No .... Post Code ....

Name ....

Address ....

....

Tel No .... Post Code ....

Name ....

Address ....

....

Tel No .... Post Code ....

Name ....

Address ....

....

Tel No .... Post Code ....

Name ....

Address ....

....

Tel No .... Post Code ....